THE HRAFNISTA SAGAS

THE HRAFNISTA SAGAS

translated by Ben Waggoner

Troth Publications
2012

© 2012, The Troth. All rights reserved. No part of this book may be reproduced or transmitted in any form or by any means, electronic or mechanical, including photocopy, recording, or any information storage and retrieval system, without prior permission in writing from the publisher. Exceptions may be allowed for non-commercial "fair use," for the purposes of news reporting, criticism, comment, scholarship, research, or teaching.

"Ohthere's Voyage" was previously published in *Idunna*, no. 77, pp. 12-24 (ISSN 1937-397X).

Published by The Troth
24 Dixwell Avenue, Suite 124
New Haven, Connecticut 06511
http://www.thetroth.org/

ISBN-13: 978-0-557-72941-8.

Cover emblem: Whale, redrawn from AM 673 4° (the Icelandic *Physiologus*), ca. 1200

Troth logo designed by Kveldulf Gundarsson, drawn by 13 Labs, Chicago, Illinois

Cover design: Ben Waggoner

Typeset in Garamond 18/14/12/10

Dedicated to Robert Russell inn silframildr,
in thanks for his generous support.
With his help, may the stories live long.

CONTENTS

Introduction viii

The Saga of Ketil Trout 3

The Saga of Grim Shaggy-Cheek 29

The Saga of Arrow-Odd 41

The Saga of An Bow-Bender 159

Appendix: Ohthere's Voyage 187

Notes 192

Bibliography 224

INTRODUCTION

Ramsta, or Ramstad, is a settlement on the 4 km-long island of Ramstadholmen, in the Foldafjord along the North Sea coast of Norway, in the present-day municipality of Nærøy. In medieval times, the settlement was called Hrafnista, and lay more or less on the boundary between the petty kingdoms of Naumudalr (Namdalen), to the south, and Halogaland, extending far to the north. A large Viking-era burial mound, known today as Ketilhaugen, shows that the area must have been a place of some importance. As late as approximately 1120, it may have been the site of a large judicial assembly of men from both Hálogaland and Namdalen.[1]

Hrafnista's significance in Old Norse literature is far out of proportion to its size. A sequence of Old Norse sagas, collectively known as the *Hrafnistasögur*, tells the story of four different members of a family that lived on Hrafnista in the 9th century. *Ketils saga hængs* (The Saga of Ketil Salmon), *Gríms saga loðinkinna* (The Saga of Grim Shaggy-Cheek), and *Örvar-Odds saga* (The Saga of Arrow-Odd) relate the lives and exploits of three successive generations of the men of Hrafnista, as they face human enemies as well as giants and various supernatural entities. *Áns saga bogsveigis* (The Saga of An Bow-bender) is mostly set elsewhere in Norway, but its hero is also descended from the Men of Hrafnista.

Örvar-Odds saga is distinguished from the others by its great length and diversity: the longer version of this saga, translated here, contains much added material, ranging from folk-tale motifs to borrowings from medieval scholarly texts. *Áns saga* is perhaps even more so the "odd one out": there are no giants or trolls (although a dwarf has a brief supporting role) and very little magic. Most of the plot deals with An's difficulties with a wicked, treacherous, but thoroughly human king, far from Hrafnista. Yet a number of motifs, and even whole episodes, link *Áns saga* with the other Hrafnista sagas.[2] Of the 123 manuscripts known to contain at least one of the Hrafnista sagas, 64 contain more than one. Twenty-six contain *Ketils saga*, *Gríms saga*, and *Örvar-Odds saga* but not *Áns saga*—but eighteen include *Áns saga* and at least one other Hrafnista saga, and eleven contain all four.[3] Thus, although the four sagas were not always copied and read as a single unit, there was still a tradition of placing them together in various combinations, as parts of the "Matter of Hrafnista".

Genre and Genealogy

The sagas of the Men of Hrafnista are traditionally classified as *fornaldarsögur*, "sagas of olden times." The word *fornaldarsögur* is not an old word; it dates from 1829-1830, when Carl Christian Rafn published the saga collection *Fornaldar Sögur Norðurlanda*, "Sagas of Olden Times of the Northlands". Later editors have added some texts to the *fornaldarsögur* corpus that Rafn did not include. While classifying this corpus as *fornaldarsögur* has long been common practice among editors and scholars, defining exactly what is meant by *fornaldarsögur* has been much discussed and debated; the *fornaldarsögur* encompass a wide range of literary materials, some of which overlap with other saga types.[4]

Fornaldarsögur are often defined by their setting: Scandinavia (although sometimes with excursions to more distant lands) in the legendary past, before the accession of Harald Fair-Hair and the settlement of Iceland. This fits most of the texts in Rafn's corpus, but not necessarily all of them, and not always to equal degrees. Stephen Mitchell's proposed definition of *fornaldarsögur* is perhaps more useful: *fornaldarsögur* are "based on traditional heroic themes", and their "numerous fabulous episodes and motifs create an atmosphere of unreality."[5] By this definition, true *fornaldarsögur* draw on the same traditions that are seen in the primary Norse mythological texts the *Eddas*, in old skaldic poems and kennings, and in later folktales and folklore. Fabulous episodes and motifs fill them: mighty heroes, greedy dragons, treacherous or helpful dwarves, huge giants, crazed berserks, vast hoards of treasure, magical workings for good or evil, and powerful enchanted weapons all figure in these sagas, and the old pagan gods themselves periodically have walk-on parts.

The Hrafnista Sagas

The Hrafnista sagas fit Mitchell's definition quite well, and at first glance they may appear to be fantasies with no basis in factual history. On the other hand, the Hrafnista sagas are more concretely localized in historical time than many of the *fornaldarsögur*. Instead of being set in the nebulous heroic past, these sagas are set just a few generations before the Norse colonization of Iceland, said to have begin in the year 870. More importantly, multiple sources name the men of Hrafnista as ancestors of many of the most prominent families in Iceland. To give a few examples: *Egils saga* claims that Kveldulf Bjalfason, the grandfather of the titular hero Egil Skallagrimson, was a nephew of Ketil Salmon, the hero of the first *Hrafnistusaga*.[6] *Gríms saga* and *Egils saga* agree that the elder Ketil Salmon had a grandson, who was also named Ketil Salmon. This second Ketil avenged the slaying of his cousin, Kveldulf's son Thorolf, and then escaped to Iceland, where he settled and raised a large and prominent family; his son Hrafn was Iceland's first Lawspeaker.[7] Kveldulf's son Skalla-Grim was also an ancestor of Bjorn, the hero of *Bjarnar saga hítdælakappa*. Through these connections, the Men of Hrafnista became ancestors of the Sturlungar, one of the most prominent and most literary families in 12th- and 13th-century Iceland.

Gríms saga also connects the men of Hrafnista with prominent persons in other sagas of Icelanders. The younger Ketil Salmon, for example, is revealed as an ancestor of Gunnar of Hlidarend, so prominent in *Njáls saga*, while another line of descent from Grim leads to Gunnar's adversary Otkel. Another leads to the family of Gudrun Osvifsdottir, the heroine of *Laxdæla saga*; another leads to the heroes of *Droplaugarsona saga* and related sagas set in the Eastfjords; and yet another leads to characters in *Gísla saga Súrssonar*. *Áns saga bogsveigis* makes An Bow-Bender an ancestor of characters in *Njáls saga*, *Víga-Glúms saga*, and *Vatnsdæla saga*, whereas *Landnámabók* and *Gísla saga Súrssonar* add another Icelandic lineage descended from An Bow-Bender by way of his grandson An Redcloak,[8] and *Bárðar saga Snæfellsáss* adds yet another, by way of An's great-granddaughter Eygerð who married Thorkel Bound-Foot.

All the *fornaldarsögur*, and indeed virtually all the sagas, include some genealogical material.[9] Even those that don't spell out a specific genealogy almost always begin with a generation or two of the hero's ancestors, or else end with statements that the hero and his hard-won bride had children, or at least the hero's companions and their brides had children, and "a great family is descended from them". In many of the *fornaldarsögur*, the ancestors and descendants of the heroes are legendary heroes themselves, sometimes with *fornaldarsögur* of their own, but with no connection to historic Icelanders. The *Hrafnistusögur* are linked with other *fornaldarsögur* through genealogy—*Gríms saga*, for instance, connects its protagonist's friend Ingjald to characters in *Egils saga einhenda*—but the number of genealogical ties to the first generation of Icelanders is noteworthy among the *fornaldarsögur*.

Why should the sagas reflect such an interest in genealogy? Uniquely in medieval Europe, Iceland had no native nobility and no kings. In fact, many of the early settlers allegedly settled Iceland because they were trying to get away from grasping and tyrannical kings. Given that medieval history dealt with the deeds of nobles and kings, Iceland had no history that medieval scholars would have considered worthwhile.[10] The problem became acute after 1262, when Iceland submitted to the Norwegian king; Icelanders must have worried that their lack of indigenous nobility would leave them at the bottom of the new social hierarchy, potentially politically powerless in the kingdom.[11] A well-known passage in one version of *Landnámabók*—a late recension, but probably copied from a very early one—makes the problem clear:

> Þat er margra manna mál, at þat sé óskyldr fróðleikr at rita landnám. En vér þykjumsk heldr svara kunna útlendum mönnum, þá er þeir bregða oss því, at vér séim komnir af þrælum eða illmennum, ef vér vitum víst várar kynferðir sannar, svá ok þeim mönnum, er vita vilja forn fræði eða rekja ættartölur, at taka heldr at upphafi til en höggvask í mitt mál, enda eru svá allar vitrar þjóðir, at vita vilja upphaf sinna landsbyggða eða hversu hvergi til hefjask eða kynslóðir.

People often say that writing about the Settlements is irrelevant learning, but we think we can better meet the criticism of foreigners when they accuse us of being descended from slaves or scoundrels, if we know for certain the truth about our ancestry. And for those who want to know ancient lore and how to trace genealogies, it's better to start at the beginning than to come in at the middle. Anyway, all civilized nations want to know about the origins of their own society and the beginnings of their own race.[12]

The accusation that Icelanders were all descended from "slaves or scoundrels" must have stung.

This is probably why genealogies were among the first texts to be written down in Iceland, beginning in the mid-twelfth century;[13] and why Saxo Grammaticus, writing around the year 1185, praised the Icelanders' zeal to preserve ancient lore, not just their own but that of all Scandinavia and even farther afield.[14] Genealogies and biographies could validate Iceland's identity as a worthy nation by showing Icelanders' connections to well-born families, even to the Scandinavian royal houses. Within Iceland, genealogies could also support leading men's and leading families' claims to high status.[15] Furthermore, genealogies determined a person's legal and social obligations, range of permissible spouses, and right to inherit property.[16] This interest in genealogy lasted long: a shorter recension of *Áns saga bogsveigis* notes at the very end that "There are still some men in Iceland, in the year 1683, who reckon their descent from the Men of Hrafnista."[17] Even in the twentieth century, at least one published Icelandic local history included genealogies that linked the *Hrafnistumenn* to modern families.[18]

An often-quoted passage in *Þorgils saga ok Hafliða*, one of the sagas in the great compilation known as *Sturlunga saga*, describes an Icelandic wedding feast in the year 1119, at which part of the entertainment includes *sagnaskemmtun*, "saga-entertainment."

> *Hrólfr af Skálmarnesi sagði sögu frá Hröngviði víkingi ok frá Óláfi liðsmannakonungi ok haugbroti Þráins berserks ok Hrómundi Gripssyni, ok margar vísur með. En þessarri sögu var skemt Sverri konungi, ok kallaði hann slíkar lygisögur skemtiligastar. Ok þó kunnu menn at telja ættir sínar til Hrómundar Gripssonar. Þessa sögu hafði Hrólfr sjálfr samansetta.*

Hrolf of Skalmarnes told a saga about Hrongvid the Viking and about Olaf King of Warriors, and the breaking into Thrain's burial mound, and Hromund Gripsson, and many verses along with it. King Sverri was amused by this saga, and he called such "lying sagas" the most entertaining. And yet men are able to reckon their ancestry from Hromund Gripsson. Hrolf himself had put this saga together.[19]

A version of this story, although not the one that Hrolf would have told, is still extant,[20] with the same fantastic escapades that are alluded to here—and it mentions that the protagonist Hromund Gripsson had kings and heroes as descendants. *Landnámabók* adds that prominent settlers in Iceland were descended from Hromund Gripsson.[21] While some listeners might be skeptical of the entertaining but fanciful legendary sagas, Icelanders evidently trusted at least some of them as evidence for the worthiness of their own ancestors. In fact, prominent Icelanders who wanted to demonstrate the worth of their ancestry were probably the ones who composed or sponsored the composition of *fornaldarsögur*, especially those that told about their own ancestors; to give just one example, the prominent Icelander Haukr Erlendsson claimed descent from many of the *fornaldarsögur* heroes (including the Men of Hrafnista) and traced several of these connections in the sagas and histories collected in *Hauksbók*, a manuscript that he wrote or had written between 1302 and 1310.[22] In addition, sagas that told of the history of a region of Iceland, and of the heroic settlers in that region, could be used to boost feelings of solidarity, consensus, and common cause among the region's people—which made them useful for chieftains trying to consolidate their power in the turbulent society of 13th–century Iceland.[23]

Many Icelandic genealogies go out of their way to trace family connections with the kings of Scandinavia.[24] Some trace families back to heathen gods such as Odin. With increased contact with continental Europe, the old gods were generally euhemerized but allowed to stay in the genealogies, which were extended farther back to the heroes of Troy, and ultimately to the Old Testament patriarchs and to Adam himself. However, Vésteinn Ólason points out that the heroes of *Ketils saga* and *Gríms saga* are free and prosperous farmers, but they have no pretensions to nobility and do not try to win a kingdom of their own. (Much the same could be said of *Áns saga*.) In the social relations that they depict, the *Hrafnistusögur* are close to the classic *Íslendingasögur*: some characters may be more prosperous and powerful than the rest, but all depend on the land and sea for their living, and all may suffer when famine comes. This contrasts with many of the later *fornaldarsögur*, in which the hero is usually of royal birth, overcomes fantastic challenges such as dragons, ogres, and sorcery instead of mundane ones such as famine, and ends up with his own kingdom to rule and a king's lovely daughter to marry.[25]

The Immanent Saga

There has been a long debate over whether the sagas should be regarded as primarily oral stories, shaped by oral transmission and transcribed more or less directly, or as primarily literary compositions, created by authors who were working with ink and parchment. Closely connected with this debate is the question of foreign influences on the sagas: just how much do the sagas owe to Christian texts, Latin learning, and translations of foreign romances, fabliaux, and other continental texts? It is beyond the scope of this essay to summarize the debate here,[26] but a consensus seems to be growing that the Icelandic sagas originated through a complex mixture of both oral and written transmission. As one scholar has summarized the situation: "the sagas may be viewed as a happy synthesis of scholastic learning acquired from books and a purely domestic artistic tradition of oral storytelling. . . The picture that seems to emerge is one of a strong, domestic oral narrative tradition coming into contact with historiographical works from abroad and flourishing by way of attempts to reproduce the methods used in them."[27]

In a seminal paper, Carol Clover presented a very plausible model that resolves the oral-written dichotomy. She noted that in cultures with a strong oral tradition, a storyteller may know many tales about a hero, but may never tell the tales in any sort of chronological order, instead choosing whichever ones suit the occasion. European scholars have tended to create written "epics" out of such short tales, either by editing written transcripts into a whole, or by asking storytellers to tell all their stories in order—a request that the storyteller may find strange and unnatural.[28] Clover calls such compositions "immanent epics": before being recorded in writing, they did not exist as formal compositions, but as a set of episodes which were all familiar to the audience, from which a storyteller could pick and choose his material. She suggests that a similar model of the "immanent saga" is the best model of saga origins. Those who wrote down the earliest versions of the sagas must have drawn on shorter tales and episodes that had been passed down orally.[29] The usual phrase for "to write a saga" is *saman setja*, "to set together"; this would well describe what the saga authors did, "setting together" selected tales, arranging them in a logical order, and reconciling (or sometimes failing to reconcile) contradictions.

The "immanent saga" model applies very well to the Hrafnista cycle, whose earliest "stratum" would have been oral stories brought to Iceland by settlers. While the question of whether the "historical Ketil Salmon" ever existed is probably unanswerable, there is no reason to doubt that some of the settlers of Iceland were descended from a family that had lived for generations on Hrafnista. Like immigrants anywhere, these settlers would have brought family stories, which would have been told and retold for a few centuries—not an improbable thing in Iceland, where even today it is not unusual for people to remember their family histories back for four or more generations. As the stories were told, they would change with every telling and every teller. No two people would know exactly the same stories or tell them in quite the same way.[30] As Gísli Sigurðsson has concluded, it is a common misconception that oral tradition maintains information accurately for centuries, or that it can be considered historically true—but it is also a misconception that oral stories cannot survive for two or three hundred years, or preserve any genuine knowledge about the past.[31]

While the word "stories" is used, some of these oral narratives were probably poems. Because Norse poetry followed strict rules of composition, and because much of it was transmitted in a social setting that highly valued accurate knowledge of rulers' deeds and lives, it has often been assumed to be more resistant to corruption during oral transmission than prose.[32] Authors like Snorri Sturluson drew on old poems (*fornkvæði*) and narrative lays (*söguljóð*) in writing their histories, as well as genealogies (*langfeðgatali*), using orally transmitted stories of known provenance to expand on them and clarify the poems' obscure meanings.[33] There is no reason why the Hrafnista material could not have been transmitted in the same fashion; Arrow-Odd's autobiographical verses in the drinking contest in chapter 27, for example, were probably transmitted orally.[34] Sagas themselves may have evolved from poems that picked up accompanying prose sections to retell or explicate them, forming a mixed composition called a prosimetrum.[35]

Evidence for this model of oral transmission of the "immanent saga", whether as prose stories, poems, or a mixture of both, comes from the fluid nature of various episodes in the Hrafnista sagas. Actions in the sagas may be attributed to two or more different people. This is probably why both *Ketils saga* and *Áns saga* begin with a surly young hero, who gives his mother a fine chair because she loves him more than his father does. This may also be the reason why *Gríms saga* and *Ketils saga* both feature a father who is forced to fight a duel with his daughter's rejected suitor, and why both *Ketils saga* and *Örvar-Odds saga* have the hero befriend a pair of warriors named Hjálmr/Hjálmarr and Stafnglámr ("Prow-Glamour"). The repetition of poetic lines in formulaic fashion may also indicate oral transmission, such as *tírarlausa / tólf berserki* ([I have killed] twelve berserks who had no honor), which appears in poems in both *Gríms saga* and *Örvar-Odds saga*.

More evidence for this model comes from looking for Hrafnista saga material in other texts. One example is the use of "Hjalmar's Death Song" in both *Örvar-Odds saga* and *Hervarar saga*[36]; both sagas describe the same battle and include substantially the same poem, but the versions exhibit enough differences to suggest that they are independent recordings of a memorized and orally transmitted poem, which must have been accompanied by enough prose to explain otherwise obscure references in the poem.[37] Some of the same formulaic phrases in "Hjálmar's Death Song" appear in other legendary "death-songs", which seem to have been a well-known poetic genre.[38] Discussing another instance of probable borrowing, Helen Leslie mentions Dragvendill, "the best of swords," which Ketil Salmon takes from his slain enemy Gusir; he passes it to his son Grim, but then it seemingly disappears. In *Egils saga*, however, the sword reappears when Egil Skallagrimsson receives it as a gift. We find out that *þat sverð hafði átt Ketill hængr ok haft í hólmgöngum, ok var þat allra sverða bitrast*—"Ketil Salmon had owned that sword and had it in duels, and it was the sharpest of all swords." This almost certainly refers to Ketil's duel with Framar at the end of *Ketils saga*, at the end of which Framar admits that *hvass er Dragvendill*, "Dragvendil is sharp." The passage suggests that the author of *Egils saga* knew the story of Ketil's duel, which must have been familiar enough to the saga writer and his audience that it did not need to be told in full.[39] Finally, skaldic kennings allude to events in the Hrafnista cycle: Snorri Sturluson records *Jólfs smiði*,

Introduction

"Jolf's handiwork" and *Gusis smíði*, "Gusir's handiwork" as kennings for arrows; Jolf's arrows appear in *Örvar-Odds saga*, and Gusir's arrows in the first three sagas in the cycle.[40] Snorri also cites *Gusis nautar*, "Gusir's Gifts", in a verse attributed to the skald Refr, who seems to have lived in the early 11th century;[41] thus at least that Hrafnista motif was known in the oral poetic tradition by that time.

Hrafnista tales and motifs may appear with different protagonists in "sagas of Icelanders", especially those that tell about the Icelandic descendants of the *Hrafnistumenn*. In *Vatnsdæla saga*, Ketil Raum marries Án Bow-Bender's daughter and has a son by her, whom he accuses of lazing around by the fire and refusing to get up and better himself—sounding rather like Ketil Salmon's father Hallbjorn.[42] Later in the same saga, Án Bow-Bender's great-grandson Ingimund is unwilling to hear the prophecies of a visiting seeress, but she speaks them anyway, and they come true—the same happens to Örvar-Odd, Ingimund's half-cousin four times removed. The hero of *Orms þáttr Stórólfssonar*, Ketil Salmon's great-great-great-grandson, is also a *kólbitr*, an unpromising lad who sits by the fire all the time, like his ancestor. Like both Ketil and Án Bow-Bender, Orm receives little love from his father in childhood, but is loved by his mother. Like Ketil Salmon, Orm first shows his real strength at the age of twelve with a great feat of harvesting hay, and when his father provokes him to exert himself, he forgets himself and injures his father as he shows his strength. Later in the tale, Orm's friend Asmund doubts the prophecies of yet another visiting seeress, who warns that he will die if he ever sets foot on or beyond North Moer in Norway—the parallel with *Örvar-Odds saga* is clear. *Egils saga* features an older brother, Thorolf, a valued retainer of King Eirek Bloodaxe, and his younger brother Egil, who is antisocial and ugly. Thorolf refuses Egil's request to go abroad with him, because he fears that his brother will be quite unmanageable. Eventually, Thorolf runs afoul of the king's treachery. This is a fairly close parallel with the main plot of *Áns saga*, with An and his brother Thorir Thane taking the roles of Egil and his brother Thorolf.[43] *Egils saga* and *Áns saga* also feature pairs of brothers who are both named Úlfr (wolf), whom the hero kills.[44] Again, the outline of a story may have been widely remembered as part of the "immanent saga," but different tellers may have attributed it to different members of the extended Hrafnista family.

References to the Hrafnista "immanent saga" can even be found outside the sagas themselves. In his *Danish History*, Saxo Grammaticus refers to Ano Sagittarius (An the Archer). His life story is quite different from *Áns saga bogsveigis*—he is not an outlaw and not a farmer, but a loyal retainer of a king—but he does commit a great feat of archery by shooting his enemy's bow without hitting the man himself, as in An's encounter with Thorir in *Áns saga bogsveigis*.[45] Saxo also refers to Arvarodd and his companion Hialmer, who battle twelve enemies on the island of Samsey[46]—an event also alluded to in the Eddic poem *Hyndluljóð*,[47] as well as in *Hervarar saga* as discussed above. Elsewhere, he lists Odd as fighting on King Sigurd Hring's side in the legendary Battle of Brávellir, an event not depicted in *Örvar-Odds saga* itself, but briefly mentioned in Odd's death-song, in *Gríms saga*, and in the fragment *Sögubrot*. These references show that at least some of the episodes that ended up in the *Hrafnistasögur* were extant before 1200, since Saxo is thought to have begun writing *Gesta Danorum* in 1185. Saxo names an Icelander, Arnoldus Tyliensis, who told stories and tales at the Danish court around 1167, and comparisons of extant legendary sagas with Saxo's *History* shows that at least some of his sources were poems or prosimetra.[48] At least some parts of the "immanent saga" of the Men of Hrafnista existed by that time.

Even more indirect evidence of this model may come from the preface to Oddr Snorrason's saga about King Olaf Tryggvason, originally written in the late 12th century. Oddr tells his audience that listening to sagas about Christian kings is better entertainment than "stepmother tales told by shepherd boys, in which one never knows whether there is truth because they always count the king least in their stories." In other words, there were oral stories circulating at the time, not necessarily only among shepherds and step-mothers but evidently not in the social circles that Oddr approved of, which failed to exalt kings properly.[49] Given that *Ketils saga* and *Gríms saga* don't mention kings at all, and that *Áns saga* puts them in a rather bad light, it's not impossible that oral stories about these ancestors were part of the "step-mothers' saga" repertoire.

Ohthere and the Hrafnista Sagas

Introduction

A final piece of evidence for the "immanent saga" model comes from details in the sagas that can be checked against contemporary sources. A number of sagas, including some that seem rather fantastic, can be shown to contain a core of information that has been corroborated by archaeology and independent written texts. If the saga was written down centuries after the events that it describes, the inescapable conclusion is that factual information, perhaps distorted and fragmented but still recognizable, must have been transmitted through oral traditions.[50]

By great good fortune, there is an independent text describing life in northern Norway in the late 9th century, during the early settlement period of Iceland and thus just a few decades after the time frame of the Hrafnista sagas. This is the Old English account of Ohthere, a Norwegian from Halogaland who gave an account of his life and travels to King Alfred the Great, around the year 890. This account was incorporated into a translation of Orosius's *Adversus paganos historiarum libri septem* (*Seven Books of History Against the Pagans*).[51] Although the version we have may have been edited somewhat, almost all scholars agree that the text is fundamentally accurate, at the very least "a remarkably good paraphrase of what a ninth-century Norwegian might have said."[52] My translation of Ohthere's account is included as an appendix to this book.

Ohthere calls himself the northernmost of all Norwegians. This would put him somewhere near the modern city of Tromsø—well over 400 miles (660 km) north of Hrafnista, as the raven flies. Still, Ohthere's life is clearly similar to life on Hrafnista: there is some agriculture (hay harvesting in *Ketils saga hængs*, a small amount of cultivation and livestock husbandry for Ohthere), but fishing, hunting, and/or whaling are more important.[54] Trade with both the south and the north is also critical: Ohthere sails from Hálogaland to the trading towns of *Sciringesheal* in south Norway and Hedeby in Denmark, and Grim and Odd sail the same coastal route to Berurjod and the Oslofjord. The archaeological record largely confirms this overall picture: grain and livestock were raised along the Norwegian coast, before and during the Viking Age, but bad years were fairly common and famine was a constant risk. Despite its own dangers, the sea was a far more reliable source of both food and trade goods—especially in the codfish spawning grounds along the coast from Troms to Møre, which included Hrafnista.[55] Minus the dragons and giants and such, the Hrafnista sagas seem to preserve accurate information on daily life and economics in coastal northern Norway.

Ohthere describes *Finnas*—not Finns, but nomadic Saami—in far northern Scandinavia, mentioning that *on feawum stowum styccemælum wiciað Finnas*, "Finns camp at a few scattered places." Ohthere also mentions *Beormas*, living on the shores of the White Sea, who *heafdon wel gebud hira land*, "had settled their land well", in contrast to the Finns' temporary camps. The account of the voyage to Bjarmaland in *Örvar-Odds saga*—minus the giants and monsters, again—is consistent with this picture: Odd and his kin find a Saami encampment of *gammar*, a word specifically meaning Saami-style huts or tents, en route to an encounter with the much more settled *Bjarmar* who have built halls. Ohthere's *Beormas* and the *Bjarmar* of *Örvar-Odds saga* are probably Karelians[56]; the name may come from a Finnish dialect word, *permi*, meaning a class of Karelian traveling merchants, or possibly from Finnish *perämäa*, "backwoods."[57]

Norse voyages to Bjarmaland were rare events, and people who made them were a rare breed—Arrow-Odd is referred to several times in his saga as "the Odd who went to Bjarmaland", suggesting that this voyage had made him famous far and wide. What made them possible at all were an extension of the Gulf Stream called the North Atlantic Drift which kept the route mostly ice-free, favorable winds from the tracks of Atlantic low-pressure systems, and strong spring currents out of the White Sea to give returning sailors a boost.[58] A number of Bjarmaland trips are recorded in various historical sources;[59] *Heimskringla*, for example, mentions Eirik Bloodaxe sailing to Finnmark and then Bjarmaland around the year 920,[60] Harald Greycloak's raid up the *Vína* (the Dvina River) around the year 970,[61] and Hakon Magnusson's victory in Bjarmaland around the year 1090.[62] In the most detailed account of a voyage to Bjarmaland, taking place around the year 1025, the leaders sail around Finnmark to *Gandvík* (the White Sea) and up the Dvina River to a market town. Here, they trade with the Bjarmians under a truce, but then plunder a burial mound and sacred site, escaping the angry Bjarmians and sailing home by the same route they came.[63] The details of the Bjarmaland expedition in *Örvar-Odds saga* could be based on the account in *Óláfs saga helga* or on other written accounts, but there is no reason why an expedition from Hrafnista could not have sailed all the way there and back, as Ohthere did. *Ketils saga* and *Gríms saga* feature voyages far along the northern coast of Norway, and Grím is said to have sailed as far as the White Sea; again, there is nothing improbable about this.

Ohthere further mentions that he himself maintains a herd of reindeer, and that he accepts tribute from the local Saami, mostly in the form of pelts and skins. Multiple sources confirm these relations between the Norse and the Saami. The Latin *Historia Norvegiae* notes that the Norse of Hålogaland "often live together with the Lapps and have frequent commerce with them."[64] *Óláfs saga Tryggvasonar* mentions Raud the Strong, a wealthy Hålogalander with a great number of Saami retainers who "followed him whenever he needed them".[65] *Egils saga Skallagrímssonar* describes additional trade, military, and tributary relations among Norwegians, Saami, and a probable Finnic-speaking people called the *Kvenir* (the *Cwenas* of Ohthere's account).[66] Norse legal codes, references in poetry, borrowed words in both languages, and further references in sagas and annals also mention the Saami and show familiarity with many aspects of their culture and daily life.[67] Modern Saami populations have genetic markers that show past interbreeding with the Norse,[68] archaeological finds of Norse coins in Saami areas attest to trade,[69] and medieval Saami burials show the influence of Norse customs.[70] In short, there is abundant independent evidence that the Norse and Saami in Hålogaland not only raided and traded, but adopted each other's folkways, and sometimes intermarried.

The Hrafnista sagas portray both hostilities and alliances between Norsemen and Saami, of much the same kinds as have been mentioned. Ketil Salmon's alliance with Bruni and killing of Bruni's rival Gusir, and his dalliance with Bruni's daughter Hrafnhild, could well have some historical basis; similar events did happen everywhere Norse and Saami came into contact. Mundal has suggested that the Saami had a custom of offering transient sexual relationships to male visitors;[71] if true, this would be reflected in Ketil's relationship with Hrafnhild. Hrafnhild herself is said to have a nose an ell across, and the Saami who claim Ketil's supply of butter are *eigi mjóleitir*, "not narrow-faced"—to this day, Saami are stereotyped as having broad faces and flat noses.[72] Nothing in *Ketils saga* would rule out identifying Hrafnhild as a Saami girl, and such intertribal relationships must have been fairly common. *Örvar-Odds saga* depicts the far north primarily as a region to plunder; the saga's "center" is in southern Scandinavia.[73] Yet Odd holds his men back from pillaging the Saami encampment, and he is the one who orders his men to give up their plunder from the Saami when a magical storm threatens them; unlike his kinsmen, Odd seems to be conscious of his family relationship with the Saami, or at least of the need to treat them humanely on a voyage that is quite dangerous enough without making enemies of them. With no family ties to the Bjarmians, Odd has no compunctions against stealing as much wealth from them as he can.

Growth of a Saga Cycle

As stories in an "immanent saga" are told and retold, they don't stay static. Every teller is free to shape his stories as he chooses, sometimes adding or deleting entire episodes. A teller may reshape his stories according to his own tastes and judgement, or to fit the pre-existing knowledge of the audience. A teller may turn a story into a comment on social, moral, or political concerns. Finally, oral tradition itself tends to determine what events count as "newsworthy" or are "tellable" as stories, and how they are to be told, even in the telling of very recent events. Thus stories are quickly shaped to fit molds that are familiar within the culture that tells them, and stories in a cultural area quickly take on elements from a common stock of motifs, themes, and set verbal formulas.[74]

In 1910, Friedrich Panzer collated over two hundred versions of a folktale generally known as "The Bear's Son", and argued that both Beowulf's fight with Grendel in the Old English epic *Beowulf*, and Grettir's fight with trolls at Sandhaugar in the Icelandic *Grettis saga*, were independent versions of the "Bear's Son" tale, with all three going back to a common ancestor. The entire "Bear's Son" tale is rather complex, but the parts of it that are paralleled in *Beowulf* and *Grettis saga* go as follows: The hero fights a supernatural enemy, who is forced to flee (sometimes losing a body part). The hero tracks the enemy to his underworld lair and enters the lair, often by lowering himself on a rope. He beheads his enemy, and in some cases a related female enemy as well, sometimes with a magic sword that he finds in the lair. He may then free a princess or princesses who have been held captive, and usually claims a hoard of treasure from the lair; unfortunately, his companions leave him in the underworld, either from fear or an unwillingness to share the princesses and treasures.

Whether Panzer's conclusions can really be justified from the evidence is controversial, and skeptical critics have found the similarities between *Beowulf*, the *Grettis saga* episode, and the "Bear's Son" folktales unconvincing and vague.[75] Supporters of the "Bear's Son" hypothesis have found a large number of additional sagas and tales that seem to parallel the basic tale, but it is at best unclear whether these parallels result from direct descent from an ancestral "old legend", or whether these simply derive from the use and reuse of a common stock of episodes and motifs.[76] Nonetheless, episodes in *Ketils saga*, *Gríms saga*, and *Örvar-Odds saga* have been claimed to fit the core of the "Bear's Son" pattern fairly closely.[77] In *Ketils saga* the "Bear's Son" section consists of the first two chapters, beginning with Ketil's unpromising childhood, and continuing through his visit to Vitadsgjafi and his fight with the giant Kaldrani (though not including his earlier visit to Midfjord and his fight with the giant Surt). In *Gríms saga*, the "Bear's Son" section would be Grim's encounter with the giantesses Kleima and Feima and their parents. Various "Bear's Son" elements appear in *Örvar-Odds saga*, although not in a unified narrative.[78]

McKinnell suggested that most of the "Bear's Son" narratives follow the basic pattern of the myths of the god Thor fighting giants and giantesses. This pattern may be summarized thus: a strong hero goes off with his companions to fight a giant; he is badly received and attacked by at least one giantess and one giant who are related to each other; and he fights them using at least some wrestling and kills them, while his companions make no useful contribution. The sagas include many variants of this schema, of which the "Bear's Son" is but one. In the "Thor pattern" proper, the hero or his associate is tricked into taking his journey; the hero is usually helped by a friendly giantess; the hero must cross a dangerous river that serves as a boundary between two worlds; the fights take place in a cave; and the hero fights by wrestling or using primitive weapons.[79] The paradigmatic version of this is the myth of Thor's visit to the giant Geirrod. The first two chapters of *Gríms saga* fit the pattern, although the order of events has shifted: in Thor's visit to Geirrod, the friendly giantess appears before the battle with the hostile giants, whereas in the saga the helpful giantess (who turns out to be Grim's abducted bride and not a giantess at all) appears after the giant fight.

Ketils saga hængs, on the other hand, fits McKinnell's "Odinnic mythic pattern", and so does the Hildir episode in *Örvar-Odds saga*. Both heroes are rescued by a friendly giant, spend the winter in the giant's household, enter a sexual relationship with the giant's daughter, and leave in the spring with a valuable reward from the giant, abandoning the giantess and later making a "conventional" marriage. The heros' children by the giantesses are sons who become mighty men but have tense encounters with their fathers when they find them; in most stories of this type, although not in *Ketils saga*, the son comes to a disastrous end and leaves no descendants.[80] The heroes of such stories are often said to be protegés of Odin, or else they are "reversed" and made into outright opponents of Odin. Ketil explicitly disavows any trust in Odin, while Odd is more ambiguous, refusing to sacrifice and expressing disbelief in the gods, but also accepting partnership with Red Grani, who suspected of being Odin in disguise. Odd's three-hundred year lifespan is also reminiscent of the very Odinnic hero Starkad the Old, who was given a lifespan three times as long as an ordinary man's.[81] McKinnell doesn't mention *Áns saga*, but the story of Án's affair with the farmer's daughter Drifa, and his later encounter with his son Thorir, fit this pattern in many ways. Drifa, though apparently human, has a giantish name;[82] Án abandons her in the spring and seemingly suffers no consequences; and he has a tense encounter with his son before they learn each others' identities. In *Örvar-Odds saga* and in others of this type, the son meets a disastrous fate; in *Áns saga* this fate may have been transferred to Án's close kinsman and follower Grim.

There are still other traditional motifs and schemas that shape the narrative of the Hrafnista sagas. *Gríms saga* closely follows another well-known folktale schema, the "Loathly Lady", in which the hero is required to embrace a hideous old woman, only to discover later that she has become beautiful.[83] The story of the death of Örvar-Odd appears again in the *Russian Primary Chronicle*, in which Oleg the prince of Kiev is said to have heard a prophecy that his favorite horse would cause his death. Oleg has his horse cared for but refuses to ever see it again; nonetheless, after his horse is dead, he himself dies when a snake crawls from the horse's skull and bites his foot.[84]

Introduction

These folktale motifs, like the dimly remembered historical events at the core of the "immanent saga", also tended to disperse along genealogical lines. This can lead to duplication of folk motifs: *Áns saga*, for example, includes a set of magic arrows that is not the same as Gusir's Gifts, the magic arrows in the other three sagas. The hero of *Orms þáttr Stórólfssonar* wrestles with a trollish enemy and rips off much of his face, like his kinsman Örvar-Odd fighting with Ogmund.[85] In another episode of this tale, Orm uses a bow and three arrows against a troll, but the arrows are useless, like Örvar-Odd fighting Alf Plank. To give yet another example, *Ketils saga* and *Grettis saga* share a large number of motifs—both heroes are of giantish descent, unpromising as youths and in conflict with their fathers, uncommonly strong, and both slayers and befrienders of giants—and Grettir the Strong is a distant descendant of Ketil Salmon.[86] Folktale motifs are not necessarily restricted to genealogical lines; the "Loathly Lady," for example, appears in *Þorsteins saga Víkingssonar*, *Hrólfs saga kraka*, and *Illuga saga Gríðarfóstra*, which are not otherwise connected with the Hrafnista sagas. Nonetheless, as Joaquín Pizarro writes, "genealogical connections have been regular conduits of thematic and structural influence between sagas."[87]

Writing the Sagas

Eventually, someone has to be the first to write down the stories. Once the saga exists primarily as a written text, pieces of other texts may become embedded in the saga. As they are copied and recopied, sagas might accrete several layers of textual additions, and here it finally becomes possible to trace the history of the saga by comparing various recensions. This is directly alluded to in the postscript to the legendary *Yngvars saga víðförla*, whose author states that he has written the saga based on accounts in the books of the monk Oddr the Wise, who had assembled it from the most noteworthy features of three different orally transmitted accounts; the author invites those with better knowledge to "add what they feel is lacking." This method of saga composition and revision seems to be a fundamentally accurate description of how the Hrafnista sagas reached the forms in which we now have them.

Scholars who see the sagas as primarily creations of authors tend to assume that any significant case of shared characters, incidents, or wording between sagas (*rittengsl*) must have resulted from copying from one manuscript to another. But such *rittengsl* could just as easily result from shared oral traditions—especially in a society where vellum manuscripts were rare and expensive, and where few if any authors had the luxury of piling up books at their elbows to consult and copy as they wrote.[88] All the same, saga authors may have heard various books being read, or may have learned passages by heart, and thus incorporated them into their writing even if copies of the books were not available to consult.

Jónas Kristjánsson has suggested that a literary relationship between sagas can only be postulated with confidence when two sagas share more than one piece of subject matter, in more or less the same order, using the same wording.[89] There are some examples of this in the Hrafnista cycle; to give perhaps the most clear-cut example, *Gríms saga* contains a passage that is very close to a passage in the legendary saga *Hálfdanar saga Brönufóstra*. In both, the hero must approach a giants' cave via an *einstigi*, a path wide enough for only one person. The path has steps or tracks (*spor*) that are too high for human legs; to climb the path, the hero must hook (*krækja*) his axe onto each step and pull himself up by the handle (*las sik svá eptir skaftinu*). In the end, the hero enters a cave with a bright fire and sees a pair of giants, male and female; he decapitates the male giant but is forced to wrestle the female until he can finally decapitate her. While these motifs are fairly widespread among legendary sagas, *Gríms saga* and *Hálfdanar saga* share not only a common sequence of events, but identical words and phrases, which suggests that in this case we may have a borrowing between written texts.

Borrowing among written texts probably accounts for the verbal similarities between *Ketils saga* and *Gríms saga*, in which both heroes attack a giant with an axe and find that *varð laus öxin. . . ok stöð hún föst í sárinu*, "the axe got loose. . . and it stuck fast in the wound."[90] *Áns saga* shows verbal influence from *Hervarar saga*; the scene in which An encounters a dwarf and forces him to make him some magic arrows has close verbal parallels with the scene in which Svafrlami forces two dwarves to forge the sword Tyrfing.[91]

Áns saga may share verbal borrowings with *Grettis saga* and *Orms þáttr Stórólfssonar*. In all three of these, the hero is not a tyical *kolbítr*, but loved by his mother much more than his father. *Áns saga* says that *Lítit ástríki hafði hann af feðr sínum, en móðir hans unni honum mikit. . . . ekki lagðist*

Án í eldaskála (He had little love from his father, but his mother loved him much. . . . Án didn't lie in the hearth-house.) *Grettis saga* has nearly identical wording: *Ekki hafði hann ástríki mikið af Ásmundi föður sínum en móðir hans unni honum mikið. . . . ekki lagðist hann í eldaskála;*[92] and *Orms þáttr* has *Ekki hafði hann ástríki mikið af föður sínum. . . en móðir hans unni honum mikið. Ekki lagðist Ormr í eldaskála.*[93] Since *Grettis saga* and *Orms þáttr* are genealogically linked with the Hrafnista sagas, it's not clear in this case whether we have direct verbal borrowings among written texts, or more traces of an oral genealogical tradition that just happened to be expressed with similar stock phrases.

The saga that shows the most obvious evidence of written composition is *Örvar-Odds saga*, which still exists in several recensions. The oldest and shortest surviving version (S) includes Odd's childhood, the seeress's prophecy, and various later Viking adventures, culminating in his career as Barkman, his marriage to Silkisif and assumption of the throne, and finally his fated death. S lacks Odd's stay with the giant Hildir, and it includes only the first of Odd's encounters with Ogmund Eythjof's Bane. Recension A, which is the one translated here, includes these added episodes.

The longer version of *Örvar-Odds saga* shows considerable evidence of borrowing from learned medieval texts, although it is not always possible to say whether or not this resulted from direct copying. The saga includes lists of Baltic countries and Russian regions that closely parallel lists in the manuscript *Hauksbók*. Written between 1302 and 1310, *Hauksbók* itself was probably not a direct source for the interpolations into *Örvar-Odds saga*, but is close to the direct source. Other geographical references seem to derive from the *Leiðarvísir* (*Itinerary*) of Abbot Nikulás, a guidebook to the main pilgrimage route from Scandinavia to Jerusalem. References to the tiger and the unicorn seem to come from other medieval encyclopedic sources; the precise source is uncertain, but it might be *Stjórn*, an Old Testament paraphrase and commentary which mentions the tiger, unicorn, and other marvellous beasts of the East.[94] Odd's explanation of thunder in chapter 5 resembles that found in the Norwegian dialog *Konungs skuggsjá*, although the wording of the two accounts are different enough that there has probably been no direct copying. Finally, the sea-monsters in chapter 21 both appear to have been borrowed from medieval bestiaries' description of the *aspidochelone*, a huge whale which drowns sailors who mistake it for an island, and which feeds by opening its jaws and exuding a scent that attracts fishes. One of the oldest surviving Icelandic manuscripts, from the mid-12th century, depicts the monster twice, once covered in vegetation and once attracting fishes to its jaws. In this saga, it looks as though these two aspects of the *aspidochelone* have given rise to two separate monsters, the *hafgufa* or "sea-steam" and *lyngbakr* or "heather-back". (Halldór Hermannson, *Icelandic Physiologus*, pp. 10-11, 19)

Aside from direct evidence of literary borrowings, a case can be made for more general influences on *Örvar-Odds saga* from other written texts, in particular from the genre of saints' lives. Odd is hardly a typical saint, and yet even before his conversion he is depicted as a "noble pagan": he refuses to sacrifice to the pagan gods, plunders pagan holy sites in Bjarmaland, and embraces the "Viking honor code" of his ally Hjalmar.[95] After Odd converts to Christianity, he makes a pilgrimage to the Holy Land,[96] rises through the ranks at the court of King Herraud, crusades against the heathen kingdom of Bjalkaland (located in the vicinity of Antioch, of all places) and ends up a king in his own right. Many of these elements, as well as similar narrative arcs in general, can be found in saints' lives, which were quite popular in medieval Iceland and which influenced the saga form considerably.[97]

Ethnography of Halogaland: Saami, Bjarmians, and Giants

The worldview expressed in the Icelandic sagas is often described as distinguishing between "center"—the inhabited lands where people speak Norse and live under a common code of law—and the wild, strange, and lawless "periphery". The same conceptual model appears at different scales: the center and periphery may be a farm and the surrounding unclaimed lands, a settlement and the mountains beyond, Norse-speaking Scandinavia and the strange countries surrounding it, or even the realm of the gods and the realm of the giants in mythology.[98] In this view, center and periphery have a complex relationship. Although each may seem hostile to the other, each needs things that the other has. Thus the boundary between them must be guarded but not impermeable: exchange must happen across it. In the mythology, for example, the gods inhabit the center, surrounded by the giants of Jötunheimr on the periphery. Yet the gods need giants—they take giants as wives and concubines, they make use of giants' services, and they take items such as the mead of poetry from the giants' realm. Giants may threaten the gods, giants may be slaughtered wholesale, and yet female giants may become gods' lovers—or even, like the goddess Skadi, become adopted into the family of gods.

The ethnographic evidence points to a similarly complex and ambivalent relationship between Norsemen and Saami in the Middle Ages. As we have seen, there is abundant evidence for close interactions and mutual influence between the Norse and Saami. However, there was evidently mistrust and violence as well. Many sources refer to the Saami's reputation as powerful magicians. In particular, the type of magic called *seiðr* is linked with the Saami in several sources; for example, Norse legal codes use expressions like *trúa á Finna*, "believe in a Saami", and *gera Finnfarar*, "make a journey to the Saami", to mean "to consult a diviner."[99] *Seiðr* could be used to divine the future, but also could be put to much more sinister uses, such as creating illusions or summoning up storms. The sagas persistently claim that marriage with Saami women could be especially dangerous; Saami women were said to have worked magic to bring about their enemies' or even husbands' downfall, such as Vanlandi's wife Drífa and Agni's wife Skjalf in *Ynglinga saga*,[100] Harald's wife Snæfrid in *Haralds saga hárfagra*,[101] and Eirik Bloodaxe's wife Gunnhild in several sources.[102]

The "otherness" of the Saami could be even greater and more sinister than this. *Seiðr*, after all, was a practice that had to be done consciously, and one that non-Saami could learn, but Saami "magic" could also result not from conscious intent but innate nature. In *Óláfs saga Tryggvasonar*, as King Óláfr Tryggvason tortures the stubbornly pagan sorceror Eyvind Kinnrifa to death, Eyvind admits that he is intrinsically unable to accept baptism because he is a spirit, incarnated by Saami sorcery.[103] In Oddr Snorrason's saga of Olaf Tryggvason, a Saami seer informs the king that he cannot withstand the "bright spirits" that follow him because he is "of a different nature"; like Eyvind Kinnrifa, the seer explains that he is inherently unable to convert to Christianity.[104]

The same complex center-periphery relationship is clearly visible in the *Hrafnistusögur*. The far north may be inhabited by strange and sometimes hostile races, but it has what the saga heroes need: rich fishing when famine strikes, opportunities for trade, and women on whom mighty sons are sired. Although Ketil and Grim encounter hostile beings on the periphery, they encounter friendly folk and ally with them as well. When Odd and his men break faith with the Bjarmians, dire consequences are set in motion which lead to the creation of Ogmund Eythjof's Bane, who kills Odd's friends one after another. On the other hand, when Odd grants help and friendship to the giant Hildir, he gains fine treasures (not all of which he can take with him) and a strong and promising son.[105] Yet some of the beings on the periphery are so far outside the order of things that they become innately magical and therefore potentially dangerous: Grim "Shaggy-Cheek" is marked with a hairy patch on his face because his mother accidentally looked at a hairy Saami man as Grim was being conceived, presumably without the Saami man consciously intending to do anything.

The most extreme outsider is Ogmund Eythjof's-Bane in *Örvar-Odds saga*. Half-Bjarmian and half-troll, he inherits magical powers from his mother, but that's not enough to make him inhuman; Ketil Salmon's father is also said to be half-troll, and the men of Hrafnista also have inherited magical skill. But the magic that he learns in Finnmark, and then the magic cast on him by the Bjarmians, fundamentally alters him and pushes him right out of the bounds of humanity: as he describes himself, *nú em ek eigi síðr andi en maðr*—"now I am no less a spirit than a human," rather like Eymund Kinnrifa. Ármann Jakobson has suggested that Ogmund may in fact be already dead, a *draugr* or *aptrganga*, and therefore unable to be killed.[106]

The single most prominent marker of the Saami as Other is the fact that the sagas don't always distinguish between them and giants. *Ketils saga hængs* presents the brothers Gusir and Bruni. Bruni is explicitly called a *grýlur*, "ogre"; his name appears as a dwarf's name in the poem *Völuspá*.[107] Gusir is said to be *Finna konungr*, "king of the Saami", in the saga—although Snorri Sturluson lists his name as a giant's name.[108] Several other texts explicitly conflate Saami people and *jötnar*, "giants", or *tröll*, "trolls."[109] Female giants and trolls in the Hrafnista sagas are also seen fishing and traveling alone. The Saami had relatively flexible gender roles; for example, women could fish, hunt, and ski—and the independence of female giants may be ultimately based on Norse reactions to Saami society.[110] Such "outsider" spouses can be extremely dangerous: in *Gríms saga*, for example, the tyrannical Grimhild from Finnmark—married to a human ruler and presumably "passing" as human, but with dreadful giant relatives in the far north—kidnaps and transforms her stepdaughter, Grim's betrothed Lopthaena. In this light, Ketil's father's demand that his son marry a Norse girl and jilt his Saami lover—whom he refers to as a troll in a fit of annoyance—makes a certain sense.

Human-giant encounter tales in the *fornaldarsögur* often end with the death of the giant or giantess in a rather grotesque way, and some modern readers may be baffled by this: as one scholar has asked rhetorically, "how could the dismemberment of unwashed, foreign-favored women possibly have been considered by any audience at any time as entertainment?"[111] Yet dealings between the human/Norse world and the giant/Saami world are far more nuanced and complex when taken as a whole. Ketil Salmon may slaughter the giantess Forad, but he also loves his troll/Saami partner Hrafnhild with apparent sincerity, resisting marriage to a Norse girl—and it is Ketil's son by Hrafnhild who goes on to be the hero of the next saga.[112]

Arnold points out that there are three main types of human-troll encounter narratives in the sagas. In the first type, the hero, fully a part of human society, takes on hostile trolls and overcomes them; the hero and his society are defined against the trollish Others. The trolls may pose active threats to the hero's interests or his society, or they may simply be in the way, but in any case, their Otherness—lack of human manners, bizarre habits, and so on—marks them for death. Arnold lists several "sagas of Icelanders" as examples: *Finnboga saga*, *Kjalnesinga saga*, *Grettis saga*, and so on. In the second type, the hero is able to move freely between human society and the non-human world, but the worlds remain distinct. Arnold gives *Bárðar saga Snæfellsáss*, grouped with the "sagas of Icelanders" but with many *fornaldarsögur*-like features, as an example.

In Arnold's third group, however, the human world and the trollish world are combined, and the Hrafnista sagas are paradigmatic examples of this.[113] The *Hrafnistumenn* descend from *Úlfr inn óargr*, Ulf No-Coward.[114] Nothing is said of him in the sagas,[115] except that he is the father of Hallbjorn Half-Troll, so presumably Ulf married or at least had a son with a "troll", beginning a long family tradition of interbreeding. Ketil's father Hallbjorn lives like a Norwegian farmer and tries to make

Ketil follow his example, urging him to take up farming chores and offering him the management of the farm, while discouraging him from traveling into the trollish north. Yet the words of the man-eating giant Surt clearly show that Hallbjörn is not only half troll, but has had past friendly dealings with the trolls of the far north. Ketil repeatedly disobeys his father, traveling to the northern wastes and encountering trolls both friendly and hostile. Hallbjörn drives Ketil apart from his troll/Saami lover Hrafnhild, in favor of a conventional, negotiated marriage with a human/Norse girl. Ketil and his Norse wife have a child, but the hero of the next saga and propagator of the "main bloodline" is Grim, Ketil's son with Hrafnhild, who has a "blood quantum" of five-eighths troll. Grim goes on to make his own excursions into trollish country.

Grim's son Odd goes through much the same father-son conflicts as his grandfather Ketil did: despite Ingjald's attempts to keep Odd on the farm, Odd heads for Bjarmaland for his own encounter with trolls and Saami, his foes and his kinsmen. The later recension of *Örvar-Odds saga* increases the strange tensions between Odd and the trolls; Odd dallies with a giantess and sires the redoubtable Vignir, who would be only three-sixteenths human. Vignir is killed by Ogmund Eythjof's-Bane, who in the older recensions of the sagas is only encountered once, but in the later recension is given a full "back-story" and is pitted against Odd repeatedly, the only adversary that he cannot defeat. We find that Ogmund was born to a Bjarmian father and an ogress mother, and he has become so much altered by Saami magic, sorcery, and sacrifices that he is no longer human. Ogmund might seem to be as Other as it is possible to be—and yet he becomes a strange double of Odd himself.[116] Both Ogmund and Odd are of mixed parentage, and both make use of magic—whether inherent in their bodies and their "genetics", such as Ogmund's monstrous ancestry and Odd's family knack for getting fair winds, or received later in life, such as Odd's arrows and shirt and Ogmund's weird transformation among the Saami and Bjarmians.

Politics and the Hrafnista Sagas

Even a work of literature that is set in a place and time far removed from its author and audience reflects what the author and audience collectively believe to be important. Whether intentionally or not, a work of literature reflects on shared ideas concerning political power, human relationships, wealth production and distribution, and so on—the "mental realities" of the society in which it is born and lives. Just as a science fiction novel or film from 1950s America may have more to say about the Cold War, Communism, or nuclear destruction than about distant planets, a *fornaldarsaga* written in medieval Iceland may comment extensively on social and political concerns at the time of its writing, whether or not its creators intended to make it do so.[117]

In 1262, Iceland formally submitted to Norwegian rule. Over the next few years, its unique form of self-government was replaced with rule by Norwegian (and later Danish) royal governors. Governors (*hirðstjóri*) often bid for their office, with the highest bidders recouping their expenses by squeezing the island for all they could get. Iceland's traditional law code, transmitted orally for centuries before being written down, was also replaced by Norwegian legal codes. Arnold suggests that the Hrafnistumenn, with their mixed blood and conflicting human and trollish urges, reflect "tensions that arise when a revered past has little place in the present."[118] He suggests that saga narratives of human-troll interaction shifted over time, from expressing concern over outside threats, to expressing concern over the loss or fragmentation of the in-group's identity.[119] Straubhaar also concludes that the Hrafnista sagas, especially *Ketils saga* and *Gríms saga*, reveal deep-seated social concerns over gender, ethnicity, access and control of resources, and class conflict at the time the sagas were written.[120]

An Icelander might respond to his country's changed circumstances by either resisting royal authority if it proved unjust and onerous, or else by trying to accommodate to it and rise through the ranks of the social hierarchy. Torfi Tulinius interprets *Örvar-Odds saga* as being fundamentally about the right way to achieve social advancement under a monarchy. While Odd is successful enough as an independent Viking, his adversary and ally Hjalmar shows him the folly of fighting over nothing but reputation, and offers him a code of honorable conduct that he can accept. Later, after Hjalmar's death, Odd accepts Christianity, and eventually comes to the court of King Herraud, starting on the lowest rank of courtly society, progressively showing his mettle, and working his way up to becoming a king in his own right. This is, perhaps, the "moral" of *Örvar-Odds saga*: heroic life outside of society may bring transient glory, but the only way to win lasting success in life is to accept social rules and authorities and integrate into the prevailing social structure. In practical terms, this meant accepting the king's rule and finding a place at court, as a number of Icelanders did, notably Odd's distant kinsman Haukr Erlingsson.[121] Tulinius goes further and suggests that Ogmund, who plays a small role in the earlier versions of the saga but who becomes a major character in later versions, is a personification of death itself—reflecting increasing preoccupation with death in the aftermath of the Black Plague, which devastated both Norway and Iceland in the 14th and 15th centuries.[122]

The other three sagas, however, take a strongly contrasting approach. *Ketils saga* and *Gríms saga* don't mention kings at all; their heroes are strong and powerful leaders, but they are not kings and have little to do with kings. *Áns saga* is more blatantly anti-monarchical; its hero grows into a prosperous farmer and respected leader, despite being outlawed by a grasping and conniving king. Arrow-Odd wins a king's daughter and a kingdom of his own to rule—but his kinsman An advises his son that "It's better to look out for your own honor than to set yourself up in a higher station and be brought down." Shaun Hughes notes that in 1362, the royal governor Smiður Andrésson outlawed a number of prosperous residents in the northern part of Iceland, who rose up and killed him. This incident, or something like it, might well have inspired the writing of *Áns saga*.[123] Icelanders reading or hearing such stories may have looked back nostalgically on a time when they had no need or desire for royal rule.

Finally, some information on the political subtext of the sagas comes from the manuscripts in which they were found. The texts that are translated here all come from the late 15th-century parchment manuscript AM 343a 4to, which contains all four of the *Hrafnistasögur* in the order they appear in this book. AM 343a includes fifteen sagas in all; nine of them are traditionally considered *fornaldarsögur*, while the other six are classified as "sagas of chivalry" (*riddarasögur*). However, all the sagas are set primarily in Scandinavia, the Baltic, and/or Russia. They may have been selected for this volume as a comment on the Kalmar Union, in which Norway, Sweden, and Denmark were united under one ruler. Many of these sagas may be read as political commentaries, implying the need for neighboring kingdoms to remain at peace, maintain a balance of power, and unite against common foes, and the need for a king to treat his retainers well and not interfere too much with their freedom of action.[124]

Notes on the Texts

The Hrafnista cycle was quite popular in medieval and modern Iceland. *Áns saga* is known from 53 manuscripts, *Ketils saga* from 63, *Gríms saga* from 68, and *Örvar-Odds saga* from 69.[125] Eleven manuscripts are known to contain all four; as mentioned above, the manuscript AM 343a 4to contains all four sagas in the same order as they appear in this book. The oldest surviving manuscript of any of the Hrafnista sagas, AM 343a was produced in Iceland, at Möðruvellir in Eyjafjörður; the handwriting of most of AM 343a also appears in a diploma dated 1461, and thus the manuscript must date from the latter half of the 15th century.[126] The texts translated here are all based on AM 343a, and were published in Jónsson and Vilhjálmsson's three-volume edition, *Fornaldarsögur Norðurlanda*. Jónsson and Vilhjálmsson's edition closely follows Rafn's 1829-30 edition, also called *Fornaldarsögur Norðurlanda*. My text of Ohthere's account was published in Janet Bately's edition of *The Old English Orosius*.[127]

This book is the first English translation of the complete Hrafnista cycle. Jacqueline Simpson published an excerpt from *Örvar-Odds saga* in 1965,[128] while the entire saga has been translated by Herman Pálsson and Paul Edwards, first published in 1970[129] and later, with minor revisions, in 1985.[130] *Áns saga bogsveigis* has been translated by Shaun Hughes[131] and by Willard Larson.[132] *Ketils saga hængs* and *Gríms saga loðinkinna* have not been formally published in complete English translation at this writing, although excerpts of both sagas have appeared.[133] Translations of both sagas exist on-line, but they contain a number of inaccuracies.[134] I have consulted all of these translations, but in the end have tried to find my own way through the texts, and do not necessarily agree with them on all points.

As is usual in saga translations, I have anglicized the spelling of Norse personal names by dropping accents and diacritics, replacing *þ* with *th* and *ð* with *d*, and dropping the masculine nominative case ending, whether *–r* or a geminate consonant. Place names have been translated by their modern equivalents when possible, and anglicized when the modern equivalent is unknown or obscure.

I thank Kay Anderson, Dan Campbell, J. Blade Canty, and Thomas DeMayo for reading and commenting on various drafts of these translations. Any errors that remain are entirely mine. I thank Zoe Borovsky, Sean Crist, P. S. Langeslag, Stefan Langeslag, Andy Lemons, Carsten Lyngdrup Madsen, and Jon Julius Sandal, who have created free electronic resources that made my own work possible. Last but certainly not least, I thank Amanda Waggoner for her unfailing love and support.

*Hafi þeir þökk er hlýddu
en sá litla sem krabbað hefir söguna.*

THE SAGA OF KETIL SALMON
Ketils saga hængs

CHAPTER I

There was a man named Hallbjorn, called Half-Troll, the son of Ulf No-Coward. He lived on the island of Hrafnista, off the coast of Romsdal. He was a powerful man, and much better off than the farmers to the north. He was married and had a son named Ketil. He was very tall, and a manly man, but not handsome.

When Ketil was several years old, he lay around in the hearth-house[1]. Worthy men felt that it was ridiculous for him to do that. Ketil was in the habit of keeping one hand on his head when he sat by the fire, and poking the fire in front of his knees with his other hand. Hallbjorn told him not to put his hand on his head, and said that matters would go better for them then. Ketil didn't answer. Somewhat later, he ran away, and stayed away for three nights. Then he came home carrying a chair on his back. It was well made. He gave it to his mother and said that he had more love from her to reward than from his father.

One day in the summer, when the weather was fine, Hallbjorn was having the hay carted, and much of it was in danger of being ruined. Hallbjorn went into the hearth-house and came up to Ketil and said, "Son, it would be best for you to help cart the hay today, because everyone is needed at haytime." Ketil jumped up and went out. Hallbjorn gave him two oxen and a serving-woman to help with the work. Ketil carted hay into the farmyard, and went at it so briskly that in the end, eight haystacks were hauled away, and everyone thought that he'd done enough. When evening came, all the hay was stored, and both oxen had dropped dead from exhaustion.

Hallbjorn said, "Now I think it would be best for you to take over the management of the estate, son, because you're a rising young man and capable at everything, but I'm growing old and stiff and no longer useful."

The Saga of Ketil Salmon

Ketil said that he didn't want that.

Hallbjorn then gave him an axe, very large and quite sharp, an excellent weapon. He said, "There is one thing, son, that I must warn you against. Once the day is done, I don't want you to go outside much. Most of all, I don't want you going north to the islands, away from the settlements." Hallbjorn explained many things to his son Ketil.

There was a man named Bjorn, who lived a short distance away. It had always been his habit to mock Ketil, and he called him Ketil the Hrafnista-Fool. Bjorn was always rowing out to sea to fish. One day, when he had rowed out, Ketil took a fishing boat and a line and a hook, and rowed out to the fishing grounds and started fishing. Bjorn was there ahead of him, and when Bjorn and his men saw Ketil, they laughed a lot and mocked him harshly. Bjorn went out the farthest, as he usually did. He and his men caught plenty of fish, but Ketil pulled up one very poor-quality ling cod and no more fish.

When Bjorn and his men had loaded their boat, they hauled in their gear and set course for home, and so did Ketil. They laughed at him. Ketil said, "Now I want to leave all my catch with you, and the first one of you to catch it shall keep it."

He grabbed the cod and threw it at their ship. The cod hit farmer Bjorn in the ear so hard that his skull was broken, and Bjorn was knocked overboard into the water and never came up again.[2] The others rowed to land, as did Ketil. Hallbjorn took the news coolly.

One evening after sunset, Ketil took his axe in his hand and went to the north of the island. When he had gone rather a long way away from the settlements, he saw a dragon flying at him from the cliffs to the north. He had coils and a tail like a serpent, but wings like a dragon. Flames appeared to blaze from his eyes and his maw. Ketil didn't think he'd seen a fish like this, or any other monster, for he would have preferred to have to defend himself against a host of men. The dragon attacked him, but Ketil defended himself well and bravely with the axe. It went on like this for a long time, until Ketil managed to strike the coils and cut the dragon in two, and it dropped down dead.

Ketil went straight home, and his father was outside in the farmyard. He greeted his son warmly, and asked whether he had heard of any hostile beings to the north on the island. Ketil replied, "I don't know how to tell stories about watching the salmon run. But it's true that I chopped a male salmon[3] in two at the middle, as he was searching for a spawning female."

Hallbjorn answered, "You must think that such trifles are of little worth, since you count such a beast with the small fish. Now I'll lengthen your name, and call you Ketil Salmon."

They stayed at home quietly. Ketil sat by the fire a great deal. Hallbjorn often went fishing, and Ketil asked to come with him, but Hallbjorn said that it was more fitting for him to sit by the fire than to go on sea voyages. But when Hallbjorn came to the ship, Ketil was there first, and Hallbjorn didn't know how to send him back. Hallbjorn went in front of the boat's bow, and asked Ketil to go behind the stern and push the boat out. Ketil pushed, but the boat went nowhere.

Hallbjorn said, "You're not like your kinfolk, and I think it'll be a long time before you get your strength. Before I got old, I was used to pushing out the boat by myself."

Ketil became angry, and pushed the boat forward so hard that Hallbjorn was knocked down onto the gravel, but the boat didn't stop until it went out onto the sea. Hallbjorn said, "You don't let me benefit much from being kin to you, since you want to break my bones. But I'll say now that I suppose you're quite strong enough, because I wanted to test your strength, and I withstood you as hard as I could, but you pushed it out as hard as ever. It seems to me that I have a good son in you."

Now they went to the fishing camp. Hallbjorn took care of the hut, and Ketil rowed out to sea. He managed to bring in a large catch. Then two hostile men rowed towards him and ordered him to give up his catch. Ketil refused, and asked them their names. One said that he was called Haeng, and the other was Hrafn, and they were brothers.[4] They attacked him, but Ketil defended himself with a club and knocked Haeng overboard and killed him. Hrafn rowed away.

Ketil went back to the hut, and his father went to meet him and asked whether he had encountered any people that day. Ketil said that he had met two brothers, Haeng and Hrafn.

Hallbjorn said, "How did your dealings with them go? I know all about them. They are bold men, and have been outlawed from the settlements for their unruliness."

Ketil said that he had knocked Haeng overboard, but Hrafn had fled.

Hallbjorn said, "Son, you're eager for big fish, so your name is well founded."

The next day they went home with their catches. Ketil was eleven years old at the time. His relationship with his father improved.

CHAPTER II

At that time, there was a great famine in Halogaland; much of the people's livelihood came from the sea. Ketil said that he wanted to go fishing and not be completely useless. Hallbjorn asked to go with him. Ketil said that he was quite able to make the journey himself.

"That's unwise, but you want to have your own way," said Hallbjorn. "But I will tell you the names of three fjords. One is called Næstifjord, the other is Midfjord, and the third is Vitadsgjafi.[5] It has been a long time now since I left two of them, and on the shore of each one there was a hut with a fire lit, back then."

That summer, Ketil went into Midfjord, and there was a fire lit in a hut. At the head of the fjord, Ketil found a large hut, and the owner wasn't home when Ketil came. He saw a great catch of fish there, and huge pits dug down into the earth. He pulled everything up out of them and scattered it every which way. In the pits he found the flesh of whales and polar bears, seals and walruses and all kinds of animals, but on the bottom of each pit he found salted human flesh. All of this he dragged out and spoiled any way he could.

When evening came, he heard a great splashing of oars. He went to the shore. The owner was rowing towards land. His name was Surt.[6] He was huge and grim-looking. As soon as the ship scraped the bottom, he stepped overboard and picked up the boat and carried it into the boatshed, and he sank into the earth almost up to his knees. He was talking to himself in a deep voice. "Something's gone wrong here," he said, "because all my possessions are scattered, and it's gone the worst with the ones that were the best, such as my human carcasses. Such a thing would be worth paying back. And it hasn't turned out well that my friend Hallbjorn stays quietly at home, but Ketil Salmon, the fireplace-fool, has come here. It would never be too much trouble for me to pay him back. It would be a great disgrace to me if I didn't get the better of him by far, since he's grown up to be a coal-biter by the fire."[7]

He turned towards the hut, but Ketil ran away and took a position behind the door with the axe raised. When Surt came to the hut, he had to bow down very low to get through the doors, and he stuck his head and shoulders in first. At that moment, Ketil struck at his neck with the axe. It sang out loudly as it cut off his head. The giant fell dead on the floor.[8] Ketil loaded his boat and went home that autumn.

The next summer he went to Vitadsgjafi. Hallbjorn tried to discourage him, and said that it would be best for him to drive the wagon at home. Ketil said that it wouldn't do for him to be untested—"and I must go," he said.

"You'll think that place is haunted, "said Hallbjorn, "but it's clear that you want to see my hearth-fires[9] and consider yourself my equal in everything."

Ketil said that he was right about that. He went straight north into Vitadsgjafi and found a hut there and camped in it. There was no lack of good fishing: he could catch fish there with his bare hands. Ketil hung up his catch in his boathouse and then went to sleep. But in the morning, when he awoke, all his fish had been taken away.

Ketil stayed awake the next night. He saw a giant go into the boathouse and wrap up a great bundle for himself. Ketil attacked him and struck at his shoulder with the axe, and the bundle tumbled down. The giant turned quickly when he was wounded, so that the axe got loose from Ketil and stuck fast in the wound.[10]

The giant was named Kaldrani.[11] He rushed to the head of the fjord and into his cave, with Ketil after him. Trolls were sitting there by a fire, and they laughed a lot and said that Kaldrani had been punished for his deeds as he deserved. Kaldrani said that the wound needed ointment more than scolding.

Ketil came into the cave and said that he was a healer. He asked them to bring him some ointment, and said that he would bandage his wound. The other trolls went farther into the cave. But Ketil pulled the axe out of the wound and struck the giant a deadly blow. Then he went straight to his hut and loaded his boat and went home right away.[12]

Hallbjorn welcomed him warmly, and asked if he had heard of anything happening. Ketill said that he had traveled a long way.

Hallbjorn said then that he was looking very disheartened—"did you stay there in peace?"

"Yes," said Ketil.

CHAPTER III

In the autumn, before Winternights,[13] Ketil readied his boat. Hallbjorn asked what he was going to do. Ketil said that he meant to go on a fishing expedition.

Hallbjorn said that no man would do such a thing—"and you're doing this without my permission." All the same, Ketil went. When he came north to a fjord, a violent gale caught him and drove him off course into the open sea, and he couldn't reach harbor. It drove him towards some cliffs on the coast of Finnmark, and he landed where there was a break in the cliffs. He made camp there and went to sleep.

When he awoke, the entire ship was shaking. He stood up and saw that a troll-woman had grabbed the prow and was shaking the ship. Ketil leaped into the boat and picked up a chest of butter, cut the mooring lines and rowed away. The gale was still blowing. A whale came swimming towards him and sheltered the ship against the wind, and it appeared to him that the whale had human eyes.[14] Then he was driven onto some rocks, and the boat was broken. He swam to one of the rocks, and he saw that there was nothing to do but swim for land. After a rest, he swam from the rock and made it to land. He found a road leading away from the beach, and came to a farm. There stood a man outside, in front of the doors, splitting wood. His name was Bruni. He greeted Ketil and spoke a verse:

> Welcome, Salmon!
> Seek shelter here
> and live with us
> for the length of winter.
> I'll betroth to you,
> unless you turn her down,
> my own daughter
> before day comes.

Ketil spoke a verse:

> Here I'll seek shelter!
> I suspect that a Finn
> wielded the windstorm
> with witchcraft and spells.
> All day I bailed,
> doing three men's work.
> The whale soothed the sea.
> I'll shelter here.

They went on inside. There were two women there. Bruni asked whether he wanted to lie next to his daughter, or alone. She was named Hrafnhild, and she was very tall and strong. It's said that she had a face an ell across.[15] Ketil said that he would prefer to lie next to Hrafnhild.

At once they got into bed, and Bruni spread an ox-hide over them. Ketil asked why he had to do that. "I've invited my Finn friends to come here," said Bruni, "and I don't want you two to be seen. They shall now come for your butter-chest."

The Finns came, and they weren't narrow-faced. They said, "This butter is a great banquet for us." Then they went away.[16]

Ketil stayed behind and enjoyed himself with Hrafnhild. He also went constantly to the archery range and learned skills. Now and then he went hunting with Bruni. In the winter, after Yule, Ketil wished he could leave. But Bruni said that he could not, because of the severe winter and foul weather—"and Gusir, the king of the Finns, lurks in the forest."

In the spring, Bruni and Ketil prepared to travel. They went to the mouth of the fjord. When they parted, Bruni said, "Take the path that I will show you, and don't go into the forest." He gave him some arrows and a broad-arrow, and told him to make use of them, if he should need them in dire straits.[17] Then they parted, and Bruni went home.

Ketil said to himself, "Why shouldn't I go by the shorter route and not be afraid of that ogre Bruni?" At once he turned into the forest, and he saw a great cloud of wind-driven snow. He saw a man coming after him in a wagon drawn by two reindeer.[18] Ketil addressed him with a verse:

> Creep from your cart
> and calm your reindeer,

traveller at twilight,
tell me your name.

The man answered:

> The noble Finns
> name me Gusir.
> I am the head
> of the whole tribe.
>
> Who is this man
> who meets me here,
> and creeps like a wolf from the woods?
> You'll speak words of fear,
> if you scurried away
> thrice in Thrumufjord.
> I think you're no hero.

They met in front of Ofara-Thruma. Ketil spoke a verse:

> Salmon I'm called,
> come from Hrafnista,
> the son of Hallbjorn.
> Why the skulking, wretch?
> I'll speak no soft words
> for the spineless Finn,
> I'll bend the bow, rather,
> that Bruni gave me.

Gusir realized who this Salmon was, because he was very well-known. Gusir spoke a verse:

> Who is on snowshoes
> at sun's rising,
> eager for fighting,
> in a fierce mood?

> We two shall strive
> to stain our arrows
> in each other's blood,
> unless bravery falters.

Ketil said:

> As half my name,
> I'm known as Salmon.
> I will defy you
> from this day forth.
> Before we two part,
> I'll prove to you
> that farmers' shafts
> have sharp points.

Gusir said:

> Ward yourself against
> sharp weapon-thunder.°   *weapon-thunder*: battle
> Shield yourself well.
> I will shoot hard.
> Soon I'll become
> your slayer, unless
> you give up all of
> your gold to me.

Ketil said:

> I will not yield
> my wealth to you,
> nor falter and flee
> before you alone.
> The shield on your breast
> will be shattered first,
> and darkness will come
> to dim your sight.

Gusir said:

> You won't enjoy
> your jewels and gold
> with a happy heart
> at your home in peace.
> Soon I'll deal out
> death to you,
> if we go out to play
> the game of arrows.°   *game of arrows*: battle

Ketil said:

> Of my gold I'll grant
> Gusir no share,
> nor be soonest
> to sue for peace.
> A sudden death
> I'd deem much better
> than cowardice
> and creeping away.

At once they bent their bows and nocked arrows on the strings and traded shots. Each arrow hit the point of the other and fell down, and so it happened with a dozen arrows from each man. By that time, Gusir had one arrow remaining. Ketil's broad arrow was also left. Gusir took his arrow, and it looked warped to him, and he stepped on it. Ketil said:

> This fearful Finn
> is fated to die,
> since he treads upon
> his twisted arrow.

At once they shot at each other, and the arrows missed each other. The broad-arrow flew into Gusir's breast, and he was killed. Bruni had made the arrow look warped to Gusir, because he was next in line for the kingship if anything should happen to Gusir, and he felt that their arrangement was less than his due.

Gusir had owned the sword named Drangvendil, the best of all swords.[19] Ketil took it from Gusir's corpse, along with the arrows Flaug, Hremsa and Fifa.[20] Ketil went back to Bruni and told him what had happened. Bruni said that the blow had struck close to home, since his brother was slain. Ketil said that he had now won the kingdom on Bruni's behalf. Then Bruni accompanied him to the settled regions, and they parted with great affection.

Nothing more is said about Ketil's journey until he came home to Hrafnista. He met a farmer and asked what ships those were, coming to the island. The farmer said that they were invited guests, and they meant to hold a funeral feast for Ketil, if nothing had been heard of him by then. Ketil traveled to the island on a broken-down boat and went into the house, and the men were glad to see him. The funeral feast turned into a welcoming party in Ketil's honor.

Ketil stayed at home for three years. Then a ship came to the island, and on it were Bruni's daughter Hrafnhild and her son by Ketil, who was named Grim. Ketil invited them to stay there.

Hallbjorn said, "Why are you inviting this troll to stay here?" He was quite exasperated and peevish at her coming.

Hrafnhild said that neither of them would come to harm from her. "I will go away, but our son Grim Shaggy-Cheek shall stay behind." He was called that because one of his cheeks was hairy, and he was born with that. Iron could not wound him on that spot.

Ketil asked Hrafnhild not to be angry at this. She said that her anger wouldn't matter much to them. Then she went home, rowing north along the coast, but she told Grim to stay there for three years, and said that they would come for him then.

CHAPTER IV

There was a man named Bard, a good farmer. He had a lovely daughter named Sigrid. She was considered to be the best prospect for marriage.

Hallbjorn told Ketil to ask to marry this woman, and so forget about Hrafnhild. Ketil said that he had no interest in marriage. He was always sad, ever since he and Hrafnhild parted. Ketil said that he would travel north along the coast.

Hallbjorn said that he himself would make a matchmaking journey on Ketil's behalf—"it's a bad thing that you want to love that troll."[21] Then Hallbjorn went on his matchmaking journey to Bard. The farmer said that Ketil had made longer and more difficult journeys than that one to ask for a woman's hand.

"Are you accusing me of lying?" said Hallbjorn.

The farmer answered, "I know that Ketil would have come here if he had any heart for it. I'm not sure that I shouldn't want to refuse you the woman."

They bargained together, and a date was set for the wedding feast. Then Hallbjorn went home. Ketil didn't ask what had happened. Hallbjorn said that many people would be more interested in wedded life than Ketil was. Ketil paid no attention. All the same, the plans went ahead, and the feasting was good.

Ketil didn't take off his clothes on the first night that they came into one bed. She didn't worry about that, and soon they resolved matters between them.

After tha,t Hallbjorn died. Ketil took over the management of the household, and many people stayed with him. Ketil had a daughter with his wife, and she was named Hrafnhild.

After three years had passed, Bruni's daughter Hrafnhild came to meet with Ketil. He invited her to live with them, but she said that she would not stay there: "Now you have forfeited our meeting and living together, by your fickleness and unfaithfulness." She went to the ship, very downcast and gloomy, and it was obvious that she was grieving deeply over parting with Ketil. Grim stayed behind.

Ketil was the most powerful of men there in the north, and men put a great deal of trust in him. One summer, he went north to Finnmark to find Bruni and Hrafnhild. They traveled in a little ship and tied up at a certain cliff, close to some others. Ketil told Grim to look for water for them. Grim went and saw a troll by the river, who barred his way and wanted to capture him. Grim was scared and ran home and told his father. Ketil went to meet the troll and spoke a verse:

What is that strange freak
who stands by the rock
and frowns above the fire?[22]
Our neighborly dealings
I know will improve.
See where the sun is rising.[23]

The troll disappeared, but father and son went home.

One autumn, some Vikings came to Ketil. One was named Hjalm, and the other was named Stafnglam.[24] They had been raiding far and wide. They asked to have sanctuary there with Ketil, and he granted them those terms. They stayed with him through the winter, highly honored.

In the winter, at Yule, Ketil swore an oath that he would not marry off his daughter Hrafnhild without her consent.[25] The Vikings wished him luck with that.

On one occasion, Ali Uppdale-Champion came there. His family came from Uppland. He asked to marry Hrafnhild. Ketil said that he didn't want to give her in marriage without her consent—"but I might talk the matter over with her."

Hrafnhild said that she didn't want to give her love to Ali, nor to bind her fate with his. Ketil told Ali how it was, and so Ali challenged Ketil to single combat. Ketil said that he would go. The brothers Hjalm and Stafnglam wanted to fight for Ketil, but he told them to hold shields in front of him.[26]

When they came to the field of battle, Ali struck at Ketil, and the shields failed to block the blow, and the sword point hit Ketil in the forehead and scratched him down to his nose, and it bled a lot. Then Ketil spoke a verse:

> Hjalm and Stafnglam,
> shelter yourselves.
> Give this old man room
> to go a bit forward.
>
> Battle-snakes° fly.   *battle-snakes*: spears
> Bold is the Dale-Champion.
> Ugly is the edge-game.°   *edge-game*: battle

> The old man's beard is seen.
> Skin tunics scrape.
> Iron-shirts quiver.
> Mail-coats shake.
> The maid's suitor is frightened.

At that moment Ketil whirled his sword around at Ali's head, and Ali brought up his shield. But then Ketil struck at his feet and cut them both out from under him, and there Ali fell.

CHAPTER V

A little while later there was a terrible famine, because the fish stayed away from land and the grain crop failed. Ketil had many people in his household, and Sigrid thought that they needed provisions in the house. Ketil said that he wasn't about to be blamed, and jumped into his ship.

The Vikings asked where he was going. "I have to go fishing," he said. They asked to go with him. But he said that he was in no danger, and told them to take care of the farm in the meantime.

Ketil came to the place called Skrofa.[27] And when he came to harbor, he saw a troll-woman on the headland, in a bare skin tunic. She had just come out of the sea and was as dark as pitch. She was squinting at the sun. Ketil spoke a verse:

> What's that ogress I see
> out on the old cape
> gaping and gawking at me?
> I have never seen
> while the sun is up
> anything more ugly.

She said:

> I am called Forad.[28]
> Far to the north
> is my home in Hrafnsey.

> I'm hated by landlubbers;
> keen is my courage,
> whatever crime I shall do.

And then she said:

> Many men came here
> meaning to fish,
> but I've sent them down to the dust.
> Who is this clown
> who's come to the skerries?

"They call me Salmon," he said.[29]

She replied, "It would be better for you to stay home in Hrafnista, rather than dragging yourself to the outer skerries alone."

Ketil spoke a verse:

> I thought the jeering
> of giant trolls
> would be arrogant,
> before we arrived here,
> from all of our travels.
> I curse the sluggard.
> I came here to fish.
>
> I don't think I'll desist,
> despite Forad's words.
> Needs drove me on;
> I have neighbors to help.
> I wouldn't sail to this skerry
> and risk sealing here,
> if we had enough
> over on my island.

She answered:

> Wide-faring warrior,
> I won't prohibit
> you from living
> longer than others,
> if you tell of our meeting
> to mighty heroes.
> I see that your will
> is wavering, little boy.

Ketil said:

> When I was a wee lad,
> I went all by myself
> often, to outlying places.
> Many night-riders
> I met on my way.
> I'm not scared of ogres' snorting.
>
> You are long-faced, foster-mother,[30]
> and you let your nose wag like an oar.
> I don't look for an awful ogre.

At that, she moved towards him, and said:

> I began my goings in Angr,[31]
> then got to Steigen, plodding.
> A clattering sword scraped.
> Then I strode to Karmoy.
> I will set blazes in Jaeren,
> blow up flames in Utstein.
> Then I'll go east to the Elfr
> ere daylight dawns upon me,
> and frolic with bridesmaids,
> be betrothed to a jarl soon.[32]

This journey was all along the length of Norway.

She asked, "What will you do now?"
"Boil meat and prepare a meal," he said.
She said:

> I will come to your campfire,
> and clutch you with desire,
> until I grab you greedily.

"Now this is what I expect from her," said Ketil.
She groped towards him. Then Ketil spoke a verse:

> I trust in my shooting,
> you trust in your strength.
> A barb will bite you,
> unless you back away.

She spoke a verse:

> Flaug and Fifa
> are far from my mind,
> and I'm not scared
> of a stab from Hremsa.

These were the names of Ketil's arrows. He nocked an arrow on the string and shot at her. She took the shape of a whale and plunged into the sea, but the arrow went under her tail flukes. Ketil heard a great shriek. He watched the giantess and spoke up: "Forad's engagement to that jarl will have to be broken off. He won't find her bed very desirable now." Then he caught some fish and loaded his boat.

One night, he awoke to a loud cracking noise in the woods. He jumped out and saw a troll-woman whose hair fell to her shoulders.[33] Ketil said, "Where do you think you're going, foster-mother?"

She stiffened at him and said, "I must go to an assembly of trolls. Skelking, king of the trolls, is coming from the Arctic Ocean in the north, and Ofoti from Ofotfjord[34], and Thorgerd Horgatroll[35] and other mighty beings from the lands to the north. Don't delay me. I don't like you, because you killed Kaldrani."

And then she waded into the sea and out into the ocean. There was no lack of staff-riding[36] on the island that night, but no harm came to Ketil from it. With matters as they stood, he went home and stayed there quietly for some time.

The next thing that happened was that Framar, a king of the Vikings, came to Hrafnista. He sacrificed to the heathen gods, and iron wouldn't bite him. He ruled a kingdom in Hunaveld, in Gästrikland.[37] He sacrificed at a burial mound called Arhaug; snow wouldn't stay on that mound.[38] His son was named Bodmod, who had a large estate next to Arhaug, and he was well-liked, but everyone wished Framar ill. Odin had ordained for Framar that no iron could bite him.[39]

Framar asked to marry Hrafnhild, and Ketil responded that she should choose a husband for herself. She refused Framar—"I didn't want to choose Ali as my husband, and so much the less will I choose that troll."

Ketil told Framar her answer, and it made him very angry. Framar challenged Ketil to a duel by Arhaug, on the first day of Yule—"and be the most worthless of all men if you don't come."

Ketil said that he would come. Hjalm and Stafnglam asked him to go with him. Ketil said that he wanted to go alone.

A short time before Yule, Ketil had himself ferried down the coast to Namdalen. He put on a shaggy cape and stepped into his skis, and went up along the valleys and through the woods to Jämtland, and eastwards through Skalkskog Forest to Hälsingland, and on eastwards through Eyskoga Forest—it divides Gästrikaland and Hälsingland, and it is twenty leagues long and three leagues broad,[40] and it's difficult to cross.

Thorir was the name of a man who lived by the forest. He offered Ketil his help and told him that evildoers lay in the woods: "The worst of them is the one named Soti. He is treacherous and hardy."

Ketil said that he couldn't do him any harm. He went into the forest and came to Soti's hut. He was not at home. Ketil made a fire for himself.

Soti came home and didn't greet Ketil, and set out food in front of himself. Ketil sat by the fire and said, "Do you always starve your guests,[41] Soti?". Soti tossed some lumps of meat at Ketil.

When they had eaten, Ketil lay down next to the fire and snored loudly. Then Soti jumped up, but Ketil woke up and said "Why are you wandering over here, Soti?"

He answered, "I'm blowing on the fire, which was almost out."

Ketil fell asleep again. Soti jumped up again, with a two-handed axe. Then Ketil jumped up and said, "You must want to butcher some big carcasses."

After that, Ketil stayed up all night.

In the morning, Ketil asked Soti to go with him into the forest, and he went. And when night fell, they lay down under an oak. Ketil fell asleep, or so Soti supposed, because he was snoring loudly. Soti sprang up and struck at Ketil so that he ripped off the hood of his cloak, but Ketil wasn't in the cloak. Ketil awoke and wanted to put Soti to the test. He jumped up and said, "Now we two should test each other's wrestling skills." Ketil shoved Soti over a log and cut his head off, and then he went his way and came to Arhaug on the evening of Yule. It was a place of sacrifice for Framar and the people of the land, for good harvests. There was a heavy snowfall. Ketil went up onto the mound and sat down facing the wind.

As men were coming to Bodmod's home, he spoke up: "Will Ketil make it to Arhaug?" The people said that it was unlikely.

Bodmod said, "There's a man that I can't make out. Go find out who he is, and invite him to our house."

They went now to the mound and didn't find Ketil, and told Bodmod what happened. Bodmod said that he must have gone up onto the mound. He went right away to the mound and up onto the top, and there he saw a large heap on the north side of the mound.[42] Bodmod spoke a verse:

> Who is this tall man
> hunkered on the mound,
> turning towards the wind?
> I find you frost-hardened,
> so afflicted a man
> that you seek no shelter or warmth.

Ketil spoke a verse:

> I am called Ketil,
> come from Hrafnista.
> I was raised under that roof.

Proud in my mind,
I can protect myself.
Yet I'd like to have lodgings.

Bodmod said:

You should get up
and go from the mound
and seek safety in my hall.
I'll offer you meals
for many a day,
if you'll have my hospitality.

Ketil spoke a verse:

I will now get up
and go from the mound,
just as Bodmod bids me.
My own brother could not
make a better offer,
though at my side he were standing.

Bodmod took Ketil's hand. And when he stood up, his feet slipped on the mound. Then Bodmod spoke a verse:

You've been challenged, son,
to go to the battle
and fight with Framar for wealth.
At an early age,
Odin gave him victory.
He's quite used to combat, I say.

Ketil became angry when Bodmod named Odin, because he didn't believe in Odin, and he spoke a verse:

I've never offered Odin
any sacrifices,

yet I've lived long.
I already know
that the noble head
of Framar is destined to fall.

Then Ketil went with Bodmod and stayed with him for the night and sat next to him.

In the morning, Bodmod asked to go with him, or else to lend him a man to go with him to meet Framar. Ketil didn't want that. "Then I will go with you," said Bodmod. Ketil was willing, and they went to Arhaug.

Framar came to the mound bellowing. Bodmod and Ketil were there first, with many men. Then Framar pronounced the laws of dueling. Bodmod held a shield in front of Ketil, but no one held a shield before Framar.

Framar said to Bodmod, "Now you shall be my foe, rather than a son."

Bodmod said that Framar had dissolved their kinship by his sorcery. And before they fought, an eagle flew out of the woods at Framar and tore off a piece of clothing. Then Framar spoke a verse:

> This eagle is ill-disposed—
> I'm not afraid of a wound—
> he sinks his tawny talons,
> tears at my blood vessels.
> The storm-carver° screams now,   *storm-carver*: eagle
> what sight does he see coming?
> I've often gladdened eagles,
> to corpse-goslings° been kind.   *corpse-goslings*: ravens

Then the eagle attacked so fiercely that he had to defend himself with his weapons. Then he spoke a verse:

> You wave your wings about,
> with weapons I'll reply to you.
> You waft about, wide-flier,
> as if warning me of danger.
> Your wits are confused, war-starling,°   *war-starling*: eagle

we two will have victory.
Turn to attack Salmon,
it's time for him to die now.

The one who had been challenged had to strike first. Ketil struck at Framar's shoulder. He stood quietly before the blow, and the sword didn't bite, but he was staggered because the blow was so powerful. Framar struck at Ketil and hit his shield. Ketil struck at Framar's other shoulder, and once again it didn't bite. Ketil spoke a verse:

> You dawdle, Dragvendil,
> with this dainty for eagles.°   *dainty for eagles*: Framar himself
> You've met harmful magic,
> can't manage to bite.
> Salmon wasn't aware that
> weapons steeled in venom
> would rebound from blows,
> if Odin blunted them.

And again he spoke a verse:

> What's with you, Dragvendil,
> why have you been blunted?
> I have struck at him now.
> You're sluggish to bite.
> You submit at the sword-meeting,°   *sword-meeting*: battle
> at the metal-clash° you give way.°   *metal-clash*: battle
> You've never failed before,
> when fighters struck each other.

Framar spoke a verse:

> The old fellow's beard's aflutter.
> His weapon fails to strike home.
> The maiden's father is afraid;
> he fears for his sword's sharpness.

> The wound-sticks° are sharpened,   *wound-sticks*: swords
> so that they may bite
> stout-hearted heroes,
> if your heart so urges you.

Ketil said:

> No sense in stirring us up;
> seldom do brave troopers
> ever care to question
> the keenness of my sword-strikes.
> Bite now, Dragvendil,
> or break otherwise.
> Both of us have bad luck,
> if you balk for a third time.

And he spoke again:

> The lass's father won't lose heart
> as long as Dragvendil is whole.
> I feel that this is certain:
> it won't fail a third time.

Then he turned the sword in his hand and brought the other edge forward.[43] Framar stood quietly, but the sword sliced into his shoulder and it didn't stop until it had gone down to his hip, and the wound gaped open at once. Then Framar spoke a verse:

> The Salmon has daring.
> Dragvendil is sharp;
> it hacked Odin's words
> as if they had not been.
> Balder's father fails now,
> it's folly to believe in him.
> Blessed be thy hands!
> Here we must be parted.

Then Framar died, but Bodmod left the dueling ground with Ketil.

Bodmod said, "Now if you think you have to give me any reward for my help, I'd like you to give me your daughter in marriage."

Ketil welcomed this proposal and said that Bodmod was an excellent companion.

After that was done, Ketil went home, and was very famous from his mighty deeds. He betrothed Hrafnhild to Bodmod. Ketil ruled over Hrafnista as long as he lived, and Grim Shaggy-Cheek ruled it after him. Arrow-Odd was Grim's son.

And here ends this saga.

THE SAGA OF GRIM SHAGGY-CHEEK
Gríms saga loðinkinna

CHAPTER I

It is said of Grim Shaggy-Cheek that he was both big and strong, and the most warlike of men. He was called Shaggy-Cheek for this reason: one of his cheeks was overgrown with dark hair, and he was born with that. Iron couldn't cut him on that spot. Grim took over the farm in Hrafnista after Ketil Salmon, his father. He became wealthy. He was also practically the sole ruler over all Halogaland.

Harald was the name of a powerful and famous hersir[1] in Viken[2] to the east. He married Geirhild, the daughter of King Solgi, the son of King Hrolf of Berg[3] in Uppland. Their daughter was named Lopthaena. She was the loveliest of women and quite accomplished. Grim Shaggy-Cheek went there in a small ship with seventeen other men and asked for Lopthaena's hand in marriage. It was agreed upon, and he was to come for the wedding in the autumn.

But seven nights before the wedding, Lopthaena disappeared, and no one knew what had become of her. When Grim came to the wedding, he missed his beloved there, since the bride had been taken, and yet he realized that her father had nothing to do with it. He stayed there for three nights, and they drank there, but with little cheer. Then he went home to Hrafnista.

It so happened that the wife of hersir Harald had died five years previously. A year later, he had married Grimhild the daughter of Josur,[4] from Finnmark in the north, and had brought her home with him. Soon it seemed as if she was ruining everything there. She was bad to Lopthaena, her stepdaughter, as was later proved. Grim wasn't much content with his condition, hearing nothing about Lopthaena, his betrothed.

It happened, as it often does, that a terrible famine came to Halogaland. Grim Shaggy-Cheek prepared to leave home and went on his journey with three men. He sailed north along the coast of Finnmark and eastward to Gandvik.[5] When he came into the bay, he saw that there were plenty of fish to catch. He drew his ship up on shore, and then went straight to a hut and lit a fire in front of himself.

When they had fallen asleep that night, they were awakened by a storm that had come, with a dark blizzard that blotted out all the light. The gale came on with such ferocity that everything froze, both outside and in.

In the morning, when they were dressed, they went out to the beach. There they saw that all their catch was gone, so that they couldn't see any sign of it. They thought that they were in a bad situation, but they couldn't get a wind to sail away. Now they went back to the hut and stayed there for the day.

In the night, Grim was awakened by laughter outside, next to the hut. He leaped up quickly and took his axe and went out. He also had with him, as he always did, the arrows known as Gusir's Gifts, which his father Ketil Salmon had given him. When he came outside, he saw two troll-women down by the ship, and each of them was picking up one end of the ship and trying to shake it apart. Grim spoke up, and recited a verse:

> Who are these, living
> in the lava field,
> bent on breaking
> this boat of mine?
> I've never seen
> a sight to compare,
> more loathsome to look at,
> than the likes of you.

The one who was standing near him spoke a verse:

> Feima is my name,
> in the north I was born,
> Hrimnir's daughter[6]
> from high mountains.

> Here sits my sister,
> stronger by half—
> Kleima[7] she's called—
> who's come to the sea.

Grim spoke:

> May Thjazi's daughters[8],　　　　　*Thjazi's daughters:* giantesses
> most dreadful of women,
> fail to flourish—
> I'll be furious soon.
> Before the sun rises,
> it's certain that I
> will butcher your flesh
> to feed the wolves.

Kleima said:

> Earlier on,
> our own father
> witched[9] the wave-flocks[10]　　　　　*wave-flocks:* fish
> away from here.
> You'll not live through this—
> unless it's fated—
> nor, safe and sound,
> see your home again.

Grim said:

> From the outset,
> I can swiftly
> promise you two
> both point and blade.
> Then Hrimnir's hags
> will have to find out
> whether barb or fist
> is better help.

Grim took one of Gusir's Gifts and shot the one who was standing in front of him, so that she died at once.

Feima said, "Now it's gone all wrong, Kleima my sister." She charged Grim. He struck at her with an axe, and it landed on her shoulder-blade. She shrieked and rushed along the beach. The blow knocked the axe out of Grim's hands, and it stuck fast in the wound. Grim rushed after her, and he got neither closer nor farther, until they came to some huge cliffs. There he saw a large cave in the cliffs, up ahead. There was a path leading upwards, only wide enough for one person, and she rushed up as if it were a level field. And as she hauled herself up the cliff by leaps and bounds, the axe fell out of the wound. Grim picked it up at once, and he was able to hook the axe into each step as he stood on the one below, and pull himself up by the handle. In this way he got up into the cave. There he saw a bright fire burning, and two trolls were sitting by the fire, a male and a female. They were lying on their backs with their feet pressed together. They were both wearing short, shriveled leather tunics. He could clearly see what they carried between their legs. The male was named Hrimnir, and the female was named Hyrja.[11]

When Feima came into the cave, they greeted her and asked where her sister Kleima was. She answered, "Guess what? She's lying dead outside on the beach, and I'm mortally wounded. And you two are lying inside, stretching out here by the fire."

The giant said, "Killing you wasn't much of a brave deed, with one of you six years old and the other seven.[12] But who did this?"

Feima answered, "That wicked man, Grim Shaggy-Cheek, has done this. He and his father are more skilled than other men at striking down trolls and rock-dwellers. But even though he's done this, he still won't ever get his wife Lopthaena. And that's funny, considering how short a distance lies between them."

Hrimnir said, "My sister Grimhild made that happen. She's the most crafty."

Then Feima grew weak from loss of blood, and she fell down dead. At that moment, Grim entered the cave and struck Hrimnir so hard that he cut off his head. Then the old hag Hyrja sprang up and ran at him, and they began to wrestle. Their fight was both hard and long, because she was the worst troll, but Grim was strong and powerful. In the end, he caught her with a hip-throw, and she fell. He cut off her head and left her dead, and went straight to his hut.[13]

CHAPTER II

The next day, the weather was good. Grim and his men walked along the beach and saw where a large whale had washed up. They went there and began flensing the whale. A little later, Grim saw twelve men walking. They came up suddenly. Grim greeted them and asked their names. The one in front said that he was named Hreidar the Reckless, and asked why Grim wanted to rob him of what was his.[14] Grim said that he had found the whale first.

"Don't you know," said Hreidar, "that I own everything that washes up here?"

"I don't know about that," said Grim, "but as it is, we'll have half."

"I'm not willing," said Hreidar. "You must do one of two things: get away from the whale, or else we'll fight."

"We'll fight," said Grim, "rather than give up the whole whale."

At once they joined battle and fought, and it was the fiercest fight. Hreidar and his men were both powerful and quick with their strikes, and in a short time, both of Grim's men fell. Then the battle was hardest, but in the end, Hreidar and all his men fell. Grim also collapsed, both from wounds and from exhaustion. There he lay among the slain on the beach, and he expected nothing but death for himself.

But when he had not been lying there long, he saw a woman walking, if you could call her that. She was no taller than a seven-year-old girl, but so fat that Grim thought that he wouldn't be able to reach around her. She was long-faced and grim-faced, bent-beaked and bare-shouldered, sooty-faced and scrawny-cheeked, foul-faced and forehead-bald. Both her hair and her skin were swarthy. She wore a short skin tunic. It hung down in the back no farther than her buttocks. She looked quite unkissable, because snot was hanging down in front of her maw.

She went to where Grim was lying, and said, "The chief Halogalanders have sunk low. Will you accept your life from me, Grim?"

Grim answered, "I can hardly do that, as hideous as you are. What's your name?"

She answered, "I am called Geirrid Gandvik-Bed. You may assume that I have some authority around the bay. Make your decision, one or the other."

Grim answered, "It's an old saying that 'everyone is greedy for life'." I'll choose to accept my life from you."

She picked him up under her skin tunic and ran with him as if he were an infant, so fast that her tunic was filled with wind. She didn't stop until they had come to a certain large cave, and when she put him down, Grim found her even more hideous than before.

"Now you've come here," she said, "and I want you to reward me for saving you and carrying you here. Kiss me now."

"I can't do that at all," said Grim, "as horrible as you look now."

"Then I won't offer you any help," said Geirrid, "and I see that you'll soon be dead."

"Then it must be so," said Grim, "although I'm really not in the mood."

He went to her and kissed her. She didn't seem to him as bad to touch as she was filthy to see. By then, evening had come. Geirrid prepared a bed and asked whether Grim wanted to lie alone or next to her. Grim said that he would rather lie alone. She said that she didn't want to make any effort to heal him. Grim saw that that wouldn't be right for him, and said that he'd rather lie next to her, if there was no other choice. He did so. First she bound all his wounds, and he seemed to feel neither burning nor soreness. He found it strange how soft-fingered she was, considering how ugly her hands appeared, since they looked to him more like vulture's claws than human hands. And as soon as they came to bed, Grim fell asleep.

But when he awoke, he saw a woman lying in bed next to him, so fair that he thought he had hardly seen anyone like her. He was amazed at how her body resembled Lopthaena, his betrothed. On the floor by the bedside, he saw where the hideous skin of a troll-woman was lying, which Geirrid Gandvik-Bed had owned. The woman was completely powerless. He stood up quickly and dragged the skin into the fire and burned it to ashes. Then he went to the woman and dripped water into her mouth, until she came to her senses and said, "Now each of us has done well: I saved your life at the beginning, but you brought me out of bondage."

"How did you come here, and how did you come to be in this condition?" said Grim.

She answered, "A little while after you had gone westward from Viken, away from my father Harald, my stepmother Grimhild met me, saying, 'Now I will pay you back, Lopthaena, because you have shown me defiance and disobedience ever since I came to the kingdom. I now pronounce that you shall become the ugliest troll-woman and go off north to Gandvik and live right next to[15] Hrimnir, my brother; and you two will have at it, both frequently and roughly.[16] The more downhearted you get, the worse you'll have it. You shall be detested by all, both trolls and men. And,' she said, 'you shall be in this bondage all your life, and never get free, unless some man should agree to these three things that you'll ask—and I know that won't happen. The first is to accept his life from you, the second is to kiss you, and the third is to lie in bed with you. You'll have it worse than everyone.' Now you've done all these things for me, as you were obliged to. I want you to bring me east, to my father in Viken, and celebrate my wedding, as was planned."

Then they went back to Grim's hut, and there were plenty of fish to be caught. A beached whale was lying in every bay. He loaded his boat, and when it was ready, he sailed from the land with the two of them in the ship, Grim and Lopthaena. He made use of the knack which his father Ketil Salmon and the other men of Hrafnista had: he hoisted the sail, and at once a favorable wind sprang up. He sailed home to Hrafnista, and the people thought that he had been snatched out of Hel.

CHAPTER III

A little later, Grim went eastwards to Viken, and Lopthaena went with him. Over to the east, Grimhild ruled nearly everything by herself. But as soon as Grim came, he had Grimhild captured, and a bag put over her head,[17] and he had her stoned to death, because he had previously told hersir Harald what had happened. Then he held his wedding to Lopthaena and went home to Hrafnista. But hersir Harald married for the third time, and married Thorgunna the daughter of Thorri.

Grim and Lopthaena had not been together long before they had a daughter who was named Brynhild. She grew up in Hrafnista and was the fairest maiden. Grim loved her very much. But when she was twelve years old, a man named Sorkvir asked for her hand. He was the son of Svadi, the son of Raudfeld, the son of Bard, the son of Thorkel Bound-Foot.[18] She didn't want to marry him, and for that reason, Sorkvir challenged Grim to single combat. Grim agreed to this. Sorkvir was from Sogn on his mother's side, and there he had estates to manage. The single combat was to be held in half a month's time.

There was a hersir in Norway named Asmund, who governed the estate called Berurjod.[19] He was married and had a son named Ingjald. Ingjald was the boldest of men, and he stayed for a long time with Grim Shaggy-Cheek, and there was deep friendship between them. Although Ingjald was older, Grim was much stronger. Ingjald married a woman named Dagny, the daughter of Asmund who was called Gnod-Asmund after his ship the *Gnod*,[20] and the sister of Olaf King of Warriors. By her he had a son named Asmund who later became the sworn brother of Odd the Far-Traveller, also known as Arrow-Odd, who fought on the side of Sigurd Hring at Bravellir.[21]

At the appointed time, Sorkvir came to the combat with eleven other men. They were all berserkers. Grim was already there, and Ingjald with him, and many farmers from Halogaland. They went to the dueling ground, and Grim had to strike the first blow. He carried the sword Dragvendil which his father had owned. The man who held the shield in front of Sorkvir was named Throst.

Grim struck such a mighty first blow that he split the shield from end to end, and the point cut Throst's left shoulder and sliced completely through the man down to his right hip. The sword plunged into Sorkvir's thigh so that it cut both legs from under him, one above the knee and the other below the knee, and he fell down dead. Grim and Ingjald turned on the ten who were left and didn't stop until they were all killed. Then Grim spoke a verse:

> Here we have
> hewn to earth
> twelve berserks,
> tainted with shame.
> Sorkvir was still
> strongest by far

of these men;
Throst was next.

And he also said:

> First I must follow
> my father's example:
> I'll never allow
> the lace-pine°, my daughter,   *lace-pine*: woman
> to wed any man
> unwillingly,
> as long as I live,
> without leaving wounds.

Grim went home after the combat, and Ingjald went back to Berurjod. A little while later, Ingjald's father died, and Ingjald took over all his holdings. He became a prominent farmer and the most hospitable of men.

CHAPTER IV

Some winters previously, Bodmod Framarsson had died. He had had one daughter with his wife Hrafnhild, who was named Thorny. Thorny's son was Thorbjorn Fish-Gills, the father of Ketil the Broad, the father of Thorny who married Hergils Knob-Arse.[22] Hrafnhild then went home to Hrafnista to live with Grim, her brother.

There was a prominent man named Thorkell, who was the jarl of the shire of Namdalen. He went to Hrafnista and asked for Hrafnild's hand, and she was given to him in marriage. Their son was Ketil Salmon, who burned Harek and Hraerek, the sons of Hildirid, inside their home, because they slandered his kinsman Thorolf.[23] After that, Ketil went to Iceland and claimed land there, between Thorsar and Markarfljot, and he lived at Hof. His son was Hrafn, the first law-speaker in Iceland. His second son was Helgi, the father of Helga who married Oddbjorn the Shipwright.[24] The third was Storolf, the father of Orm the Strong[25] and Hrafnhild who married Gunnar Baugsson; their son was Hamund, father of Gunnar of Hildarend,[26] and their daughter was Arngunn who married Hroar the Priest of Tunga;[27] their son was Hamund the Lame.

The Saga of Grim Shaggy-Cheek

Vedrorm, the son of Vemund the Old, was a powerful hersir.[28] He asked to marry Brynhild, the daughter of Grim Shaggy-Cheek, and she accepted him. Their son was Vemund, the father of Vedrorm who escaped from King Harald east to Jamtland and cleared a forest to settle there. His son was Holmfast, and Vedrorm's sister was named Brynhild; her son was Grim, who was named for Grim Shaggy-Cheek. These kinsmen, Grim and Holmfast, went on Viking raids to the west and killed jarl Asbjorn Skerry-Burner in the Hebrides. As booty, they took his wife Olof and his daughter Arneid. Holmfast was allotted Arneid, and he gave her to his father Vedrorm. She was his concubine until Ketil the Noisy took her and brought her out to Iceland. Arneidarstad in the East Fjords is named for her.[29] Grim married Olof the daughter of Thord Waddler, who had been the jarl's wife. Grim went to Iceland and claimed Grimsnes all the way to Svina Lake. He lived at Ondverdunes for four winters, and later at Burfell. His son was Thorgils, who married Helga, the daughter of Gest Oddleifson[30]. Their sons were Thorarin, at Burfell, and Jorund, who lived at Mideng. Grim died in single combat by Hallkelsholar, killed by Hallketil, the brother of Ketilbjorn at Mosfell.[31]

Grim Shaggy-Cheek stayed at Hrafnista, as was said earlier. Late in his life, he and his wife had a son named Odd. Ingjald fostered him at Berurjod. He was later called both Arrow-Odd and Odd the Far-Traveller.

Grim was thought of as a great man. He was physically strong and the boldest of men, but mostly kept to himself. He died of old age.

And here ends the saga of Grim Shaggy-Cheek, but here begins Arrow-Odd's saga, a great saga.

THE SAGA OF ARROW-ODD
Örvar-Odds saga

CHAPTER I

There was a man named Grim, who was called Shaggy-Cheek. He was called that because he was born with a hairy cheek. That came about in this way: when Grim's father Ketil Salmon and Bruni's daughter Hrafnhild went to bed together, as was described earlier, Bruni spread a hide over them, since he had invited many Finns to his house. In the night Hrafnhild looked out from under the hide and saw the cheek of one of the Finns, and it was hairy all over. And because Grim had this mark later, people suppose that he must have been conceived at that moment.

Grim lived at Hrafnista. He was wealthy and highly influential, all around Halogaland and farther-flung places. He was married, and his wife was named Lopthaena. She was the daughter of Harald, a hersir from Viken[1] in the east.

One summer, Grim made ready to travel eastward to Viken after the death of his father-in-law Harald, because he had large holdings there. When Lopthaena found out about this, she asked to go with him, but Grim said that that could not be, "because you're pregnant."

"I want nothing more than to go," she said.

Grim loved her very much, and he indulged her. She was lovelier and more accomplished than any woman in Norway. They prepared to travel in style.

Grim sailed out of Hrafnista in two ships, heading eastwards into Vik. But as they sailed past the district called Berurjod,[2] Loptaena said that she wanted the sail lowered, because she realized that she was in labor. And so it was that the ships put in to shore.

A man named Ingjald lived there. He was married, and he and his wife had a son, young in age but handsome in appearance, who was named Asmund. When Grim's party landed, men were sent up to the farm to tell Ingjald that Grim and his wife had arrived in their land. Ingjald had a team of horses yoked to a sleigh and went to meet them himself, and he offered them all the hospitality that they needed and that they would accept. They went home to Ingjald's farm. Lopthaena was brought directly to the women's quarters, and Grim was brought into the main house and seated in the high seat. Ingjald thought that nothing was too good for Grim and his people. Lopthaena's labor pains grew worse, until she delivered a boy-child. The women took him and declared that they had never seen such a handsome child.

Lopthaena looked at the boy and said, "Carry him to his father. He must name the child," and so it was done. The boy was sprinkled with water[3] and given a name, and called Odd.

Grim stayed there for three nights. Then Lopthaena said that she was ready to travel, and Grim told Ingjald that he wanted to get ready to leave.

"I believe," said Ingjald, "that I would like to receive a certain honor from you."

"That's fitting," said Grim. "Choose your own reward, because I'm not short of money to pay out."

"I have enough money," said Ingjald.

"Then take something else," said Grim.

"I want to ask to foster your child," said Ingjald.

"I don't know how Lopthaena feels about that," said Grim.

But she answered, "I advise you to accept it, as it's a good offer."

Then they were brought to their ships, but Odd stayed behind in Berurjod. They went on their way until they had come to Viken in the east, and they were there for as long as they thought necessary. Then they prepared to leave, and they had a favorable wind until they sailed past Berurjod. Grim ordered the sails to be lowered.

"Why shouldn't we be on our way?" said Lopthaena.

"I thought that you'd want to meet your son," said Grim.

"I looked at him when we parted," she said, "and it seemed as if he wouldn't look on us Hrafnista people with loving eyes. We two should be on our way."

Grim and his wife came home to Hrafnista and settled down on their farm, but Odd grew up with Asmund at Berurjod. Odd took up the skills that were customary for men to learn. Asmund served him in every way. He was more handsome and accomplished than most men. Odd and Asmund swore brotherhood between them. Every day they were at the archery targets, or swimming. No one could equal Odd in any achievement. Odd never played at games, like the other young men. Asmund always went with him. Ingjald esteemed Odd more highly than Asmund in every respect.

Odd had every man whom he found to be skilled make arrows for him. He didn't take care of them afterwards, and they scattered all over the floor and the benches and got underfoot. Many people got scratched when they came inside in the dark or sat down. This one thing was making Odd unpopular. Men told Ingjald that he should speak with Odd about this. Ingjald found Odd one day at mealtime.

"There's just one thing, my foster-son, that's making you unpopular," said Ingjald.

"What's that?" said Odd.

"You don't take care of your arrows, as other men usually do," said Ingjald.

"I'd think you had the right to complain," said Odd, "if you had gotten me something to keep them in."

"I'll get that for you," said Ingjald, "whatever you want."

"I think you'll fail to get it," said Odd.

"That won't happen," said Ingjald.

"You have a three-year-old buck goat, black in color," said Odd. "I want you to have him slaughtered, and flay the whole skin off, with the horns and hooves."

It was done as Odd had asked, and he was brought the skin when it was ready. He put his arrows inside, and he didn't stop until the skin was full. He had many more and longer arrows than other men. He got himself a bow to match.

Odd was dressed in this way: he wore a red scarlet tunic every day, and had a gold headband tied around his head. He had his quiver wherever he went. Odd wasn't accustomed to making sacrifices, because he trusted in his own might and main, and Asmund followed him, but Ingjald was the greatest man for sacrifices. The sworn brothers Odd and Asmund often sailed out to sea.

CHAPTER II

There was a woman named Heid.[4] She was a prophetess and seeress and knew in advance about things that had not happened yet, by means of her uncanny wisdom. She went to feasts and told men in advance about how the winter would turn out, and about their fates. She had fifteen boys and fifteen girls with her. She was at a feast not far from Ingjald.

One morning, Ingjald was up early. He went to where Odd and Asmund were sleeping, and said, "I want to send you two out of the house today."

"Where should we go?" said Odd.

"You two should invite the seeress here, because a feast is to be held here," said Ingjald.

"Then I won't make that trip," said Odd, "and I won't thank you at all, if she comes here."

"You must go, Asmund," said Ingjald, "because I have your consent."

"I'll do something," said Odd, "that will seem no better to you than this seems to me now."

Now Asmund went and invited the seeress there, and she promised to come, and came with all her following. Ingjald went to meet her with all his men and invited her into his house. They prepared for divinations[5] to take place that night. And when the people had eaten their fill, they went to sleep, but the seeress and her retinue went to her night-journeying divinations. Ingjald came to her in the morning and asked how her prophecies had gone.

"I believe," she said, "that I have become certain of that which you would all like to know."

"Then I shall assemble the men on their seats," said Ingjald, "and get information from you."

Ingjald was the first man to come before her. "It is well, Ingjald," she said, "that you have come here. I can tell you that you shall dwell here until old age, with great honor and worth, and that will be most welcome to all your friends."

Then Ingjald went away, and Asmund went up. "It is well," said Heid, "that you have come here, Asmund, for your glory and honor will spread far and wide through the world. You won't have to deal with old age, but you will seem to be an excellent companion and a great champion, which you are."

Then Asmund went to his seat. All the people went to the seeress. She told each one what was destined for him, and they all were content with their lot. Then she told about how the winter would go, and many other things that people didn't know before. Ingjald thanked her for her prophecies.

"Have all those in your household come here now?" she said.

"I suppose that almost all of them have come now," said Ingjald.

"What's lying there on the far bench?" said the seeress.

"Some cloak is lying there," said Ingjald.

"It looks to me as if it stirs from time to time as I look towards it," she said.

Then what had been lying there sat up and spoke up, and said, "It's exactly what you think it is—this is a man, and it's the man who wants you to shut up right now and not babble about my business, because I don't believe what you say." Odd had a stick ready in his hand, and he said, "I'll bring this stick down on your nose if you prophesy anything about my affairs."

She said, "All the same, I'll tell you, and you'll listen." Then this song came to her lips:

> Don't frighten me
> with firewood sticks,
> Odd of Jaederen,
> argue as we may.
> The tale will prove true
> told by the seeress.
> She knows beforehand
> all the fates of men.
>
> You'll not fare over
> fjords so broad,
> nor light out far
> over land and sea,
> though waves should well
> and wash over you—

your body shall burn
at Berurjod here.

Filled with venom,
a viper shall wound you,
flashing from Faxi's
faded skull.
An adder will lash
your leg from below,
when, oh hero,
you've had a full life.

"I must tell you, Odd," she said, "as may seem good to you to know, that a great age is in store for you, much greater than other men's. You shall live for three hundred years and travel from land to land, and always be thought the greatest man wherever you go. Your path will lead throughout all the world, but no matter how far you shall travel, here you shall die, at Berurjod. A horse stands here in a stall, gray with a dark mane. The skull of that horse, Faxi, shall be the death of you."

"You make the most wretched prophecies about my affairs of any old crone," said Odd. He jumped up as she was speaking her prophecy, and brought the stick down onto her nose, so hard that blood poured down on the ground.

"Take my baggage," said the seeress. "I want to go away from here, because I have never before been treated this way, with men beating me."

"You mustn't do that," said Ingjald, "for there's compensation for every wrong. You shall stay here for three nights and receive fine gifts."

She took the gifts, but left the feast.

CHAPTER III

After that, Odd told Asmund to come with him. They took Faxi and put a bridle on him, and led him until they came to a certain small dale. There they dug such a deep pit that Odd had to struggle to get out of it. Then they killed Faxi and dropped him down into the pit. Odd and Asmund brought the largest stones they could carry and piled them over him, and they poured sand between every stone. There they raised a burial mound that Faxi lay under. And when they had finished their work, Odd said, "I suppose I'd have to say that trolls must have a hand in it, if Faxi gets up out of that. I think I've thwarted the fate that he would be the death of me."

They went home afterwards and met Ingjald. "I want a ship as a gift," said Odd.

"Where will you go?" said Ingjald.

"I suppose I'll leave Berurjod," said Odd, "and never come back as long as I live."

"You mustn't do that," said Ingjald, "because that way you'd do what feels worst to me. What men do you want to have with you?"

"We two shall travel together, Asmund and I," said Odd.

"I want you to send Asmund back quickly," said Ingjald.

"He'll no more come back than I will," said Odd.

"You're doing this wrongfully," said Ingjald.

"I'll do what I think you'd like least, because you invited the seeress here, and you knew that that was the worst thing for me," said Odd.

Now Odd and Asmund prepared for their journey, and they went to meet Ingjald and bid him farewell. They went to the ship and pushed it out, and then they rowed away from the land.

"Where should we go?" said Asmund.

"Wouldn't it be a good idea to seek out my own kinfolk in Hrafnista?" said Odd.

But when they had rowed out to some islands, Odd spoke up: "Our journey will be hard if we have to row all the way north. Now we'll have to find out whether I have any of our family luck. I've been told that Ketil Salmon would hoist the sail when becalmed. Now I'll put that to the test and hoist the sail."

And as soon as they had hoisted the sail, they got a favorable wind, until they arrived at Hrafnista early in the day. They beached their ship and went straight to the farm. Odd had no other weapons than the quiver that he carried on his back, but his bow was in his hand. When they came to the farm, a man stood there outside and greeted the arrivals warmly, and he asked their names.

"I'm not sharing that with you," said Odd.

Odd asked whether Grim was at home. The man said that he was. "Then call him to come outside," said Odd.

The man went in and told Grim that two men had arrived outside—"and they said that you should go out."

"Why can't they come inside?" said Grim. "Ask them to come in."

The man went outside and told them what he had been told. "You must go inside a second time," said Odd, "and tell Grim to come out and meet us."

The man went and told Grim.

"What sort of men are they?" said Grim.

"They are handsome men and very tall. One of them has a large animal skin on his back."

"You're saying that these men who have come here must be the sworn brothers, Odd and Asmund."

Then Grim went outside, along with everyone who was inside, and he welcomed Odd and Asmund warmly. Grim invited them into his house, and they accepted.

As soon as they had sat down, Odd asked about his kinsmen, Gudmund and Sigurd. They were related in this way: Gudmund was Odd's brother, the son of Grim and Lopthaena, and Sigurd was Grim's sister's son. They were promising men.

"They are anchored north of here, in the lee of the island, and they intend to go to Bjarmaland," said Grim.[6]

"I want to meet them," said Odd.

"I want you to stay here this winter," said Grim.

"First I have to go and meet them," said Odd.

Then Grim traveled with him, until they came to an island to the north. Gudmund and Sigurd were anchored there in two ships. Their kinsman Odd called for them to come onto land. They welcomed him warmly, and as soon as they had heard the news, Odd said, "Where have you two decided to travel?"

"To Bjarmaland," said Gudmund.

"Asmund and I want to go with you," said Odd.

But Gudmund had heard word of them in advance, and he said, "There's no way that you can travel with us this late in the summer,[7] kinsman Odd. We've already prepared for our journey. Come with us in the summer, wherever you want."

"That's well said," said Odd, "but I think I just might get a ship when summer comes, and have no need to be your passenger."

"That makes no difference—you won't go with us," said Gudmund, and with that they parted.

CHAPTER IV

Now Odd accepted his father's invitation to stay at home, and Grim seated him next to himself on the high seat, with Asmund next to Odd. Grim offered them every hospitality. Gudmund and Sigurd anchored there by the island for half a month, since they were never able to leave.

It happened one night that Gudmund tossed in his sleep. The men advised that he should be awakened. Sigurd said that he should enjoy his dreams. Then Gudmund woke up.

"What have you dreamed?" said Sigurd.

"In my dream, I appeared to be anchored here by the island," said Gudmund, "but I saw a white bear lying up on the island, in a ring around it. Right here, up above the ships, the beast's rump and head met. It was so fierce that I have never seen anything like it, for all the beast's hair was standing on end. It seemed as if it might leap out onto the ships and sink them both at any moment, and then I woke up. Now you must interpret my dream."

"I don't think it needs much interpretation," said Sigurd, "because while you saw the bear-beast lying there looking so fierce that all its hair seemed to be standing up, and you thought that it would sink the ships, I can clearly see that that is the fetch[8] of our kinsman Odd, and he must be angry with us. He must be as hostile towards us as that beast looked to you. I can tell you that we'll never be able to leave, unless he goes with us."

"He won't want to go now, even if we ask him," said Gudmund.

"What should we do then?" said Sigurd.

"My advice," said Gudmund, "is for us to disembark and invite him to go with us."

"But what will become of the voyage if he doesn't want to go?" said Sigurd.

"Then we shall give him the second ship, rather than not have him go," said Gudmund. Now they disembarked and found Odd and invited him to go with them. He said that he certainly did not want to go.

"We're willing to give you the second ship now. Come with us," said Gudmund.

"Then I'll go," said Odd, "and I'm all ready now."

Grim went to the ships with them. "Here are treasures that I want to give you, Odd my son," said Grim. "These are three arrows, and they have a name; they are called Gusir's Gifts."

He gave the arrows to Odd. Odd examined them and said, "These are the greatest treasures." They were feathered with gold, and they launched themselves from the bowstring and returned to it, and there was never any need to search for them.

"Ketil Salmon took these arrows from Gusir, the king of the Finns," said Grim. "They pierce anything that they're aimed at, because they were crafted by dwarves."

"I've never received any gifts that seemed as beautiful to me as these," said Odd. He thanked his father, and they parted in friendship.

Odd stepped aboard the ship and ordered his men to sail away from the island. They hoisted the sail on Odd's ship, and did the same on the other. Now they got a favorable wind and sailed together, northwards along the coast of Finnmark. Then the wind subsided, and they put into an anchorage and stayed there for the night. There were many Finnish huts[9] up on land there.

In the morning the men on Gudmund's ship landed, and they ran into every hut and pillaged the Finns, who took it badly and cried out a great deal. The men on Odd's ship decided that they wanted to land, but he wouldn't allow it.

Gudmund and his brother came to the ships at evening. Odd said, "Were you on land?"

"I was," he said, "and I've done what I found to be the most fun, making the Finns weep. Will you be wanting to come with me in the morning?"

"Far from it," said Odd.

They stayed there for three nights, and then they got a favorable wind. There is nothing further to tell about them until they came to Bjarmaland. They steered their ships up the river called the Dvina. Many islands lie in the river. They anchored alongside a certain cape that projects from the mainland. They saw what was happening on land: men were coming out from the forest and gathering in one place.

Odd said, "Gudmund, what do you suppose that those men on land are up to?"

"I don't know," he said. "What do you think, kinsman Odd?"

"I suppose that there must be a great sacrifice here," he said, "or else an inheritance feast. Now, Gudmund, you must guard the ships, and Asmund and I will go onto land."

When they came to the forest, they saw a large house there. It was almost completely dark. They went to the doors and took up positions there and saw many things happening. Men were seated on both benches. They saw that a vat was standing against the far doors. It was so bright there that there was no shadow except where the vat stood. A great hustle and bustle was to be heard inside.

"Can you make out anything of what the people are saying here?" said Odd.

"No more than birds twittering," said Asmund. "Do you think you can make any of it out?"

"No better than you," said Odd. "You can see that one man is serving drink to both benches, and that makes me suspect that he must know how to speak Norse. Now I'll go inside and take up the position that I find most advantageous. You wait here for me in the meantime."

He now went inside and took up a position by the doors, until the servant's path took him there. The servant didn't notice anything before he was seized, and Odd swung him up over his head. The servant shouted out loud and told the Bjarmians that a troll had captured him. They leaped to their feet and grabbed him from the other side, but Odd dragged them along with the servant. In the end, Odd and Asmund hung on to the servant, and the Bjarmians didn't have the confidence to rush out after them.

They came to the ships with the servant, and Odd sat him down on a bench next to him and asked him for information, but he stayed quiet.

"You don't need to keep quiet," said Odd, "because I know that you can speak Norse."

Then the servant said, "What do you want to ask me?"

Odd said, "How long have you lived here?"

"Several years," he said.

"How do you like it?" said Odd.

"My time staying here has been the worst I've ever spent," said the servant.

"What can you tell us," said Odd, "about what we might do that the Bjarmians would hate the most?"

"I'm glad you asked," he said. "A burial mound stands along the Dvina River. It's made of two substances, silver and earth. A double handful of silver must be brought there for every man who leaves the world, and the same when he comes into the world, along with just as much earth. You would do what the Bjarmians would consider the worst thing, if you were to go to the mound and carry off the money."

Odd called Gudmund and Sigurd and said, "You and your ship's crews should go to this mound, according to this servant's instructions." They made ready to travel and went onto land, but Odd stayed behind and guarded the ships, keeping the servant next to him.

CHAPTER V

Now they traveled until they came to the mound, and they packed up bundles for themselves, because there was no shortage of silver. When they were ready, they went to the ships. Odd asked how it had gone, and they said it had gone well, and that there was no lack of plunder there.

"Now you two should take the servant," said Odd, "and keep a careful watch on him, because his eyes kept straying towards the land, as if he didn't find his stay with the Bjarmians to be as bad as he claimed."

Now Odd went to the mound, and Gudmund and Sigurd guarded the ships. They sat together and sifted out the silver, and the servant sat between them. They didn't notice anything, until he had dashed up onto the land and they didn't have him any more.

There is this to tell about Odd and his men: They arrived at the mound, and Odd said, "Now we must pack bundles for ourselves, each man as much as he can carry, so that we may go on our way fully loaded."

It was getting light when they left the mound. They traveled until it was light. Then Odd planted his feet.

"Why aren't you walking?" said Asmund.

"I see a huge mob coming out of the forest," said Odd.

"What do we do?" said Asmund. Now they all saw the mob.

"This is not going well," said Odd, "because my quiver is down on the ship. I'll turn back to the forest and cut myself a club with this broadaxe that I'm holding, and you should go out onto that cape that juts out into the water." They did so, and when Odd came back, he had a huge club in his hands.

"What do you think that mob means?" said Asmund.

"I think," said Odd, "that the servant must have gotten free from Gudmund and Sigurd, and that he must have brought news of us to the Bjarmians, because I figured that he didn't find this place as bad as he let on. We must now deploy our men across the peninsula."

The men now rushed at them, and Odd recognized the servant at the forefront of the ranks. Odd addressed him and said, "Why did you steer us wrongly?"

The server said, "I wanted to figure out what pleased you best."

"Where did you go?" said Odd.

"Onto land," he said, "to tell the Bjarmians about your plans."

"How did they like it?" said Odd.

"I put your case before them so well," he said, "that they want to hold a market with you."

"We'd certainly like that," said Odd, "when we get to our ships."

"The Bjarmians wouldn't think it too much if they could have the market held right here."

"What should we trade?" said Odd.

"They want to trade weapons with you, giving silver weapons in exchange for iron weapons."

"We don't want to strike that bargain," said Odd.

"Then we'll have to fight this battle," said the servant.

"It's up to you," said Odd.

Then Odd told his men that they had to fling every man of theirs who was killed out into the river—"because they'll work sorcery on our men, as soon as they get any of the dead." The battle broke out at once. Odd broke through the ranks wherever he attacked, and the Bjarmian fighters were felled like brushwood, and their battle was both fierce and long. The fighting ended when the Bjarmians fled. Odd pursued the fleeing host, but soon turned back and reviewed his own men. Few had fallen, but a mob of the natives had been killed.

"Now we should divide the spoils," said Odd. "Let's pack up bundles of silver weapons."

They did so, and went to their ships at once. But when they came there, the ships had disappeared. Odd felt rather short of friends in that place.

"Now what do we do?" said Asmund.

"One of two things has happened," said Odd. "They must have laid up the ships in a hidden anchorage off the islands—or else they've betrayed us worse than we suspected."

"That can't be," said Asmund."

"I'll make a test," said Odd. He went to the forest and kindled a fire up in a tall tree. It swiftly caught fire and burned so that the flame shot up into the air. Next they saw that the ships were coming to land. There was a joyous reunion of the kinsmen, and they set a course away from there with their plunder, and nothing is said of their travels until they came to Finnmark, into the same anchorage where they had stayed before.

But when night fell, they awoke to hear a crash up in the air, so mighty that they had never before heard the like. Odd asked Gudmund and Sigurd if they had ever heard any mention of such things. And as they were discussing this among themselves, there came another crash, no softer than the first. Then came a third, and it was the loudest.

"What do you think is the reason for this, Odd?" said Gudmund.

Odd said, "I've heard it said that two winds may be in the air at the same time and collide with each other, and there may be great crashes when they come together.[10] Now we should brace ourselves for some severe storms coming."

They brought cross-bands around the ships and took other necessary precautions, according to Odd's prediction. No sooner had they made preparations than the storm blew up so fiercely that it drove them away from land. They weren't able to get the mast down, and were incessantly blown eastward. The gale was so strong that it seemed certain that the ship would sink out from under them.

Gudmund called out from his ship to Odd and said, "What should we do now?"

"There's only one thing to do now," said Odd.

"What's that?" said Gudmund.

"Take all the loot from the Finns and throw it overboard," said Odd.

"What good will that do them?" said Gudmund.

"We'll let the Finns figure that out themselves," said Odd.

This was done: all the loot from the Finns was broken up. At once they saw that it was driven forward along one side of the ship, and back along the other, until it all came into one mass, and then that was driven violently against the wind, so that it was soon out of sight. Shortly after that, they saw land, but the wind kept up and drove them to the land. Most of them were exhausted, except for Odd and his kinsmen and Asmund.

Now they reached land. It isn't said how long they had been at sea. They unloaded their ships. Odd advised them to haul their ships up onto shore and build strong defenses around them. At once they set about doing it, and they built a hut for themselves. When they had finished this, they explored the land. Odd thought that it must be an island. They saw that there was no lack of game, and they shot animals for food as they needed them.

One day, when Odd had gone into the forest, he saw a huge bear. He shot at it and didn't miss. When the beast was dead, he flayed off the skin. Then he had a splint set lengthwise in its mouth. He let that stand in the middle of a path, and the bear faced towards the mainland. Odd enjoyed himself very much on the island.

One evening, when they were standing outside, they saw something happening on the mainland. Men were assembling together on a cape. It happened that the men were both large and small.

"Who do you think those men must be, kinsman Odd?" said Gudmund.

"I don't know," said Odd, "but I'll find out by going to land and learning what's being discussed there."

Odd told Asmund to go with him. They went to the beach and pushed out a boat, and rowed in under the cape, and pulled in the oars and listen to what the people were saying. The one who was the chieftain spoke up: "It's just as you suspected. Some children have come to the island that we own, and they are doing us great injury. So I have come here to advise that these intruders on our lands be killed. I have a ring on my hand. I will give it to the one who will put them to death."

A woman stepped forward in the assembly and said "We women are fond of finery, so give me the ring."

"Yes," said the giant, "it's a good reward for your expedition."

Now Odd and Asmund went until they came home, and they told what had happened, as they had heard it. In a little while, they saw the woman wading from the mainland out to the island. She was wearing a skin tunic and was very tall, and so hideous that they thought they'd never seen such a creature. She went to the ships and seized both prows and shook them so hard that the men were afraid they'd be completely broken up that way. Then she went up onto the island, and Odd ducked behind the bear's back. He had previously laid coals in the beast's mouth. Now he took an arrow and shot it from behind the animal. She saw the arrow flying towards her and brought up her palm to block it, and it bit no more than if it had struck a stone. Then Odd took Gusir's Gifts and shot one, as he had the first. She brought up her other palm, and the arrow flew right through her palm and into her eye and out the back of her head. Still she kept walking. Odd shot a third arrow. She brought up her other palm to block it, spitting in it first, but the arrow flew just as the previous one had, plunging into her eye and out the back of her head. She turned around and splashed back to the mainland and said that her journey hadn't gone smoothly. Now they stayed on the island in peace for a while.

CHAPTER VI

One evening, as they were standing outside by their hut, they saw that a host of people was assembling out on the cape, in the same way as before. Odd and Asmund rowed to the mainland and pulled in the oars.

The chieftain spoke up on the cape. "It's a great wonder that we can't contrive the death of these children," he said. "I sent the boldest of women there, but they have a beast that blows out arrows, and flames shoot out of its nose and mouth. Besides, I've become so sleepy that I have to go home." And Odd and Asmund did the same.

On the third evening, they saw the same thing happening on the mainland, and Odd and Asmund rowed there and listened in. The same chieftain spoke up on the cape: "It's as you thought: we've passed sentence on these children before, and it's come to nothing. But now I've been given a vision."

"What do you see happening now?" said his comrades.

"I see," he said, "that two children have come here in a boat and are listening to what we say. I'll send them a message."

"Now we must get away as fast as we can," said Odd. And at that moment a stone flew from the cape and crashed down where the boat had been. They rowed back. Then the chieftain spoke up: "This is a terrible shame. Their boat is still whole and so are they. I'll throw another stone and a third, but if they escape each time, I'll leave them in peace." The third stone was so huge that Odd and Asmund's boat was swamped.[11] Then they rowed away, and the giant spoke up: "They are still whole and so is their boat, and now I'm so sleepy that I can't wake up." And the giants went home.

Then Odd said, "Now we'll go and beach our boat."

"What do you want to do now?" said Asmund.

"I must find out where those people have their home."

They went up on land and came to a cave, and a fire was burning there. They took up positions and saw that trolls were seated on both benches. There sat an ogre on the high seat. He was both huge and hideous, with hair as long and black as whale baleen, an ugly nose and evil eyes. A woman sat next to him, and what was said about the looks of one can be said about both.

The chieftain spoke up. "Now I am given a vision, and I look out to the island, and now I know who has come there. They are kinsmen, sons of Grim Shaggy-Cheek, Odd and Gudmund. I see that the Finns have sent them here, intending for us to put them to death, but we aren't able to bring that about, because I see that Odd is fated to have a much longer lifespan than other men. Now I will give them a favorable wind away from here, just like the one the Finns gave them to send them here."

Odd said in a low voice, "Of all men and trolls, you give the most wretched gifts."

"I see also that Odd has those arrows called Gusir's Gifts. For that I will give him a name, and call him Arrow-Odd."

Odd then took one of Gusir's Gifts and nocked it on the bowstring, wanting to pay him back for the wind. But when the chieftain heard the whine of the arrow coming at him, he dodged it and jumped up onto a rock, but the arrow struck the woman under the arm and came out under the other arm. She leaped up and flew at the giant and pulled his hair. The trolls on both benches leaped up, and some helped him, and some helped her. Odd shot another of Gusir's Gifts into the giant's eye and went back to the ships, and the brothers welcomed Odd and Asmund warmly. "But where did you go for so long, Odd?" said Gudmund. Odd spoke a verse:

> I set out, going
> with Gusir's Gifts
> between the cliffs
> and the coals burning.
> I shot out the eye
> of an awful troll,
> and pierced the breast
> of the boulder-Freyja.°   *boulder-Freyja*: giantess

"I expected that you'd achieve a great deal," said Gudmund, "since you were away for so long. But did anything more happen on your journey?"

"A name was given to me," said Odd, and he spoke a verse:

> There I won the name
> that I wanted to have,
> which the ogres called
> from the crags to me;
> they said they'd gladly
> give Arrow-Odd
> a wind for sailing
> away from here.

"We were promised a wind to carry us away from here, and I was told that it would be no gentler nor easier than the one that the Finns sent to bring us here."

They now prepared for their journey with no less hope of success than before, and left at once. As soon as they got away from land, a gale like the previous one blew up, so that it drove them over the seas and kept on blowing from the east without ceasing. The gale didn't let up until they came to the same anchorage where they had formerly been driven away from land. All the Finnish huts up on the land were wrecked.

As soon as they got a favorable wind, they sailed away and came to Hrafnista when the winter was well advanced. Grim was glad to see them and invited them to his home with all their men, and they accepted his invitation. They put all their shares of wealth into Grim's keeping and stayed there over the winter.

CHAPTER VII

Odd was so famous for this voyage that it seemed as if no other voyage like it had been made from Norway. There was much good cheer over the winter there, and much feasting. But when spring began, Odd asked his kinsmen what they wanted to do. "You should decide for us," they said.

"I want to go raiding," said Odd. He told Grim that he wanted to have four ships made ready to sail. When Grim heard that, he worked hard at the task, and told Odd when the ships were ready.

"Now," said Odd, "I want you to direct us to some Vikings that you think would be easy for us to handle."

Grim said, "There's a Viking named Halfdan who anchors by the Elfar Skerries[12] in the east, and he has thirty ships."

When they were ready, they set sail southward along the coast of Norway. When they came to the Elfar Skerries, they laid up their ships in an anchorage. Halfdan wasn't far away. As soon as Odd and his men had pitched their tents, he went off with a few men to the place where the Vikings were anchored. Odd saw a huge dragon ship in the fleet. He called out to the ships and asked who was in command of them. The men on the ships loosened the edges of the awnings over them, and said, "Halfdan is the name of the man who commands these ships. Who wants to know?"

"His name is Odd."

"Are you the Odd who traveled to Bjarmaland?"

"I've been there," said Odd.

"Why did you come here?" said Halfdan.

"I want to know which of us is the better man," said Odd.

"How many ships do you have?" said Halfdan.

"We have three ships," said Odd, "and all of them are large, with a hundred men on each one. I will come here in the morning to fight you."

"We won't lose any sleep over that," said Halfdan.

Odd rowed away and came back to his men and told them about their arrangement. "Now we have a lot of work to do," said Odd, "but I've thought up a plan for us. We must carry our valuables onto land, and load our ships as lightly as possible. But we must cut down two trees for each ship, the tallest and most branched that we can find." And they did so.

When they were ready, Odd said, "Gudmund and Sigurd, I think that you two should sail along the other side of the dragon-ship." They did so, rowing silently to where the ship lay before them in the bay. Odd rowed out alongside the dragon ship, and when they had surrounded the ship on both sides, the Vikings didn't realize what was happening until they had rolled the trees down onto the dragon-ship. A man climbed up every branch and knocked out the awning-pegs. Odd and Asmund cleared paths ahead of them, and they had cleared the dragon-ship of men all the way back to the afterdeck before Halfdan could get to his feet. They killed him there, on the afterdeck.

Odd gave Halfdan's men two options, to hold battle or submit to him, and they quickly made the choice to submit to Odd. From them, he chose the ones who seemed most vigorous. Odd kept the dragon-ship for his own, and another ship besides, but he gave all the other ships to the Vikings. He took all their money for himself. He gave a name to the dragon-ship and called it *Halfdan's Gift.*

Then they sailed home to Hrafnista, having won a great victory, and stayed there over the winter. But when spring came, Odd prepared to sail away from land. When they were ready, Odd asked his father, "Where can you direct us to a Viking who has some honor?"

Grim said, "Soti is the name of the Viking whom I will direct you to. He is anchored in the south, off Skien.[13] He has thirty ships, all of them large."

CHAPTER VIII

The kinsmen steered five ships away from Hrafnista and southwards to Skien. When summer came, Soti heard about Odd's journey and went to meet him, travelling day and night until they found each other. Soti then had a headwind, and he spoke up: "Now we must arrange our ships in line alongside each other, and I will place my ship in the middle, because I've heard that Odd is a great warrior, and I guess that he'll sail directly at our ships. But when they come and lower their sails, we'll form a ring around their ships and not let any mother's son escape."

Now it's time to tell about Odd's plan. "I see what Soti and his men are planning," he said. "They think that we'll sail directly at their ships."

"Wouldn't that be rather unwise?" said Gudmund.

"I won't spoil Soti's plan," said Odd, "but I'll counter it with another plan. First, I plan to sail my dragon-ship towards Soti's position. We must move everything behind the mast." They did so, and the dragon-ship *Halfdan's Gift* rushed forward. It was protected with iron plates all the way forward to the ramming prow, but it rode on the rear of the keel. "I mean to sail at Soti's dragon-ship", said Odd, "but you should sail behind. I think it's possible that their mooring lines might break."

Odd sailed the dragon-ship as fast as it could go. Soti didn't suspect anything until the ship bore down on him and broke the lines between the ships. Odd and Asmund rushed ahead of the sail, fully armed. They attacked Soti and his men from the flank and leaped down onto Soti's dragon-ship, and they'd cleared the dragon-ship of men and killed Soti before Gudmund and his men could arrive. Then Odd gave the Vikings the choice to accept a truce from him or fight a battle, and they chose to have peace with Odd. Odd took the dragon-ship, but gave the Vikings the other ships. Now they sailed home to Hrafnista with a great store of wealth. Grim welcomed them, and they stayed there over the winter, highly honored.

When the year began, Odd and his men prepared their ships to leave, and he picked a great host of men to voyage with him. Odd gave Gudmund and Sigurd the dragon-ship *Soti's Gift*. He had the dragon-ship *Halfdan's Gift* painted all over, and he had both the dragon-head and the weathervane decorated with gold. When they were ready to go, Odd went to meet his father Grim and said, "Now you must direct me to the greatest Viking you know."

"There are two things to consider," said Grim. "You are highly accomplished—but you think that no one will dare to defend himself against you. But now I will direct you to the two Vikings whom I know to be the greatest and most accomplished in all respects. One is named Hjalmar the Bold-Hearted, and the other is Thord, called Prow-Glamour."

"Where are they," said Odd, "and how many ships do they have?"

"They have fifteen ships," said Grim, "and a hundred men on each one."

"Where are they based?" said Odd.

"There is a king in Sweden named Hlodver," said Grim. "They stay with him in the winter, but set out in warships in the summer."

They left as soon as they were ready. Grim went with them to the ships, and the father and son parted with much affection.

CHAPTER IX

As for Odd and his men, the story goes that they sailed away from Hrafnista as soon as they had a favorable wind. Nothing is said about their voyage until they came to Sweden, where a cape juts from the mainlaind into the sea. There they spread awnings over their ships. Odd went up on land to see what was happening, and there lay fifteen ships anchored along the other side of the cape, with tents pitched on land. He saw that there were games going on outside, by the tents. Hjalmar and Thord were in command of the ships.

Now Odd went back to his own ships and told the news. Gudmund asked what they should do.

"We'll divide our forces in half," said Odd. "You must steer your ships around the cape and shout a war-cry at the men on land. But I will land with half our forces and move inland, along the edge of the forest, and we shall shout another war-cry at them. Maybe they'll be a bit surprised then. It occurred to me that they would flee to the forest, and we wouldn't need to deal with them any further."

But as for Hjalmar and Thord's reaction, it's said that when they heard the war-cry of Gudmund and his men, they never paid any attention to it. And when they heard another war-cry from up on land, they stayed where they were all the while. When it was over, they resumed their games. The two forces turned around and went back along the cape, and Odd and Gudmund met. "I wasn't sure," said Odd, "whether these men we've encountered here would be so timid."

"What do you intend to do now?" said Gudmund.

"It's easy to see that we won't take these men by surprise here," said Odd. "We'll stay here along the cape through the night and wait for morning."

The next morning, they landed with all their forces to find Hjalmar. As soon as Hjalmar's men saw raiders coming onto land, they armed themselves and went out to face Odd. When they met, Hjalmar asked who was in command of this force. Odd answered, "There's more than one chieftain here."

"What's your name?" said Hjalmar.

"I'm called Odd, the son of Grim Shaggy-Cheek from Hrafnista."

"Are you the Odd that went to Bjarmaland a little while ago? Why have you come here?"

"I want to know which of us is the better man," said Odd.

"How many ships do you have?" said Hjalmar.

"I have five ships," said Odd, "but how large a force do you have?"

"We have fifteen ships," said Hjalmar.

"Our forces are very unequal," said Odd.

"Ten ship's crews shall stay here," said Hjalmar, "and we'll face each other man for man."[14]

Now both sides prepared for battle and drew up their lines, and fought until the day was over. When evening came, peace-shields were held up,[15] and Hjalmar asked Odd how he felt he had done that day. He said that he felt it had gone well.

"Do you want to play this game again?" said Hjalmar.

"I don't plan on doing anything else," said Odd, "because I haven't encountered better fighters or hardier men. We must begin the battle at daylight."

It was done as Odd had said. Men bandaged their wounds and went to their tents in the evening. The next morning, both sides drew up their battle-lines and fought all day. When the day was over, peace-shields were brought up. Then Odd asked how Hjalmar felt the battle had gone that day. He said that he felt it had gone well.

"Do you want us to hold this game for a third day?" said Hjalmar.

"We'll file down to the steel,"[16] said Odd.

Then Thord spoke up: "Can we expect to win a lot of wealth on your ships?"

"Far from it," said Odd, "we haven't gained any money this summer."

"I think I've never seen bigger fools deal with each other than us here," said Thord, "because we're fighting over nothing but pride and reputation."

"How do you want to proceed?" said Odd.

"Don't you think it would be a good idea for us to become partners?" said Thord.

"I would like that very much," said Odd, "but I don't know how Hjalmar feels about it."

"I want to live only by those Viking laws which I've previously kept," said Hjalmar.

"When I hear them, I'll know how agreeable they'll be to me," said Odd,

Hjalmar said, "The first thing to say is that I and my men will never eat raw meat, because it is the custom of many men to wrap flesh in cloth and call it boiled, but their custom seems more fitting for wolves than men. I will never rob merchants or farmers—no more than necessary to have fresh meat on my ships when I need it. I will also never rob women, even if we find them on land with great stores of wealth. And I shall never bring a woman to my ships unwillingly, and if a woman can say that she came here against her will, then the man who abducted her shall forfeit nothing less than his life, whether he is powerful or humble."

"Your laws seem good to me," said Odd, "and they won't stand in the way of our partnership."

Now they swore fellowship. It's said that they had just as many men all together as Hjalmar and Thord had had, before they met.

CHAPTER X

After that, Odd asked if they knew where they could expect to get money. Hjalmar answered, "I know that five berserkers are anchored off Zealand, bolder than most other men whom we have heard of. One is named Brand, the second is Agnar, the third is Asmund, the fourth is Ingjald, and the fifth is Alf. They are all brothers and have six ships, all large. How do you want to arrange our travels now, Odd?"

"I want to head for where the berserkers are," said Odd.

They came to Zealand in fifteen ships, and found out that the berserkers were on land, having gone to meet their concubines. Odd went up on land by himself to find them. When they met, a battle broke out, and in the end he felled them all and wasn't wounded. But when Odd had gone on land, Asmund missed him. He said to Hjalmar, "Yes, we mustn't fail now that Odd's gone on land, and we mustn't be idle in the meantime."

Hjalmar now sailed with six ships to where the Vikings were anchored, and a battle broke out. Odd came down from the land at the same moment that Hjalmar captured the ships. Each told the other what had happened. Both men had gained wealth and honor for themselves.

Now Hjalmar invited Odd and Asmund to come to Sweden with him, and Odd accepted. But the Halogalanders, Gudmund and Sigurd, traveled north to Hrafnista with their men. They agreed to meet up by the Göta River in the east.

When Hjalmar and Odd came to Sweden, King Hlodver gave them a lavish welcome, and they stayed there through the winter. Odd was so highly esteemed that the king felt that no one could equal him in any respect. Odd had only been there a short while when the king gave him five estates.

The king had a daughter named Ingibjorg. She was more lovely than any woman and most accomplished in all the skills that a woman might pride herself on having. Odd always asked Hjalmar why he didn't ask for Ingibjorg's hand in marriage, "because I see that you're in love with each other."

"I've asked for her," he said, "but the king doesn't want to marry his daughter to a man who doesn't have the rank of king."

"Then we should assemble our forces in the summer," said Odd, "and give the king a choice: either fight with us, or give you his daughter."

"I don't know about that," said Hjalmar, "because I've had this place as a base for a long time."

They stayed there peacefully over the winter. But in the spring they set out on a raid, as soon as they were ready.

CHAPTER XI

Nothing is said about their journey until they met up at the Göta River, and discussed amongst themselves where they should head that summer. Odd said that he was most eager to sail west over the sea. Now they had twenty ships, and Odd captained the dragon-ship *Halfdan's Gift*. They came to Scotland and raided there, harrying and burning everywhere they went, and they didn't stop until they had imposed tribute on the land. From there they went to Orkney and conquered it, and stayed there over the winter. In the spring they went to Ireland and raided there, both by sea and on land. Odd never went anywhere without Asmund. Children and women and men fled to the woods and forests, concealing their valuables and their persons.

One day, Odd and Asmund were on land together. Odd was wearing his quiver on his back and carrying a bow in his hand, and they wanted to search for some people if they could find them. Odd didn't notice anything until a bowstring twanged and an arrow flew out of the woods. It didn't stop before striking Asmund. He fell, and soon died.

Odd felt this to be such a terrible, wicked event, that he felt that he had never suffered such harm in his life. He now went inland, leaving Asmund behind. Odd was in such a bad mood that all he wanted was to do all the harm he could think of to the Irish.

He came to a clearing and saw a great many people there, both women and men. He saw a man stand up, wearing a velvet tunic; he had a bow in his hand, but his arrows were stuck in the ground next to him. It looked to Odd as if he was surely about to leave, so that he would have to search for him to take revenge later. So he took one of Gusir's Gifts, nocked it on the string, and shot at this man. The arrow hit him in the belly, and he fell down dead at once. Odd shot at one man after another, killing three other men there, and the people fled into the forest.

Odd was in such a fury against the Irish that he intended to do them all the evil that he could. He went down a wide road through the forest. Every bush in his way he tore up by the roots. He tore up one bush that was looser than the others. He saw a trapdoor underneath, and he pulled it up and went down into the earth there. There he found four women in an underground house. One of them was by far the prettiest. He seized her by the hand at once, wanting to pull her out of the chamber.

She spoke up. "Turn me loose, Odd," she said.

"What sorcery do you know," he said, "finding out whether I am called Odd or something else?"

"I knew who you were as soon as you came here," she said. "I also know that Hjalmar is with you, and I'll know to tell him if I go to the ships against my will."

"You'll go all the same," said Odd.

The other women held on to her and wanted to hold her back, but she told them to leave off. "I will make a deal with you, so that you'll let me go in peace," she said, "because I have no lack of wealth."

"I certainly don't want your wealth," said Odd, "because I'm not short of gold or silver."

"Then I will have a shirt made for you," she said.

"It's all the same," said Odd. "I have enough shirts and shirt-making."

"You must have fine ones," she said, "but none like the one that I'll have made, because it will be embroidered with gold and made of silk.[17] I will have such powers go with the shirt that you won't have had such powers before."

"Let me hear them," said Odd.

"You shall never get cold wearing it, neither at sea nor on land. Swimming shall not weary you, and fire shall not harm you, and hunger shall not strike you, and iron shall not bite you. I will make it with all these qualities, except for one."

"Which one is that?" said Odd.

"Iron will bite you if you're fleeing," she said, "even if you're wearing the shirt."

"I usually want to achieve something in battle other than fleeing," said Odd. "But when will it be completed?"

"Next summer," she said, "at exactly the same time of day as it is now, when the sun is in the south. Then we two will meet here in this same clearing."

"If you don't accomplish this," said Odd, "has it occurred to you how much of a chance I will give you Irish then? I have to pay them back for their evil, since they've killed Asmund."

"Don't you think you've avenged him," she said, "since you've killed my father and my three brothers?"

"I don't think he's been avenged at all," said Odd. Their bargain was made as they had agreed, and with that, they parted.

Odd now traveled to where Asmund lay. He picked him up and laid him on his back and walked to the sea carrying him. Hjalmar had landed there with all his men and intended to search for Odd. They met a short distance from the ships. Hjalmar asked what had happened, and Odd told him.

"Have you avenged him at all?" said Hjalmar.

A song came to Odd's lips:

> I ran down the wide
> wagon's track,
> seized my sturdy
> staves of the bowstring.°   *staves of the bowstring:* arrows
> All of my gold
> I'd give, to have
> Asmund alive,
> alongside me.

"What's our plan now?" said Hjalmar. "You must want to pillage and do all kinds of damage here."

"Far from it," said Odd, "because now I want to leave as soon as possible."

The Vikings were quite amazed at that, but Hjalmar said that it had to be as Odd wished. They raised a burial mound in honor of Asmund. The Vikings disapproved of this so much that as they avoided Odd's gaze, they made accusations behind his back. He acted as if he didn't know.

Now they sailed out of the west until they came to Laeso.[18] A jarl who isn't named was anchored there, and he had thirty ships. They agreed to fight, and at once there was a hard battle. Odd cleared himself of the accusations of cowardice that the Vikings had made in Ireland. Odd and Hjalmar won victory in that battle.

From there they sailed to Denmark, and they heard the news that a host had been raised in order to avenge the five berserkers whom they had killed, before they went west to Ireland. Two jarls were in command of the force. Their encounter ended in this way: they killed them both, and imposed tribute on the land.

CHAPTER XII

Now their forces split up. Gudmund and Sigurd sailed north to Hrafnista, and they settled there peacefully, wishing to give up raiding. Odd stayed behind in Denmark over the winter, but Hjalmar went to Sweden with his men. They agreed to meet on Skaney in the east in the spring. Both of them stayed at home quietly that winter.

When spring came, Hjalmar and Thord Prow-Glamour set out from the east at the agreed time for their meeting. When they met, Hjalmar asked where Odd wanted to sail that summer. He said that he wanted to go to Ireland.

"You didn't want to raid there last summer," said Hjalmar.

"Nonetheless, I shall go there this summer," said Odd.

They sailed away from land, and they had a favorable wind until they came to Ireland. Odd said, "Now we'll pitch our tents here, and I will go onto land alone."

"I'll go with you," said Hjalmar.

"I want to go alone," said Odd, "since I've agreed to meet certain women in the woods."

Now Odd traveled until he came to the same grove that he and Olvor had agreed on, and she hadn't come. He was filled at once with great anger against the Irish, and meant to go through the land plundering everything that he could. But when he had traveled for a little while, he heard wagons coming towards him. There he met Olvor, and she greeted him first: "Now I don't want you to be angry with me, even though I am later than I promised."

"Is the shirt ready?" said Odd.

"Of course," she said. "You must sit next to me. I want to see how the shirt fits you." He did so; he took it and unfolded it and put it on, and it was a perfect fit for him in every respect.

"Do all the powers that we agreed on go with the shirt?" said Odd.

"That's true," she said.

"Whether or not it is," said Odd, "did you make this treasure by yourself?"

A song came to her lips:

> A silken shirt I offer,
> in six places it was made:
> one arm sewn in Ireland,
> the other by the Finns;
> Saxon maids struck the loom,
> Scots maids spun the thread,
> Welsh brides did the weaving,
> warped by riff-raff's mother."[19]

Then a song came to Odd's lips:

> It did not seem
> like a stout byrnie,
> or frigid iron rings
> falling about me,
> when this silk shirt,
> sewn with gold,
> fell over me firmly,
> fitting my sides.

"How do you like the shirt now?" she said.

He said he liked it very much.

"Now you must choose a reward for making the shirt," said Odd.

"This land has been at risk of invasion," she said, "ever since my father was killed. As matters stand, the land is under my rule. For that reason I choose this reward: for you to stay here for three winters."

"Then we two must strike another bargain," said Odd. "You must go with me and be my only woman."

"You'll think I'm saying this because I'm eager for a man," she said, "but I'll accept that."

Then Odd looked around and saw a troop of men near him. He asked whether those men had been assigned to take his head. "Far from it," she said. "These men are to be your escort to the ships. Now you shall travel with greater honor than last summer."

Odd turned and went down to the ships with this escort, and he met Hjalmar in his tent. Odd asked Hjalmar to stay there for the next three winters, and he agreed. Odd now married Olvor. In summer they sailed there in warships and killed the Vikings that were raiding there. When they had stayed there for the agreed time, they had destroyed all the Vikings in Ireland, both near and far; some were killed and some ran away. By then Odd was so sick of being there that it was no use trying to hold him back.

Olvor and Odd had begotten a girl-child, and she was named Ragnhild. Olvor and Odd had to decide what to do with her: Odd wanted to keep her with him, but Olvor didn't want that. It got to the point that Hjalmar had to decide this, and he wanted the girl to grow up with her mother.

When they were ready, they sailed away and came to England. They had heard that the Viking named Skolli was anchored there, with forty ships. When they had tied up in an anchorage, Odd stepped into a boat, meaning to find Skolli and talk with him. And when they met, Skolli asked Odd why they had come to that land.

"I intend to hold a battle with you," said Odd.

"What wrong are you paying me back for?" said Skolli.

"None," said Odd, "except that I want to have your wealth and life, before you raid the king who rules this land." He was named Edmund.

"Are you the Odd who went to Bjarmaland a long time ago?" said Skolli.

"The same," said Odd.

"I'm not stupid enough to pit myself against you," said Skolli. "You must want to know why I'm attacking King Edmund."

"That would be good," said Odd.

"This king killed my father and many of my kin from this land, and then settled down in the kingdom. Sometimes I manage to take half of the land, and sometimes a third. Now I would think you would win greater fame by joining forces with me, and we could kill King Edmund and bring the kingdom under our rule. I will swear to this with witnesses."

"Then you should get eight freemen from this land to witness the oath."

"So be it," said Skolli.

Odd went to his ship and met Hjalmar, and told him that if matters went as Skolli had said, they would join forces with him. Now they slept through the night, and in the morning they landed with all their forces. Skolli had been busy in the night, and he had come down from the land with the free farmers, and they swore an oath to him. After that, they joined forces and went up on land and traveled over it with war-shields. They fired and burned everywhere they went. The inhabitants fled and found the king. The two forces met in the southern part of the land. A battle broke out between them at once, and they fought for three days. In the end, King Edmund fell there. Odd and his men subjected the land to their rule and stayed there over the winter.

In spring, Skolli offered to give them the land. But Odd wouldn't accept—"I suggest that you offer it to Hjalmar."

But Hjalmar didn't want it. "Then my advice is that we give the land to Skolli," said Odd. He accepted, and he decreed that they could always stay there whenever they wanted, whether in winter or summer. They readied twenty ships to sail away, and nothing is said about their journey until they came south to Skien.

CHAPTER XIII

There were two kings, one named Hlodver and the other named Haki. They were anchored off Skien with thirty ships. When Odd and his men had brought their ships to land, ten ships came rowing at them. When they met, there were no taunts, because fighting broke out between them at once. Odd's side had twenty ships. They had such a hard sea-fight that Odd had hardly ever found himself in a tougher fight. But when their fight ended, Odd's side had won ten ships.

Then Odd spoke up: "These men were much more frightening in stories."

"Do you think so?" said Hjalmar. "Those were their messengers who were sent to find us."

And when they had rested for a little while, twenty ships came rowing at them from the shore. At once such a fierce and hard battle broke out that Odd and his men had never been in a situation where they had encountered such men before, neither at sea nor on land. The battle ended with both kings falling, along with all their men. But it's said that by then, Odd and Hjalmar had so few men that they sailed away in one small vessel, and they came to the rocks that are called the Elfar Skerries. Inlets run in among the skerries, which are called the Crane Inlets. They saw two ships anchored there, and there were black awnings over both of them. It was early summer.

"Now I want us to go on our way without being noticed," said Hjalmar, "because the Vikings are lying quietly under their awnings."

"I can't enjoy not having a word with the men that I meet on my way," said Odd.

Now Odd called out and asked who was in command of the ships. A man stuck his head out from under the awning and answered, "His name is Ogmund."

"Which Ogmund are you?" said Odd.

"Where have you been, that you haven't managed to hear of Ogmund Eythjof's Bane?" said the man on the ship.

"I haven't heard of you," said Odd, "and I've never seen anyone as hideous as you." As for this man's appearance, it's said that he had black hair, with a shock of hair hanging down in front of his face where the bangs should be. Nothing of his face could be seen except for his eyes and teeth. At the time, he had eight men with him who looked much the same. Iron couldn't bite them. They were more like giants than men, on account of their size and wickedness.

Then Ogmund spoke up: "Who is this man who's bowing to me?"

"His name is Odd," he said.

"Are you that Odd who went to Bjarmaland a long time ago?" said Ogmund.

"That's the man who's come here," said Odd.

"I'm glad," said Ogmund, "because I've been searching for you for most of my life."

"What do you have in mind for me?" said Odd.

"Would you rather fight at sea or on land?" said Ogmund.

"I'll fight at sea," said Odd.

Then Ogmund and his men took down the awnings from their ships. Odd and Hjalmar prepared for battle elsewhere, and they carried stones onto their ship. When they were both ready, a fierce battle broke out, and the ships came side to side. They had a long hard fight. When it had gone on for a while, Ogmund raised peace-shields and asked Odd how he felt it was going. Odd said that he felt that it was going badly.

"Why is that?" said Ogmund.

"Because I've always fought with men before, but now I think I'm dealing with demons," said Odd. "I struck at your neck, which I could reach most easily, with this sword that I was holding, and it didn't touch you."

Ogmund answered, "Either of us might say the same, that he has to deal with trolls no less than men. I struck at your neck, which I could reach most easily, using the sword whose blows have never been blocked before, and it didn't bite. Do you want us to fight longer, or do you want us to part? For I can tell you how our battle will go: your sworn brothers, Hjalmar and Thord, will fall here, with all your men. All my champions will also fall, and the two of us will be left. But if we fight to the end, then I will fall before you."

"I'll keep playing this game," said Odd, "until all our men and yours have fallen."

Now they clashed shields together a second time and fought, until three were left standing: Thord, Hjalmar, and Odd. Ogmund and eight of his men were also still standing.

Ogmund spoke up: "Do you want us to part now, Odd? I say now that our losses are even, since it will go as I told you. But a life much longer than other men is fated for you. You also have that shirt, so that you can't be hurt."

"It seems better for us to separate first," said Odd, "if you won't make any accusations of cowardice behind my back."

"Why not separate?" said Ogmund. "I say that we're even."

Odd said that he wanted to get out of the inlets. They did so, and anchored beside a certain island. Odd said that there were three tasks for them to take care of: one was to go into the forest and shoot an animal, and the second was to guard the ship. "I'll start a fire," said Hjalmar, "and take my turn at the cooking." Odd went into the forest, and Thord watched over the ship.

But when they came back, Thord had disappeared. They searched for him and found the boat where it was tied up. Now they searched for Thord and found him sitting in a ravine on a hillside, dead.

"This is such a terrible thing to happen," said Odd, "we haven't suffered such harm since Asmund died."

They searched for what had caused his death, and they found an arrowhead sticking out from under one arm, and feathers sticking out from under the other arm.

"That wicked Ogmund must have thought that his losses weren't equal to ours," said Odd. "We two must head for the inlet at once to find them."

They did so, but Ogmund was quite gone. They searched for him for a whole week, thoroughly and completely, in the skerries and through the woods, islands and promontories, and never found him or heard news of him. Then they sailed to where Thord was, and they brought him to Sweden and raised a mound for him. They went home to Uppsala and told the king what had happened. The king welcomed them generously, and they stayed there quietly. At the height of summer, the king invited them to stay there—"and I will give you ships and men to sail out from this land so that you may amuse yourselves."

CHAPTER XIV

Now it is said that Odd and Hjalmar readied two ships, and had forty men on each ship. They sailed away from land. It so happened that the wind pushed them back, and they sailed towards a certain island called Samsey. There are inlets there called the Munar Bays. They sailed their ships into an anchorage and spread awnings over them.

It happened that the weathervane[20] on Odd's ship had fallen into the sea that day. When morning came, Odd and Hjalmar went up onto land to cut wood for a new one. Hjalmar was wearing all the armor that he bore in battle, as he usually did. Odd left his quiver behind, down in the ship, but he wore his shirt both day and night. All their men were asleep, and they didn't suspect anything until Vikings came at them. The man who led them was named Angantyr. There were twelve of them together, all brothers, and they had no other men. They had traveled far and wide from their home, and never encountered resistance. Now they came to where Odd and Hjalmar's ships were. They charged on board fighting, and to make a long story short, they killed every mother's son on the ships.

Then the brothers began to speak, and said, "We still have to decide whether our father Arngrim lied to us again, when he told us that these men were such hardy and powerful Vikings that no one could withstand them. We've seen to it that they all made the worst showing and turned out to be useless. Let's go home and kill that old shit of a father, and let him have that for his lies."

"It's one of two things," some said, "either Odd and Hjalmar are highly overrated, or else they've gone onto land, since the weather is good. Now we must go on land and search for them, rather than go back without having been tested."

The twelve brothers now did so, and the berserk fury came upon them and they howled as they went. The berserk fury also came upon Angantyr, which had never happened before. This went on until Odd and Hjalmar came down from the forest. Odd stopped and planted his feet. Hjalmar asked what was the matter with him. Odd said, "There's a strange sound in front of me. It sounds sometimes like bulls bellowing or dogs howling, but sometimes it's like screaming. Do you know anything about these men who make such a noise by their natures?"

"Yes," said Hjalmar, "I know these twelve brothers."

"Do you know their names?" said Odd.

Then a song came to Hjalmar's lips:

>   Hervard, Hjorvard,
>   Hrani, Angantyr,
>   Bild and Bui,
>   Barri and Toki,
>   Tind and Tyrfing,
>   the twin Haddings,
>   bairns who were born
>   in Bolm to the east,
>   the sons of Arngrim
>   and Eyfura.
>
>   I know these men,
>   most malevolent
>   and least willing
>   to work good deeds.
>   They are berserks,
>   brimful of evil;
>   they cleared two ships
>   of trusty men.

Then Odd saw where the berserkers were going, and there was a song on his lips:

>   I see men coming
>   from Munarvagr,
>   greedy for battle,
>   in gray tunics.
>   They are screaming
>   in scorn and anger.

> Our ships on the beach
> are barren and empty.

Odd said, "This doesn't look good, because I left my quiver and bow behind, down in my ship. All I have is a a wood-axe in my hand." Then he spoke a verse:

> Then I felt fear
> for the first time,
> when these screamers
> stormed from their ships
> and walked on the island
> wailing and howling.
> I know these men,
> most deceitful,
> and the most willing
> to work evil deeds.

Odd went back into the forest and cut a club for himself, and Hjalmar waited for him. When he came back, the berserkers came at them. Hjalmar said this:

> Never tremble before
> the trees of battle,°   *trees of battle:* warriors
> though the struggle may seem
> savage to us.
> We this evening
> with Odin shall lodge,
> two sworn brothers,
> but the twelve will live.

Odd added:

> Just one word
> I will refute:
> They this evening
> with Odin shall lodge,

> twelve berserks,
> but we two will live.

Then a song came to Angantyr's lips:

> Hardy warriors
> have come hither,
> heroes from the roller-wood.°   *roller-wood*: a ship
> Fallen are your
> fellow travellers,
> faring to Vidrir's hall.°   *Vidrir's hall*: Odin's hall, home of slain warriors

Then Odd said:

> Raging warriors
> are arriving here,
> twelve all together,
> tainted with shame.
> One brave warrior
> should battle against one,
> unless his heart
> should happen to fail him.

"Who are these men we've found here?" said Odd.

"Angantyr's the name of the commander of this force," they said. "We are twelve brothers, the sons of Jarl Arngrim and Eyfura from the east, from Flanders."

"Who wants to know?" said Angantyr.

"One of us is Odd, the son of Grim Shaggy-Cheek, and the other is named Hjalmar the Bold-Hearted."

"It's a good thing that we've met," said Angantyr, "because we've been looking for you far and wide."

"Have you been to our ships?" said Odd.

"We went there," said Angantyr, "and everything went our way."

"What do you intend, now that we've met?" said Hjalmar.

"I think," said Angantyr, "that one man should fight against one man here, as you said before. I propose that Odd should fight me, because you have that shirt whose maker swore to you that no iron would bite you, but I have the sword Tyrfing which the dwarves smithed, and they swore that its stroke would never be blocked, neither by iron or by stone. We'll divide our men in half; seven will go somewhere else, and I will stay here with four other men. By myself, I'm equal to the two Haddings, and Tyrfing's worth one more man."

Then Hjalmar spoke up. "I want to fight Angantyr, because I have this mailcoat, and I have never been wounded wearing it. It is made with fourfold layers of rings."

"Then you're doing the wrong thing," said Odd, "it will turn out well for us if I fight Angantyr, but it's not certain otherwise."

"Whatever happens, it's my choice," said Hjalmar.

Then Angantyr spoke up: "If any of us get away from here, I don't want anyone else to steal our weapons. I want to keep Tyrfing in a mound with me, should I die. Odd shall have his shirt and his arrows, and Hjalmar his mailcoat." They agreed that the survivors should raise a burial mound for the others.

Now the two Haddings advanced first, but Odd struck each of them with a blow from his club, and they didn't need any more. One after another of those whom Odd had to fight rose up, and in the end he killed all who were intended for him. Odd took a rest. Then Hjalmar stood up, and one of the berserks faced him. They didn't exchange blows for long before he fell. Then another stood up, and then a third and a fourth. Then Angantyr rose up, and they had a long, hard fight. In the end, Angantyr fell before Hjalmar.

Hjalmar went over to a hillock and sat down and fell over. Odd went to him and spoke a verse:

> What's happened, Hjalmar?
> Haggard is your face.
> Dire wounds, I say,
> are wearying you.
> Your helmet's been hewn,
> but your hauberk's at your sides.
> Now your life, I say,
> is leaving you.

"Now what I told you has turned out to be true: it wouldn't go well for us if you fought Angantyr."

"That doesn't matter," said Hjalmar, "everyone has to die sometime." And he spoke this verse:

> I have sixteen wounds,
> slashed is my mailcoat,
> darkness before my eyes,
> it's too dim to walk.
> Angantyr's weapon
> wounded me to the heart,
> the bitter point
> in poison was tempered.

"Now I've suffered such a loss that I can never hope for it to be made right, as long as I live," said Odd. "Your fight has ended badly. We would have won a great victory here, if I had had my way."

"You must sit down," said Hjalmar. "I want to sing you a lay and send it home to Sweden." He recited this:

> Let not the ladies
> of our land say
> that I fell back
> before the blows.
> The wise-minded lady
> who lives in Sigtuna
> won't laugh me to scorn
> for skulking away.

> I went away
> from women's singing,
> sailed out with Soti,
> seeking joy.
> I sped on my journey
> to join the host,
> left my dear friends
> for the last time.

The dear daughter
of the doughty ruler
led me onward
to Agnafit.
What she told me
proved a true story:
that I would not
ever return.

I turned away
from tender Ingibjorg,
on the destined day
we chose our doom quickly.
The girl will grieve
for this gallant man:
no more shall we two
meet again.

Take these tokens—
I tell you my wishes—
my helm and hauberk
to the hall of the king.
His daughter's mind
will be moved with grief,
to see my mail shirt
sheared from my breast.

Five farms, all told,
in fief I held,
but I had no love
for life ashore.
Now I must lie,
with little strength,
struck by a sword
on Samsey.

Take from my fingers
the fair gold ring
and give it to
the girl Ingibjorg.
The lady will mourn
for her loyal man:
no more shall we two
meet again.

I see in Sigtuna
the seated women
who tried to detain me
from travelling far.
No more shall mead
or men's friendship
make Hjalmar happy
in the hall of the king.

"I also want you to bear my greetings to all our benchmates, and I will name them by name:

We drank and talked
many days together,
Alf and Atli,
Eyvind, Trani,
Gizur, Glama,
Gudvard, Starri,
Steinkell, Stikill,
Storolf, Vifill.

Hrafn and Helgi,
Hlodver, Igul,
Stein and Kari,
Styr and Áli,
Ossur, Agnar,
Orm and Trandill,

Gylfri and Gauti,
Gjafar and Raknar.

Fjolmund, Fjalar,
Frosti and Beinir,
Tind and Tyrfing,
the twin Haddings,[21]
Valbjorn, Vikar,
Vemund, Flosi,
Geirbrand, Goti,
Guttorm, Sneril.

Styr and Ari,
Stein and Kari,
Vott, Veseti,
Vemund, Hnefi.
We all sat once
on the same bench,
lively and cheerful—
I'm reluctant to leave.

Svarfandi, Sigvaldi,
Saebjorn and Kol,
Thrainn and Thjostolf,
Thorolf and Sval,
Hrappi and Hadding,
Hunfast, Knui,
Ottar, Egil,
Ingvari as well.

"Now," Hjalmar said to Odd, "I want to ask you not to lay me in a mound next to evil beings such as the berserks, because I think much better of myself than them."

"I will grant what you ask for," said Odd, "because now it looks to me as if you're fading fast."

"You must take the ring from my hand," said Hjalmar. "Bring it to Ingibjorg, and tell her that I send it to her on my dying day."

A song came to Hjalmar's lips:

> The battle-leader
> and his band of jarls
> gladly drink ale
> at Uppsala together.
> Some grow sleepy
> from swilling beer—
> but here, what wearies me
> are weapon-tracks.°

weapon-tracks: wounds

> A raven soars from the south,
> from a stately tree,
> and an eagle flies,
> following him.
> I've fed the eagle
> on my final day;
> now he may sup
> on my spilled blood.

And after that, Hjalmar died.[22]

Odd dragged the berserks together into a single heap a short way from the sea, and bent saplings around them. He laid their weapons and clothes next to them, taking nothing away. He piled turf around the outside, and poured on sand afterwards. Then he picked up Hjalmar and laid him across his back. He went down to the sea and laid him down on the beach, but he went out to the ships and carried every man who had fallen to land, and built another mound there for his own men. And it's said by the men who have been there that one can still see this landmark, which Odd built, in the daytime.

CHAPTER XV

After that, Odd laid Hjalmar in a ship and left that land. Odd had to use the skill which had been granted to him: he hoisted the sail in calm weather, and sailed home to Sweden with the dead Hjalmar. He landed where he wanted to, beached his ship, laid Hjalmar on his back and went home to Uppsala carrying him, and laid him down in front of the doors of the hall. He entered the hall, carrying Hjalmar's mailcoat and helmet in his hands. He laid them down on the hall floor before the king, and told him news of what had happened.

Then he went to where Ingibjorg was sitting on a chair. She was sewing a shirt for Hjalmar. "Here is a ring Hjalmar sent you," said Odd, "with his greetings, on his dying day."

She took the ring and looked at it, but didn't answer. She sank back against the chairposts and died at once.

Odd burst out laughing and said, "Few things have gone well for a while, so we have to make the best of it. They must enjoy each other in death, which they could not do alive."

Odd picked her up and carried her in his arms, and laid her in Hjalmar's arms before the hall doors. He sent men into the hall for the king, and asked him to see how he had arranged matters. After that, the king welcomed him warmly and seated him in the high seat next to him. After he had rested, the king said that he wanted to hold a funeral feast for Hjalmar and Ingibjorg, and to have a mound raised for them. The king had everything done as Odd said. The helm and mailcoat that Hjalmar had owned were brought forward, and the people felt that his valor and vigor had been of great worth. Now they were both laid in the same mound. Everyone came to witness this momentous occasion, and Odd had it done with highest honor.

Odd stayed quietly that winter with King Hlodver, but in the spring the king gave him men and ten ships. Odd went out that summer to seek out Ogmund Eythjof's Bane once again, and he didn't find him anywhere.

CHAPTER XVI

This went on until autumn, when Odd came to Gotland. There he heard of a Viking named Saemund; it was said he was harder to beat than other men. He had sixty-five ships. Odd and his men came there with ten ships, and as soon as they met, a battle broke out, so long and fierce that nothing was held back. By the evening, all of Odd's ships were cleared of men, and he alone was left standing. Odd jumped overboard when it was almost dark. A man saw him swimming away from the ships. He seized a javelin and threw it after him. It pierced Odd's calf and stuck in the bone. Odd realized that what he was doing would be fleeing. He swam back towards the ships, and the Vikings saw Odd and pulled him up into their ship. Saemund ordered them to put fetters on his feet and tie his hands with a bowstring. It was done as he had said.

Now Odd sat in fetters, and twelve men were found to watch over him. Saemund had himself ferried to land and had a tent pitched for him. Odd said to the men assigned to guard him, "Would you rather I entertain you, or do you want to entertain me, since it's so lonely here?"[23]

"It seems that there's little happiness in store for you," said the man in charge. "You're in fetters, and marked for death in the morning."

"I'm not worried about that," said Odd. "Everyone must die sometime."

"Then we choose you to entertain us," they said.

He sang them songs, and didn't stop until they were all asleep. Then Odd went to where an axe was lying on the deck. He managed to turn it so that the edge faced upwards. He turned his back to it and rubbed his hands against it until he was loose. Then he put his hands to the fetters and got them off him. When he was free, he found the deck to be roomier. He went to where the men were sleeping, and jabbed them with the axe-handle and ordered them to wake up—"You were sleeping like fools, and the prisoner's gotten loose." Then he killed them all. He picked up his quiver and stepped into a boat and got away to the land. Then he went into the forest and pulled the javelin out of his leg and bandaged his wound.

Now there is to tell about Saemund: he awoke in his tent and sent men out to the ship where the guards were. Odd had left, and all the guards were killed. They grieved for their friends in that place and told Saemund what had happened. He went everywhere, throughout Gotland, to search for Odd, but Odd went elsewhere to search for Saemund.

It happened early one morning that Odd came out of the woods. He saw Saemund's tent on land, but the ships were floating in the harbor. He turned back into the forest and cut himself a club. He went straight down to the tent and smashed it down onto Saemund and his men. He killed Saemund, and fourteen other men along with him. Then he gave the men on the ships the choice to submit to him and make him their chieftain, and that's what they chose. Odd sailed home to Sweden, still with few men, and he stayed there over the winter.

CHAPTER XVII

Odd sent messengers north to Hrafnista and asked his kinsmen for help, and asked for Gudmund and Sigurd to come from the north in spring. They were glad to hear that, and went to find Odd. And when they met, there was a joyous reunion.

Now they prepared their ships for the journey, and they steered south towards lands where the seas were shallow, because Odd had rarely gone there before. They raided in the south, all through Brittany, France, and Flanders,[24] making great raids. There is nothing to tell about their journey, until they wrecked their ships on a certain land. They went onto land with their forces. When they came onto land, they saw a building in front of them. It was built in a rather different way from the houses they had seen before. They went up to the house. It was made of stone, and it was open.

Odd said, "Sigurd, what do you suppose that this house must be, here where we are?"

"I can't figure it out," he said. "What do you think, kinsman Odd?

"I don't know," he said, "but I guess that men built the house, and will be coming here to visit. We shouldn't go inside, with things as they are."

They sat down outside, next to the house. After a little while, they saw that people were coming to the house, and that noises went with them. They had never heard the like before. "I suppose," said Odd, "that the people of this land are quite peculiar. I shall wait here until the people come out of this house."

It went as Odd guessed: time passed, and people left the house. One of the locals came up to where Odd was sitting, and said "Who are these?"

Odd told him the truth. "But what is this land to which we have come?"

The man said that it was called Aquitania.

"But what's the meaning of this house, which you've been in for some time?"

"We call it either a minster, or a church."

"And what was that noise you were making?"

"We call that the Divine Office," said the local man. "But what are you doing here? Are you really heathens?"

Odd answered, "We know nothing about any faith, other than believing in our own might and main, but we don't believe in Odin. But what faith do you have?"

The local man said, "We believe in the one who has shaped the heavens and the earth, the sea, the sun and the moon."

Odd said, "Whoever made all that must be great. I think I can understand that."

Now Odd and his fellows were shown to their lodgings. Odd and his men stayed there for several weeks and had discussions with the locals. They asked whether Odd and his men wanted to accept the true faith. It happened that Gudmund and Sigurd accepted the faith. Then Odd was asked whether he wanted to accept the faith. He said that he would give them this option: "I will accept your customs, but live my life in the same way as before. I'll never sacrifice to Thor or Odin or other idols, but I have no desire to stay in this land. So I'll rove from land to land, and sometimes be among heathens, and sometimes among Christians." Still, it was decided that Odd would be baptized. They stayed there for a while.

One day, Odd asked Gudmund and Sigurd if they wanted to leave. They said, "We've stayed here, and it's seemed like the best place for us."

"Then we disagree," said Odd, "for I've stayed here, and it has become most hateful to me." So he didn't take leave of his kinsmen; he stole away by himself, and they stayed behind with all their men.

As he went away from the town, he saw a great crowd of men coming towards him. One man was riding, and the others were walking. These men were dressed in a showy way, and none of them held a weapon. Odd stood next to the road, and the men passed by him, and each one was talking with another. Then Odd saw four men rushing forward, all holding knives in their hands. They rushed at the man who was riding and chopped off his head. Then they ran back the way they had come, next to Odd, and one of them carried the head of the slain man in his hands. Odd realized that these men must have committed a foul deed. He rushed after them and chased them, but they ran off to the woods and rushed down into an underground chamber in the earth. Odd rushed into the chamber after them. They resisted, but Odd attacked them, and he didn't stop until he had killed them all. Then he cut off their heads and tied their hair together, and then went out, carrying the heads with him, and also the head that they had brought there.

Odd went back to the town. The others had come to church with the body that had been killed. Odd threw the heads into the minster and said, "There before you is the head of the one who was killed, and I have avenged him." They felt that what Odd had done was a most worthy deed.

Odd asked what man that had been whom he had avenged. They said that this man was their bishop. Odd said, "Then it was better to do that, than not."

They kept a close watch on Odd, because they didn't want him to go away at all. But as much as he hated staying there, he hated it even more when he found that they were keeping watch on him, and all he did was brood on how to get away.

It finally happened that he stole away one night. He traveled from land to land, and eventually he came to the Jordan River. There he took off all his clothes, including his shirt. He went into the river and washed himself as much as he liked. Then he got out of the river and put on his shirt, and it kept all of its powers as before. Now he went away from there, carrying his quiver on his back, and still travelling from land to land. His situation got to the point that he was living out in the forest, so that he had no other means of support than shooting animals or birds to feed himself, and that's how matters stood for a while.

CHAPTER XVIII

It's said that Odd came one day to some cliffs and a large chasm, where a great waterfall was flowing and making a huge roar. He wondered whether anyone could get over it, and didn't see how. He sat down, and he hadn't been there for long before he was suddenly seized. A vulture had come there flying and clutched Odd with its claws, so hard that he had no warning of its coming. This beast flew with Odd over many lands and seas. In the end, the vulture flew to a sheer cliff and settled on a tuft of grass that grew on the cliff. This creature's young were there. It turned Odd loose, and he was well and uninjured because his shirt had protected him, both against this vulture's claws and everything that has been previously told.

Odd was right next to the vulture chicks in the nest. A high cliff towered above, and below there was a sheer drop to crashing waves. There was no way for Odd to get out, except to let himself fall down into the sea and risk his life. There was no place to reach level ground nearby, because he couldn't see any end to the cliffs. The chicks were still little. The vulture was seldom at home in the nest, and it was always searching for food. Odd tied the chicks' beaks shut, but hid himself in a cleft in the precipice by the nest. The vulture brought more fish and birds, and human flesh, and flesh of all sorts of wild animals and livestock. Eventually it happened that it brought boiled meat to the nest. And as soon as the vulture went away, Odd would eat, but he hid himself in the meantime.

One day, Odd saw a huge giant, rowing towards the nest in a stone boat.[25] He said in a loud voice, "It's an evil bird that's in the nest, because it's in the habit of stealing away my freshly boiled meat, day after day. Now I've got to try and pay it back somehow. When I took those oxen from the king, I didn't mean for this bird to have them."

Odd stood up and killed the chicks, and called out to the giant: "Here's everything that you're looking for. I've seen to it."

The giant got up into the nest and took his meat and carried it down to the boat. He said, "Where's that little baby that I saw here? Come out and don't be frightened, and come with me."

Odd showed himself, and the giant picked him up and let him down into the boat. He then said, "How should the two of us kill this noxious creature?"

Odd answered, "Take fire and place it in the nest. When the vilture comes back, I think it just might fly so near that the flame will jump to its feathers, and then we'll triumph over it."

It happened just as Odd had guessed, and they killed the vulture. Odd cut off its beak and claws and kept them with him. He stepped into the boat, and the giant rowed away.

Odd asked the giant his name. He said that he was called Hildir, a giant from Giantland. He said that he had a wife named Hildirid, and by her a daughter named Hildigunn. "I also have a son who is named Godmund, and he was born yesterday. There are three of us who are brothers; one's named Ulf, and the other is Ylfing. We have agreed to assemble this summer. Whichever one has accomplished the boldest deed, and who has the most savage dog, shall be king over Giantland. The dogs will fight at the assembly."

Odd said, "What do you think about your chances of becoming king?"

Hildir answered, "I'm afraid that one of them will get it for sure, because all my life I have been the least of us, and so it will still be."

Odd said, "What would you prefer?"

Hildir replied, "I'd choose to be king, but that's quite unlikely. Ulf owns a wolf that's the fiercest animal anywhere, and no dog dares to fight with him. Ulf has killed the beast called a tiger, and he has the beast's head as evidence. But my brother Ylfing is even harder to beat, because he owns a white bear that shows no mercy. Ylfing has killed the beast called a unicorn. But I haven't done any deed to compare with theirs, and I don't have a dog that can compete with theirs."

"It's a good thing that you've told me," said Odd, "and some advice might be had that would help, if the man were of good will."

Hildir said, "I've never seen any baby as small as you who was more impertinent, nor shrewder, because I think I can say that you're nothing but smart. I think you're the greatest treasure, as snappish as you are. I'll bring you to my daughter Hildigunn, and she'll have you for a plaything, and mother you and raise you just like Godmund my son."

After that, Hildir set to the oars and rowed home to Giantland, and Odd felt the boat went dreadfully fast. When he came home, he showed the baby that he had found, and told his daughter to take care of him like her own child and no worse. When Hildigunn took Odd and he stood next to her, he hardly reached the middle of her thigh, and yet Hildir was as much taller than she as would be expected for a man. When Hildigunn picked up Odd and set him on her knee, she turned him around in front of her and said,

> A little tyke
> with a tuft of whiskers.
> Godmund was bigger
> at his birth yesterday.

Then she laid him in a cradle next to the giant baby, and sang a lullaby over them, and treated him well. When he seemed restless in the cradle, she laid him in bed next to her and wrapped her arms around him. In the end, Odd played all the games he liked, and things went very well between them. Odd told her that he was no child, although he was smaller than the people who were born there. These people are called giants because they are much larger and stronger than any other sort. They're more handsome than most other men, and no smarter.

Odd stayed there over the winter, and in spring he asked Hildir how well he might treat the man who showed him a dog that could beat his brothers' dogs. Hildir answered, "I would owe him the richest reward. But can you tell me anything about this?"

Odd said, "I can show you the dog, but you yourself must capture him."

Hildir answered, "I'll catch him, but you must bring him into my sight."

Odd said, "This beast lies in Vargeyjar,[26] and it's called a grizzly bear. Its nature is to lie hibernating all winter, but in summer it gets up, and then it is so ravenous and fierce that it spares nothing that lies in front of it, neither beast nor man. I think it likely that this beast would beat your brothers' dogs."

Hildir said, "Come with me to this dog. If it turns out as you say, then there will be a rich reward for you when I claim my kingdom." They made ready to leave at once.

Hildigunn said to Odd: "You must be planning to come back from this journey."

He said that he wasn't sure.

"That would be even worse for me," she said, "because I love you much, even though you're little. And there's no need to hide the fact that I'm pregnant, though it might seem even more unlikely that you'd be capable of that, as puny and worthless as you are to look at. There's no one else but you who could be the father of this child that I'm carrying. But though I love you so much that I don't think I can bear to lose you, all the same, I don't want to hinder you from going where you want, since I see that it's not in your nature to stay here with us any longer. And don't doubt that you'd never get away from here, unless I was willing. But instead, I will bear with grief and sorrow, crying here and sighing there, as is my lot, rather than have you not be where you want to be. What do you want me to do with our child?"

"You shall send him to me," said Odd, "if it's a boy, as soon as he is ten years old, because I hope that there will be some manhood in him. But if it's a girl, then raise her here and look after her, because I won't be interested."

"It's entirely your decision," she said, "like everything else between us. Now travel safely and well." She wept bitterly, but Odd boarded the ship.

Hildir set to the oars. Odd thought that using the oars would be slow going, because they had a long way to go. He made use of the knack that the men of Hrafnista were gifted with: he hoisted the sail, and a favorable wind blew up right away, and they sailed forward along the coast. It wasn't long before Hildir leaped up in the boat, fumbling at Odd with his hands. He clutched at him and shoved him down, and said, "I'll kill you if you don't stop this witchcraft you're working, because all the land and mountains are rushing past like ocean waves, and this ship will sink beneath us."

Odd said, "You shouldn't worry about that, since you're dizzy because you aren't used to sailing. Now let me stand up, and you'll find out that I'm telling the truth."

The giant did as Odd asked. Odd lowered the sail, and at once the land and the mountains were still. Odd told him not to be surprised, even though it would often look this way to him if they were sailing, and he said that he could stop whenever he wanted. Hildir listened to what Odd said, and decided that this journey was quicker than rowing. Then Odd hoisted the sail and sailed, and Hildir was calm.

There is nothing to tell about their journey until they came to Vargeyjar and went up on land. There was a huge pile of boulders. Odd told Hildir to reach into the pile as far as he could and see if he could catch anything. He did so, sticking his arms into the rockpile all the way up to his armpits, and said, "Hey, there's something strange in here. I'll grab it with my rowing glove." He did so, and he pulled the bear out by the ears.

Odd said, "Now you should go with this dog, just as I told you. Bring him home with you, and don't turn him loose before the assembly when you're fighting your dogs. You must not give him food before summer. Let him stay in the house alone, and tell no one that you've captured him.

But on the first day of summer you shall fight him against your brothers' dogs. If he doesn't do the job, come to this place next summer. I'll give you another plan, if this one doesn't work out."

Hildir had suffered wounds all over his hands. He said "I'd like to make a pact with you, Odd, to come to this place at the same time next summer." Odd agreed to that.

Now Hildir went home with the beast and arranged everything as Odd had said. Odd went another way, and nothing is said about his doings or deeds until he came to the place they had agreed on, the next summer. Odd arrived first, and went a little way into the forest. He didn't want to let Hildir see him, because he didn't want to risk meeting him; he realized that the giant would want to take vengeance if everything hadn't gone the way he had told him.

Not much later, he heard oars splashing, and saw that Hildir was coming. He went up onto land holding a cauldron full of silver in hand, and two very heavy chests in the other. When he came to the place which they had agreed on, he waited there for a while, and Odd didn't come.

Then the giant said: "It's too bad that you didn't come, foster-son Odd, because I don't have leisure to delay here any longer, since my kingdom is unguarded while I am away, I want to leave these chests which are full of gold, and the cauldron full of silver. You'll have the money even if you come later. I'll lay a stone slab over them, so the wind won't blow them away. In case you don't see it, I'll lay these treasures on top: a sword, helmet, and shield. But if you're anywhere nearby, so that you can hear my words, I want to tell you that I became king over my brothers. I had by far the most savage dog, for it bit both of my brothers' dogs to death, as well as many men who wanted to help the dogs. I brought out the beak and claws of the vulture, and that was thought to be a much braver deed than my brothers had accomplished. Now I'm the sole king over the land that we brothers owned. I must leave and go home to my kingdom. Come to see me, and I won't treat you stingily, which is proper. I also want to tell you that my daughter Hildigun has given birth to a boy named Vignir, and she says that you fathered him on her. I'll raise him with loving care. I'll teach him skills and do everything for him as if he were my own, and raise him until he is ten, and then send him to you, as you and she had decided earlier."

Then he rowed away in his boat. As soon as he had left, Odd stood up and went to where the money was under the slab. It was such a huge rock that many men could never move it. So Odd only got the treasures that lay on top of the slab. Still, those were great treasures. Having taken them, as has been told, Odd went into the woods and forest.

CHAPTER XIX

One day, Odd came out of the forest. He was very weary, and he sat down under an oak tree. He saw a man walking, wearing a blue-flecked cloak[27] and high shoes, and carrying a reed-sprout in his hand. He wore golden gloves. He was of medium height and was noble in appearance; he let the hood of his cloak fall in front of his face. He had a large mustache and a long beard, which were both red. He turned towards where Odd was sitting and greeted him by name. Odd welcomed him and asked who he might be. He said that his name was Grani, and that he was called Red Grani.[28]

"I know you well, Arrow-Odd," he said, "and it's a good thing that I've found you, since you're the greatest warrior and a brave man, even though now you have no following and you're not travelling at all in the style of a mighty man. Still, it's too bad for such a man that things should go so badly for you."

"I've traveled this way for a long time," said Odd, "so that I haven't had to rule over men."

"Do you want to swear brotherhood with me?" said Red Grani.

"It's hard to turn a good offer down," said Odd, "and I'll accept it."

"You won't still be luckless in the end," said Red Grani. "I want to tell you that two champions are anchored off the land here, and they have twelve ships. They are my sworn brothers. One of them is of Danish descent and is named Gardar, and the other is Sirnir, whose family is from Gotland. I don't know that there have ever been any greater warriors, better accomplished at most things, before now. I shall bring you into sworn brotherhood with them. You shall have the most say out of all of us, but my advice will still be the most fitting for us. But where would you want to go, if this were to turn out as I've said?"

"It's always on my mind that I want to find Ogmund Eythjof's Bane, who is called by another name, Shock."

"Stop, stop," said Red Grani, "and don't say that, because there's no man as hard to deal with as Ogmund. If you find Ogmund a second time, you'll get much worse from him than before. Don't set your heart on finding him any longer."

Odd replied, "I want to avenge Thord, my sworn brother, and I'll never give up until I find him, if I'm fated to."

"You'll want me to tell you," said Red Grani, "how Ogmund came to be what he is. After that, I guess you won't think there's any hope for him to be beaten by human beings, if you know all about how he was raised.

"The first thing to tell is that there was a king named Harek, who was ruling Bjarmaland when you went there on your raid. You know what harm you did to the Bjarmians. When you had left, the Bjarmians felt they had gotten the worst of it, and they were quite eager to avenge it if they could. This was what they came up with: they got an ogress from underneath a huge waterfall,[29] full of spells and sorcery, and put her in bed with King Harek, and he had a son by her. He was sprinkled with water and given his name, and called Ogmund. From an early age, he wasn't like most humans, which was to be expected on account of his maternal descent—and besides that, his father made a lot of sacrifices to the pagan gods. As soon as Ogmund was three years old, he was sent to Finnmark, and there he learned all sorts of incantations and spells. When he had learned them fully, he went home to Bjarmaland. At the time he was seven years old and as tall as a full-grown man, physically powerful and difficult to deal with. He hadn't improved his appearance while staying with the Finns, because he was colored black and blue, and his hair was long and black, and a shock of hair hung down before his eyes, which might be called a forelock. Then he was called Ogmund Shock. The Bjarmians meant to send him against you and kill you, though they realized that many things had to be done before you could be sent to Hel. They devised another plan, and had Ogmund enchanted so that no ordinary iron might bite him. Next they made sacrifices to him, and turned him into such a troll that he wasn't like any human being.[30]

"There was a certain Viking named Eythjof. He was the greatest berserk and champion, so that no fighter seemed greater than he, and he never had fewer than eighteen ships on a raid. He didn't stay anywhere on land, but stayed out on his ships in both winter and warm summer. Everyone was terrified of him wherever he went. He conquered Bjarmaland and claimed tribute. By then, Ogmund had acquired eight followers. They all wore woolen jackets, and iron didn't bite them. They were named Hak and Haki, Tind and Toki, Finn and Fjosni, Tjosni and Torfi. Ogmund joined forces with Eythjof, and they went raiding together. Ogmund was ten years old at the time. He was with Eythjof for five years. Eythjof loved him like a son, so much that he couldn't let any harm come to him, and for his sake he exempted King Harek from paying tribute from Bjarmaland. Ogmund gave Eythjof no better repayment than this: he killed him while he was asleep in his own bed. That was easy for him to do, because Eythjof had laid him in the same bed next to him and not let any harm come to him, and he meant to adopt him as his son. He left Eythjof's men, and they went wherever they liked, but Ogmund kept two fully-crewed ships. Even since then, he's been called Ogmund Eythjof's Bane.

"And that same summer, you fought them in Tronuvagr, and Ogmund was fifteen years old at the time. He didn't like it that he hadn't taken any revenge on you, and that's why he murdered Thord Prow-Glamour, your sworn brother. After that he went to meet his mother the ogre, who was called Grimhild while she was among men, but by that time she had turned into a monster.[31] She's human in appearance above the neck, but has an animal's body below, and she has such incredibly huge claws and an enormous tail that she kills both people and livestock with them, and wild animals and dragons. Ogmund urged her to destroy you. Now she's been lurking in the forest with the beasts, and has come out of the north to England and is searching for you. Now I've told you about Ogmund, as clearly as possible."

Then Odd spoke: "I think it's likely that most men would find it hard going to deal with him, if he is as you say. Still, I'm driven to find him."

"He's even worse that I have described him," said Red Grani, "because you might call him a spirit, rather than a human, so that I don't think that he'll ever be killed by men. But let's go to the ship first."

And so they did. When they came to the sea, Odd saw many ships afloat there. They went out to the ships, where Odd saw two men who excelled all the others. They stood up to meet Red Grani and greeted their sworn brother. He sat down between them and invited Odd to sit.

Red Grani said, "Here is that man whom you two sworn brothers must have heard about, whose name is Odd and who is called Arrow-

Odd. I want him to be our sworn brother. He alone shall have the most say out of all of us, because he has the most experience in raiding."

Sirnir answered, "Is this the Odd who traveled to Bjarmaland?"

"It's true," said Red Grani.

"Then I believe it'll be a great help to us for him to be our sworn brother," said Sirnir

"I am quite pleased with that," said Gardar. They bound themselves with oaths.

Then Red Grani asked where Odd was thinking about heading. "First," said Odd, "let's go west to England." So they did: they sailed there until they came to land. They spread awnings over their ships and lay there for some time.

CHAPTER XX

One fine day, Sirnir and Gardar went onto land to amuse themselves, and many men went with them, but Odd stayed down on the ship. Red Grani was nowhere to be seen. The weather was quite hot, and the sworn brothers took off their clothes and went swimming in a lake. There was a forest nearby. Most of their men were having fun. But later in the day, they saw a huge beast coming out of the woods. She had a human head and enormous tusks. Her tail was both long and thick, and her claws were incredibly large. She carried a sword in each talon, shining and long. As soon as this monster charged at the men, she howled horribly loudly and killed five men in her first attack. Then she struck with each sword, and thirdly bit with her tusks, and she struck down two men with her tail, and killed every man she struck. In a short time she had killed sixty men.

By that time, Gardar was dressed. He turned to face the monster, and struck at her at once with a sword, so hard that the sword in one of her talons was knocked into the lake. But she struck at Gardar with the sword in her other talon, so that he fell down to the ground. She leaped down onto him. At that moment, Sirnir came at her with his sword drawn. That sword was named Snidil, the best of all swords, so that its strikes were never blocked. He struck at the beast and knocked her other sword out into the lake. At that moment, the monster knocked him down under herself, so that he fell in a faint.

The men who got away rushed to the ships and told Odd that the sworn brothers and many other men had fallen, and said that no one could deal with the monster. They said, "Odd, you must sail away from this land at once. Let's save ourselves as fast as we can."

"That would be a terrible disgrace," said Odd, "if we should leave without avenging my sworn brothers, as valiant men as they were. I'll never do that."

Then he took his quiver and went on land. When he had gone a short distance, they heard a horrible howling. A moment later, Odd saw where the monster was going. He nocked one of Gusir's Gifts on the bowstring and shot it into the beast's eye and out the back of her neck. The monster rushed him so furiously that he couldn't use his bow. She brought both claws down onto his chest, so hard that he almost fell backwards—but the shirt helped him as it always did, so that the claws didn't wound Odd. Quickly and boldly, he drew the sword that he was girded with and cut off the beast's tail, which she had meant to strike him with. He held his other hand in front of him so that she couldn't manage to bite him. But when the monster felt the loss of her tail, she ran to the woods howling. Odd shot another of Gusir's Gifts. It entered the beast's back from behind and pierced the heart and came out through the chest. The monster fell to the ground. Then many men who hadn't dared to come near the beast before rushed at her and beat her and chopped at her. With all that, the beast was dead. Odd had the beast burned, but had his sworn brothers brought to the ships and healed.

They sailed away at once and stayed in Denmark over the winter. They set out raiding for many summers, and raided throughout Sweden, Germany, France, and Flanders,[32] until Sirnir and Gardar grew tired of raiding and settled down in their own kingdoms. Red Grani went with them, for he had come down from the land when they were ready to sail, after Odd had beaten the monster. Red Grani seldom stayed with them when they were in any danger, but he was the shrewdest advisor when needed, and he seldom dissuaded them from doing great deeds.

CHAPTER XXI

Now Odd set out raiding with three well-equipped ships. He set out once again to search for Ogmund Eythjof's Bane. Ten years had now passed since Odd had left Giantland.

One evening, Odd was anchored along a promontory and had pitched his tent on land. He saw a man rowing a small boat. He pulled at the oars mightily, for he was incredibly strong in appearance. He rowed so fast towards Odd's ships that any of them would have broken if it were in the way. Soon he landed and went to where the tents were, and asked who was in command of the ships.

Odd said that he was—"but who are you?"

He said that he was named Vignir. "Are you the Odd who traveled to Bjarmaland?"

"It's true," said Odd.

"I have nothing to say to you," said Vignir.

"Why is that?" said Odd.

"Because I can hardly imagine that you're my father," said Vignir, "seeing as how you look like such a puny little shit."

"Who is your mother?" said Odd. "And how old are you?"

"My mother's name is Hildigunn," said Vignir. "I was brought up in Giantland, and I've grown up there, and now I'm ten years old. She told me that Arrow-Odd was my father, and I thought that he would be the mightiest of men. But now I see that you look like the worst weakling, and that's how you'll turn out to be."

Odd said, "Do you think that you'll do many more deeds of bravery, or greater ones, than I've accomplished? But I acknowledge you as my kinsman. Be welcome with me."

"I'll accept that," said Vignir, "although I find mingling with you and your men to be the least manly thing to do, because they look almost more like maggots than men to me. I find it quite likely that I will accomplish greater deeds than you, if I live long."

Odd told him not to despise his men.

In the morning they made ready to sail. Vignir asked where Odd wanted to head for. He said that they wanted to search for Ogmund Eythjof's Bane.

"You'll get no good from him, even if you find him," said Vignir, "because he is the worst troll and monster that's ever been created in the northern half of the world."

"It can't be true," said Odd, "that though you challenged me and my men about our size and strength, now you're so afraid that you don't dare to look at or meet with Ogmund Shock."

"You've no need to question my courage," said Vignir, "and I'll pay you back for your words sometime, and it won't feel any better to you then, than it does to me now. But I'll tell you where Ogmund is. He's gone into the fjord called Shadow, in uninhabited Helluland[33]. He and his companions are there, nine of them all together. He's gone there because he doesn't care about finding you. Now you can seek him in his home, if you want to, and find out how it goes."

Odd said that it should be so.

They sailed until they came into the Greenland Sea, and turned south and west along the coast. Then Vignir said, "Now I shall sail my ship ahead of you today, and you set your course to follow behind." Odd told him to take charge, and Vignir set their course.

That day they saw two crags coming up out of the sea. Odd was amazed at that. They sailed between the crags. When the day had passed, they saw a large island. Odd ordered them to head for it. Vignir asked why they needed to do that. Odd ordered five men to go onto land and look for water. Vignir said that this wasn't necessary and said that no one from his own ship should go. But when Odd's men landed on the island, they were there for only a short while before the island sank and they all drowned. The island was overgrown with heather. They didn't see it come up afterwards. And the crags had disappeared as soon as they looked that way. Odd was astonished at this and asked Vignir what this meant.

Vignir said, "I think it's safe to say that your wits are in proportion to your size. Now I will tell you that these are two sea monsters. One is called the sea-steam, and the other is the heatherback. The heatherback is the largest of all whales in the world, and the sea-steam is the worst monstrosity that grows in the sea. Its nature is to devour both men and ships, whales and everything that it catches. It dives under water for days, and when it sticks up its head and nose, it stays up for no less time than the tide. Now when we made passage through the sound, we went between its jaws, and its nose and the lower jaw were those crags that appeared to you in the sea, and the heatherback was that island that sank down.[34] Ogmund Shock has used his sorcery to send these beasts to kill you and all your men. He thought more of us would have perished than the ones that have now drowned, but he supposed that the sea-steam would devour us all. I sailed through its jaws just now because I knew that it had just come up. Now we've managed to see through Ogmund's tricks, but I still believe that you'll suffer worse than anyone at his hands."

"We have to risk that now," said Odd.

CHAPTER XXII

Now they sailed until they came to Helluland, and they put into Shadow Fjord. When they had tied up, the father and son went onto land and walked until they saw a stronghold standing, looking very strongly built to them. Ogmund Shock and his companions came out of one wing of the stronghold. Ogmund greeted Odd cheerfully and asked why he had come.

"You don't need to ask about that," said Odd, "because I want to take your life."

"It would be best for the two of us to come to a favorable settlement," said Ogmund.

"No," said Odd, "that shall never be, because I was thinking about it—and then you murdered my sworn brother Thord Prow-Glamour, and treated him shamefully."

"I did that," said Ogmund, "because I didn't feel that our losses were even. But now, even though you've found me, you'll never manage to defeat me while I'm in the stronghold. Now I propose to you that you and your son should fight together against our company. Or else we'll discuss this in the stronghold."

"That's what we'll do," said Odd. "I'll fight against you, Ogmund, and Vignir against your company."

"That won't happen," said Vignir. "Now I'll pay you back for the challenge you laid on me the first time we met, that I wouldn't dare to face Ogmund."

"You and I will regret this exchange later," said Odd, "though for now, it's up to you."

At once they began to fight, close to the sea. The fighting was fierce when Ogmund and Vignir went at it, because both were physically powerful and the most skilled in combat. Vignir came at Ogmund so fiercely that Ogmund dashed northwards along the sea-cliffs, and Vignir rushed after him, all the way until Ogmund leaped over the cliffs onto a grassy ledge, and Vignir followed him, forty fathoms down. They seized each other and grappled with such inhumanly powerful attacks that they tore up earth and stones like loose powdery snow.

Now we must turn to Odd. He had a huge club in his hands, because iron didn't bite any of Ogmund Tussock's companions.[35] He struck so hard with the club that in a little while he had killed everyone he faced, and he wasn't very tired and not wounded; his shirt was the cause of that. Then the desire seized Odd to search for Vignir and find out what had happened to him. He went forward along the cliffs until he came to the spot directly above where Vignir and Ogmund were fighting. And at that moment, Ogmund threw Vignir so that he fell, and in an instant he bent down over him and bit his windpipe in two. Thus Vignir lost his life. Odd said that he felt that that was the most terrible sight, and it grieved him the most.

Then Ogmund said, "Now it would seem to me, Odd, that it would have been better for you if we two had reached a settlement, as I asked. For now you have suffered a killing from me that will never be made good, since your son Vignir is dead, whom I think would have been the boldest and strongest man in the Northlands, because he was ten years old. He would have beaten me if I were an ordinary man, but now I'm no less a spirit than a human. But he squeezed my body so hard that he has broken nearly every one of my bones, so that they're all scraping inside my skin. I would be dead, if it were in my nature. But I'm not afraid of any man in the world except you, and I'm fated to get something bad from you, sooner or later. Now you have your own son to avenge."

Odd grew terribly angry, and he sprang down over the cliff and landed standing on the ledge. Ogmund reacted quickly and stepped off the cliff and plunged headfirst into the sea, so that white foam splashed up. Ogmund didn't come up again, as far as Odd could see. In that moment, Odd and Ogmund parted, and Odd was most displeased with it. He went straight to his ships and sailed away. He set a course for Denmark and found his sworn brother Gardar, and Gardar welcomed him most warmly.

CHAPTER XXIII

Odd stayed in Denmark that winter, and in the spring he and Gardar set out on a raid, sending word to Sirnir in Gautland. He came to meet them, and Red Grani joined them on the journey. Red Grani asked Odd where he wanted to head. He said that he wanted to search for Ogmund Eythjof's Bane and see if he could be found.

"I think it's true that you're acting like a carthorse," said Red Grani. "He goes most often to the place where he's treated worst. You seek out Ogmund, but every time you two meet you've gottten both shame and harm from him. And you have no need to suppose that Ogmund has gotten any better since you parted. But I can tell you where he has gone to. He has gone east to the giant Geirrod[36] in Geirrodargard, and has married his daughter Geirrid. They are both the worst trolls, and I don't encourage you to go there."

Odd said that they had to go, all the same.

At once all the sworn brothers prepared to travel to the eastern realms. When they came east to Geirrodargard, they saw a man sitting in a boat fishing. That was really Ogmund Eythjof's Bane, wrapped in a shaggy cape. When he and Odd had parted, Ogmund had gone into the eastern realms and become the giant Geirrod's son-in-law, and he forced all the kings in the eastern realms to pay him tribute in this way: they all had to send him their own mustaches and beards, every twelve months. From them, Ogmund had made the same cape made that he was wearing just then.[37]

Odd and his men headed for the boat, but Ogmund steered away, rowing very powerfully. The sworn brothers all leaped into one ship and rowed after him very mightily, and each one picked up two oars, but Ogmund Shock rowed so powerfully that he neither pulled away nor drew nearer to them, and this went on until they came to land. Then Ogmund leaped onto the land, abandoning his boat between the tide-marks. Odd was the quickest of his men to get onto land, and Sirnir was next, and they both rushed after Ogmund. But when Ogmund saw that they would meet each other, he spoke up, and said a verse:

> I ask Geirrod
> with the gods' favor,

> the keenest of champions,
> to come rescue me
> and save my wife
> soon, like the others;
> now I must have
> his help and support.

The old saying "speak of the devil and he will appear" turned out to be true. Geirrod came there with all his people, fifteen in all. Then Gardar came, followed by the sworn brothers' men. The fiercest battle broke out. Geirrod struck such mighty blows that in a little while he had killed fifteen men before Odd's eyes. Odd searched for Gusir's Gifts. He took Hremsa and nocked it on the string and shot. It hit Geirrod in the chest and came out between his shoulders. Geirrod charged forward despite the shot, and dealt death to three men before he fell dead to the earth. Geirrid was also a savage killer, for she killed eighteen men in a short time. Gardar turned to face her and traded blows with her, and in the end, Gardar sank down dead on the field. When Odd saw that, he became fiercely angry. He nocked one of Gusir's Gifts on the string and shot Geirrid in her right armpit, and it came out through her left armpit. They couldn't see that she paid any attention to that. She charged forward into the battle lines and killed five men. Odd shot the next one of Gusir's Gifts. It pierced Geirrid's small intestines and came out through her loins, and she died a short time later.

Ogmund was also making no small slaughter, because he had killed thirty men in a short time, before Sirnir turned to face him. They attacked each other fiercely, and soon Sirnir was wounded. A little later, Odd saw that Sirnir was falling back before Ogmund. He turned to face him, but when Ogmund saw that, he turned to flee and ran most vigorously, and Sirnir and Odd were behind him. Each one ran as fast as he could. Ogmund was wearing his good cape, and when they drew even with him, Ogmund threw away the cape and spoke a verse:

> Now I must cast
> my cape away,
> made of mustaches
> of mighty kings,

with beautiful lace
on both sides sewn;
it's a great grief
to give it up.

They're following me
at full speed;
Odd and Sirnir
slip from the battle.

As soon as Ogmund's load was lightened, he got away. Odd took heart then, and he was faster than Sirnir. And when Ogmund saw that, he turned to face him and they fought. Their wrestling and fighting were both fierce and long, because Odd had no strength against Ogmund, but Ogmund couldn't get him off his feet.

Then Sirnir came up with the sword Snidil drawn, and he meant to strike at Ogmund, but when Ogmund saw that, he pushed Odd in front of the blow. Sirnir held himself back. So it always went that Ogmund used Odd as a shield, and nothing came of Sirnir's attacks, but even though he hit Odd, Odd wasn't wounded because of his good shirt. On one occasion, Odd put both his feet down on an earth-fast stone, so forcefully that Ogmund was about to fall to his knees. At that moment, Sirnir struck at Ogmund. There was no time for Ogmund to push Odd in front of the blow. The blow landed from behind on the buttocks,[38] and Snidil cut what it hit. Sirnir cut off such a huge piece of Ogmund's thighs that no horse could pull a larger load. At that, Ogmund started so much that he sank downwards right where he was.[39] Odd gripped his beard with both hands with such strength that he ripped off all his beard, and the flesh underneath it down to the bone, and along with that, his entire face with both cheeks, up through the forehead and back to the middle of his skull. And there it ended when the skin tore, and Odd kept what he was holding. The earth closed up over Ogmund's head, and so their encounter ended.

Odd and Sirnir went to their ships, and they had suffered terrible losses. It was the greatest grief for Odd to lose his sworn brother Gardar. Red Grani had also disappeared, so that Odd and Sirnir never knew what happened to him once they found Ogmund in the boat. It had happened again, as it often did, that he had rarely put himself at risk, but all the advice he gave was the boldest. The sworn brothers didn't see Red Grani again, as far as anyone knows. Men felt that he must really have been Odin.

The sworn brothers sailed away, and men still felt that Odd had gotten nothing good from Ogmund. He had lost Gardar, his sworn brother and the boldest man who had ever been. Yet Odd and his men had achieved a great deal by killing the evil beings who had been with Ogmund, both at that time and formerly.

Geirrid had had a son by Ogmund Eythjof's Bane, who was named Svart. He was three years old at this point in the saga. He was huge and likely to grow up to be a wicked man.

CHAPTER XXIV

When Odd came home to Gotland with his sworn brother, Sirnir invited him to stay there over the winter. Odd accepted. As winter passed, he became deeply dejected, and he brooded on the grief that he had suffered at the hands of Ogmund Shock. Yet he realized that he couldn't endanger his sworn brother by fighting Ogmund any longer, because he thought that he would suffer great loss. He decided to steal away alone in the dead of night. He traveled on trading ships to wherever they had to to go. Sometimes he traveled through woods and forests, and he found his way over very high mountain roads, carrying his quiver on his back. He traveled through lands far and wide, and in the end, the only food he had was the birds that he shot for himself. Then he wrapped birchbark around his body and legs, and made a large birchbark hood for his head. He didn't look like other men; he was much larger than all other men, and completely covered in birchbark.

Nothing is said about him until he came out of the woods and saw an inhabited district before him. He saw a large farm standing there, and there was another farm a short distance away. It occurred to him that he might head for the smaller farm; he had never tried that before. He went to the doors. There was a man splitting planks in front of the doors, short in stature and white-haired. He greeted the newcomer warmly and asked his name.

"I'm called Barkman," he said, "and what's your name?"

Arrow-Odd's Saga

The man said his name was Jolf. "You must be wanting to stay here tonight," he said.

"I accept," said Barkman.

Now the old man brought him into the main room, and an old woman was sitting there on a seat. "Here is a guest," said the man. "You must see to him, since I have much work to do."

The old woman whined loudly, and said that he often offered lodging to men—"but there's nothing to bring him."

Now the old man left, and the old woman and Barkman stayed behind. And in the evening, when Jolf came inside, the table was set before them. When a dish was brought out to the side where Barkman was seated, he laid down an excellent knife. There were two rings on the knife handle, one of gold and the other of silver. And when Jolf saw that, he reached for the knife and examined it. "You have a good knife, comrade," said the old man, "but how did you come to have this treasure?"

Barkman said, "When I was young, quite a lot of us were salt-burners together, when a ship ran aground where we lived. The ship shattered in pieces, and the sailors were washed ashore, starving. We quickly did away with them, and I was allotted this knife as my share of the spoils. And if it seems at all useful to you, old man, then I will give you the knife if you'd like."

"You give the finest gifts of any man," said the old man, and he showed the knife to his wife. "Here's something to see," he said, "this knife is no worse than the one that I used to have."

After that, they began eating. Later, Barkman was shown to his bed, and they went to sleep for the night. Barkman didn't wake up before Jolf had left and his sleeping place was cold. Then he spoke up: "Wouldn't it be best to get up and go away, and look somewhere else for breakfast?"

The old woman said that the man wanted him to wait for him at home.

It was around midday when the man came home, and Barkman was up. The tables were set before them. Dishes were brought out to the table, but on the side where the old man was sitting, he laid out three arrows with stone points next to the dishes. They were such large and well-made arrows that Barkman thought that he had never seen finer arrows if this type.[40] He picked one up and looked at it. "This arrow is well made," he said.

"If they seem well-made to you," said the old man, "then I'll give them to you, if you'd like."

Barkman smiled at that and said, "I don't believe I'll need to haul these stone arrows on my back."

"You never know when you'll need them, Odd," said the old man. "I know that you're called Arrow-Odd, and that you're the son of Grim Shaggy-Cheek, from Hrafnista in the north. I also know that you have three arrows called Gusir's Gifts. You'll find it strange if the time comes when Gusir's Gifts won't help you, and these stone arrows would be useful."

"Since you knew that my name is Odd and you didn't say anything, and you also knew that I have the arrows named Gusir's Gifts," said Odd, "maybe you know what you're talking about. I will certainly accept the arrows." And he put them into his quiver.

"What can you tell me about this, old man," said Odd, "does a king rule this land?"

"Yes," said the old man, "and his name is Herraud."

"Who is the mightiest man with him?" said Odd.

"There are two," said the old man. "One is named Sigurd, and the other is Sjolf. They sit in the king's high seat and are the greatest warriors."

"Does the king have children?" said Odd.

"He has one pretty daughter named Silkisif."

"Is she beautiful?" said Odd.

"Yes," said the old man, "there's no one as lovely as she, neither in Russia nor in more distant lands."

"What do you think, old man," said Odd, "how would they receive me if I went there? You must not tell who I am."

"I can keep my mouth shut," said the old man.

They went to the king's hall, but then the old man put his foot down and didn't want to go any farther.

"Why are you stopping now?" said Odd.

"Because I'll be clapped in fetters if I come inside," said the old man, "and I would be happiest if I could get away."

"Yes," said Barkman, "we should both push our way in together, and I won't permit anything other than for you to come with me." He grabbed him, and then they went into the hall. As soon as the king's retainers saw the old man, they mobbed him, but Barkman held him up, so that they all bounced off.

Now they turned and went into the hall until they came before the king. The old man greeted the king well, and the king accepted his greeting warmly. Then the king asked who he was leading behind him. "I can't find that out," said the old man, "and he has to say who he is himself."

"I'm called Barkman," he said.

"What sort of man are you, fellow?" said the king.

"I know that I'm older than anything," he said, "and I have neither wits nor memory about me. I've lived out in the woods for a long time, almost all my life. But 'beggar's errands are brief ones,' king, and I want to ask you for lodging over the winter."

The king answered, "Do you have any sort of skill?"

"Far from it," he said, "because I'm less skilful than other men."

"You've no mind for any?" said the king.

"I can't do anything, and I don't feel like trying," said Barkman.

"Then this is turning out to be quite hopeless," said the king, "since I have sworn an oath to accept only those men who have some sort of skill."

"I can never do anything that's of use to others," said Barkman.

"You'll have to learn how to collect game when men are hunting," said the king. "Maybe I'll go and do this some time."

"Where will you show me to sit?" said Barkman.

"You shall sit along the outside of the hall, on the lower-ranking side, where the slaves and freedmen eat."

Now Barkman went out with the old man, and after that he went to the seat that he'd been shown. Two brothers were sitting there; one was named Ottar and the other was Ingjald. "Come here, fellow," they said, "you shall sit between us," and he accepted. Each of them sat at his knee and asked questions about every land that they could think of. No one else knew what they were talking about.

Odd hung up his quiver on a peg over his seat, but laid his cudgel under his feet. They kept asking him if they could take care of his bag, which looked like a great filthy thing, but he said that he would never let it be taken from him, and he never went anywhere without taking it with him. They offered to make a deal with him, for him to take the bark off his arms, "and we'll give you proper clothing."

"That can't be," he said, "because I've never worn anything else, and I'll never have anything else as long as I live."

CHAPTER XXV

Now Barkman stayed there, and he always drank little in the evening and went to bed early. So it went until the fall, when men had to go hunting. That evening, Ingjald said that it was expected "that we be on our feet early in the morning."

"What's happening then?" said Barkman.

Ingjald said that they were going hunting. They lay down for the night, and in the morning the brothers got up and called to Barkman and couldn't manage to wake him up, he was sleeping so soundly. He didn't wake up until every man who wanted to go hunting had left.

Barkman spoke up: "What is it now? Why are the men ready to leave?"

Ingjald answered, "They're not only ready, everyone's left. We've been trying to wake you all morning. We'll never manage to shoot an animal today."

Then Barkman said, "Aren't Sjolf and Sigurd exceptionally skilled men in all respects?"

"We'd see," said Ingjald, "if anyone competed against them in something."

Now they came to the mountain, and an animal went dashing off, right past them, and the brothers drew their bows. But when they tried to shoot the animals, they never hit a single one.

Then Barkman said, "I've never seen anyone shoot as clumsily as you two. How did you manage to do that so badly?"

They said, "We've told you that we'd be clumsier than other men. We weren't ready this morning, and now we have the deer that the others have stirred up and frightened."

Barkman said, "I can't see that I could do this any more clumsily. Let me have the bow, and I'll try." They did so. He drew the bow, and they warned him not to break it, but he drew the arrow so that the point was behind the bow, and broke the bow in two pieces.

"Now you've done it," they said, "and this is a great harm to us. We'll probably never manage to shoot an animal all day."

"It hasn't begun well," he said, "but how promising does my staff look to you for a bow? And are you at all curious to find out what's in my bag?"

"Yes," they said, "we're terribly curious about it."

"Then you two should spread out your cloaks, and I'll pour out what's inside."

They did so, and he poured the contents down onto the cloaks. Then he brought up his bow and nocked an arrow on the string and shot over the heads of all the men who were hunting. He behaved that way throughout the day, only shooting the animals that Sigurd and Sjolf were pursuing. He shot all his arrows except for six, the old man's stone arrows and Gusir's Gifts. He never missed an animal all day, and the brothers ran alongside him and found it great fun to see what he had shot.

In the evening, when the men came home, every man's arrows were set out on the table before the king. Every man had marked his own arrows, and the king could see how many animals each man had killed that day. Now the brothers said, "Barkman, go inside for your arrows, which will be laid on the table before the king."

"You two go," he said, "and claim the arrows for yourself."

"That's no good to us," they saud, "because the king knows what we're capable of—that we're worse shots than other men."

"Then we'll all go together," he said.

Now they went inside before the king. Barkman spoke up: "Here are the arrows that we partners will claim as our own."

The king looked at him and said, "You're a great archer."

"Yes, lord," he said, "because I'm used to shooting animals and birds for food."

And after that the men went to their seats. Now some time passed.

CHAPTER XXVI

One evening when the king had gone to sleep, Sigurd and Sjolf got up, each one with his own horn, and went and invited the brothers Ottar and Ingjald to drink. They told them to take the horns and drink them down. And when they had drunk, they came with another pair of horns, and the brothers took them and drank.

Then Sjolf said, "Is your companion always lying in bed?"

"Yes," they said, "he finds that more promising than drinking all his wits away, like we do."

Sjolf said, "Is he an excellent shot?"

"Yes," they said, "he's just as gifted at that as anything else."

"Could he shoot as far as the two of us?" said Sjolf.

"We think he could shoot much farther and straighter," they said.

"We'll wager on that," said Sjolf, "and we'll stake this ring that weighs half a mark, but you two must stake two rings of the same weight."

It was agreed that the king and his daughter would be there to watch their shooting, and they would take the rings ahead of time and give them to the one who won them. And so they made their wager. They slept for the night. But in the morning, when the brothers awoke, they realized that their wager hadn't been at all sensible. There was nothing for it but for them to tell Barkman.

"This wager looks completely hopeless to me," he said, "since though I managed to shoot animals, that's not much, compared with contending against such archers. Still, I must try, since you two have wagered money."

Now the men began drinking. After the time for drinking was over, the men went outside, and the king wanted to see the shooting. Sigurd went forward and shot as far as he could. A stake was set down where his arrow landed, and Sjolf went to the spot that was staked. Then a spearshaft was stuck in the ground, and a golden gaming piece was set down on top, and Sjolf shot the piece off. Everyone felt that he had shot well and said that there was no need for Barkman even to try.

"There's often luck for an unlucky man," said Barkman, "and I'll certainly try."

Now Barkman stepped up and shot one arrow, standing where Sigurd had stood. He shot up into the air, so that the arrow fell a long distance. It came down and hit the game-piece, pierced it through the center, and stuck into the spear-shaft, so that the piece didn't stir at all.

"As good as the first shot was," said the king, "that is a far better shot. I can say that I have never seen such good shooting."

Barkman took another arrow and shot it so far that no one saw where it landed. Everyone said that the game was won. After that, the men went home, and the brothers took the ring. They gave it to Barkman. He said that he didn't want to take their money yet.

Several days passed, and again, one evening, when the king had gone out, Sigurd and Sjolf went with their own horns and invited Ottar and Ingjald to drink. They drank the horns down. Then they brought them another two.

Then Sjolf said, "Barkman is still lying around and not drinking."

"He's better behaved than you in every way," said Ingjald.

"I guess," said Sjolf, "that he must have rarely been in the company of mighty men, and he must often have lurked out in the woods and forest in poverty. But would he be able to swim well?"

"Both of us think that he's equally gifted at most matters that are considered accomplishments," they said, "and we think that he's pretty good at swimming."

"Would he be a better swimmer alone than both of us?"

"We think he's a better swimmer," said Ottar.

"We must wager on it," said Sjolf. "We two will stake this ring that weighs a mark, but you two must stake two rings that weigh half a mark each."

It was agreed that the king and his daughter should watch their swimming, and everything was agreed on like the first time. They went to sleep for the night. In the morning when they awoke, news of their wager was going around the benches.

"What's this chatter?" said Barkman. "Did you two make another wager last night?"

"Yes," they said, and they told him what the wager was.

"This has turned completely hopeless," said Barkman, "because I'm not at all good at swimming. I didn't have any endurance even when I practiced it often, but now I haven't been in cold water for a long time, and too much money has been staked."

"Yes," they said, "there's no need for you to try unless you want to. It doesn't matter, even though we'll pay for our foolishness."

"I'll never refuse to try," said Barkman, "since you have shown me great honor. The king and Silkisif shall see that I will certainly compete in swimming."

The king and his daughter were told, and men went to the lake, which was large and nearby. When they came to the lake, the king sat down and his retainers sat with him, but the brothers went swimming in their own clothes, and Barkman in the outfit which he usually wore. They came for him as soon as they left the shore, and they dunked him and held him under for a long time. Eventually they let him up, and they rested. They came at him a second time. He reached out to them and seized one of them with each hand, and shoved them underwater and held them down for such a long time that it seemed unlikely that they'd come up. He allowed them a short rest, and then he seized them a second time and dunked them, and then a third time, and he held them under for so long that no one thought that they would come up alive. But in the end, they all came up. Both of the king's high-seat companions had blood streaming from their noses, and they couldn't get to land without help. Barkman picked them up and tossed them onto the land. Then he went back to swimming and played many games, such as men usually played while swimming. In the evening, he came out onto land and went to meet the king. The king asked, "You're not like other men in skills, in archery and swimming, are you?"

"You've now seen all the skills I have," said Barkman; "my name is Odd, if you want to know that, but I can't explain anything to you about my family."

Silkisif gave him the ring. Then the men went home. Ottar and Ingjald said that Odd should have all the rings, but he didn't want that—"you two should have them yourselves."

Some time passed, not a long time. The king was very anxious about who the man with him could possibly be.

CHAPTER XXVII

There was a man named Harek who was there with the king. The king held him in high esteem. He was an old man who had fostered the king's daughter. The king always conversed with him about this matter, but he said that he didn't know. He said that he thought it likely that this man must come from a great family.

One evening, when the king had gone to sleep, Sjolf and Sigurd went out before the brothers and brought them two horns, and they drank them down. Then Sjolf spoke up: "Is Odd the Great lying down?"

"Yes," they said, "that's more sensible than drinking away all your wits, as we do."

"That must mean that he's more used to lurking in woods or by lakes, than to drinking with good men. Would he be a great drinker?"

"Yes," they said.

"Would he be a greater drinker alone than both of us together?"

"We think he would drink much more," said Ottar.

"We'll wager on that," said Sjolf, "and we'll stake a ring that weighs twelve ounces, but you two must wager your heads." They made this agreement among themselves, as before.

In the morning, Odd asked what everyone was talking about. They told him. "Now you've made such a stupid bet," said Odd, "you might have gained a great deal from the previous wagers, but now your heads are at stake, but it's not certain that I'd be better at drinking, in the way that I'm taller than other men. All the same, I'll try drinking with them."

Soon the king was told that he was to judge the drinking contest, and the king's daughter had to sit nearby with her foster-father Harek.[41] Sigurd and Sjolf came out and came before Odd.

"Here's a horn," said Sigurd, and there was a song on his lips:

> Odd, you didn't hew
> Hamdir's tunics°   *Hamdir:* a legendary warrior; his *tunics:* chainmail
> when the armored foes
> fell back from battle;
> barns were blazing,
> battle was raging,
> when over the Wends
> the king won victory.

Sjolf brought him another horn and told him to drink it down, and spoke a verse:

> Odd, you weren't there
> at the edge-reddening,°   *edge-reddening:* battle
> when the mightiest men
> we made to perish;

> I brought away six wounds,
> and bore eight more still,
> but you scavenged food,
> sitting at home.

Then they went to their seats. Odd stood up and went before Sigurd and brought him a horn, and brought another to Sjolf, and spoke his own verse to each of them before he went away:

> Listen, you two,
> to my lay of praise,
> Sigurd and Sjolf,
> you seat-companions,
> I must present you
> with savage work,
> taught-twisted praise
> for twin cowards.
>
> Sjölf, you sprawled
> on a sod floor,
> chicken-hearted,
> achieving nothing,
> while I was out
> in Aquitania;
> I fought four men
> and finished them off.

They drank the horns down, and Odd went to sit down. Then they came before Odd again, and Sjolf gave him a horn and spoke a verse:

> Odd, you've wandered,
> whining for charity,
> taking away
> the table scraps,
> but I alone
> from Ulfsfjall came,

bearing in hand
a hewn shield.

Sigurd brought him another horn and said this:

Odd, you weren't there,
out with the Greeks,
when in Saracen-land
our swords we reddened;
we made a mighty
music of iron,
in the bloody battle
brave men fell.

Now Odd drank the horn down, and they went to sit down. Then Odd got up and went with his horn to each of them and said this:

You were gossiping
with the girls, Sjolf,
while we left barns
burning all around;
fierce Hadding
we fought to the death,
and Olvir lost
his life at our hands.[42]

Sigurd, you were lounging
in the ladies' quarters,
while we battled
the Bjarmians twice;
we came to the combat
as keen as hawks,
while you, soldier,
snoozed under the covers.

Now Odd went to sit down, and they drank the horns down. The people found this excellent entertainment, and they gave it their full attention.

After that, Sigurd and Sjolf came before Odd and brought him the horns. Then Sjolf said,

> Odd, you weren't there
> on Atalsfjall,
> when we made off
> with the marsh-flame;°   *marsh-flame*: gold
> we made bonds
> for berserk fighters,
> when the king's host
> was killed in battle.

Now Odd drank the horns down, and they sat down. Odd brought them horns and said this:

> Sjolf, you weren't there,
> where one might see
> byrnies of brave men
> all blood-smeared;
> arrows sprang back
> from shirts of mail—
> you were off rambling
> through the royal hall.

> Sigurd, you were lost,
> when we laid waste
> to six high-sided
> ships, off Hauksnes;
> and you weren't there
> in the west with Skolli,
> when we claimed the life
> of the king of England.

Now Odd sat down, and they brought him horns without speaking any poetry. He drank them down, and they sat down. And now Odd brought them horns and said this:

> Sjolf, you weren't there
> when swords we reddened
> off Læso Island
> at the earl's expense;
> you were cuddling
> a calf and a slavegirl,
> bundling between them
> and babbling wildly.[43]
>
> Sigurd, you weren't there
> when I slew on Zealand
> the battle-hardened brothers
> Brand and Agnar,
> Asmund and Ingjald,
> Alf was the fifth.
> You dawdled at home
> in the hall of the king,
> buggered like a bitch[44]
> and blathering lies.

Now he went to sit down, and they stood up and brought him the horns. Odd drank them both down. Then he brought them horns, and said this:

> Sjolf, you weren't there,
> at Skidam in the south
> where the princes
> pressed helms together;
> we waded in gore
> washing our ankles;
> I wakened up war,
> you weren't there.
>
> Sigurd, you weren't there,
> in the Swedish skerries
> when we paid Halfdan
> for his hatred in full;

>   the round shield-rims
>   of his wrath-stirrers°   *wrath-stirrers*: warriors
>   were hacked by swords;
>   he himself was slain.

Now Odd sat down, and they brought him the horns. He drank them down, but they went and sat down. Then Odd brought them horns and said,

>   We aimed our ash-wood[45]   *ash-wood*: ship
>   towards Elfarsund,
>   untroubled, contented,
>   to Tronuvagar—
>   there lay Ogmund
>   Eythjofsbani,
>   slowest to retreat,
>   sailing two ships.
>
>   We let shields
>   be shaken, bashed
>   by heavy stones
>   and honed swords.
>   Three of us lived,
>   and they had nine.
>   Captive crow,
>   why so quiet now?

Then Odd went to his seat, and they brought him horns. He drank them down and brought them more horns and said this:

>   Sigurd, you weren't
>   on Samsey isle,
>   when I bandied
>   blows with Hjorvard:
>   twelve, all told,
>   against two of us.

> I won the fight,
> then for a while rested.
>
> I went through Gotland,
> grim in my mind,
> for seven days all told,
> before Saemund I found;
> before I went away,
> well did I know
> how to end the lives
> of eighteen men;
> but you, poor lout,
> late in the evening,
> went stumbling off
> to the slavegirl's bed.

There was loud cheering in the hall at Odd's words. The brothers drank down their horns, but Odd sat down. The king's men were listening to this entertainment. They brought the horns to Odd again, and he made short work of them both. After that, Odd stood up and came before them. He realized that the drinking and everything else were taking such a toll on them that they were too far gone to make poetry. He gave them the horns and said this:

> You won't seem
> like worthy men,
> Sigurd and Sjolf,
> swains of the king,
> if Bold-Hearted
> Hjalmar is mentioned,
> who could most keenly
> cut with his sword.
>
> The hero Thord charged
> ahead of the shield-wall,
> wherever we had
> to hold our battles;

Halfdan forced him
to fall to the ground,
he and his soldiers
stilled the hero.

Asmund and I were
often together,
friends in childhood
and foster-brothers;
often I've handled
the hafts of spears,
whenever two kings
clashed in battle.

I've raided in Saxony,
in Sweden as well,
Ireland and England
and also Scotland,
Frisia and France
and Flanders to boot;
I've done harm
in all of them.[46]

Now I have listed
my loyal companions,
who once went roving
and raiding with me;
braver followers
in the battle's fury
will surely never
be known again.

Now I have named
the noble deeds
that we dared to do
in days gone by;
having won victory,

we heroes returned
to the seat of honor—
now Sjolf may speak!"

Odd sat down in his seat, but the brothers collapsed right there, dead drunk. There was no more drinking for them, but Odd drank for a long time. After that, men lay down and slept for the night.

In the morning, when the king seated himself in the high seat, Odd and his companions had gone outside. He went to a lake and washed himself. The brothers saw that the bark sleeve on one of his hands was torn, and a red sleeve was hanging out. There was a gold ring on his arm, and it wasn't hammered out thinly. At once they tore all the bark from him. He didn't resist. Underneath, he was dressed in a red velvet tunic trimmed with lace, and his hair hung down to his shoulders. He had tied a gold headband around his head, and he was the most handsome of all men. They took him by the hands and led him into the hall before the king's high seat and said, "We think we're not quite sure who it is that we've had here in fosterage."

"That may be," said the king. "Who is this man who's been concealing himself from us?"

"My name is Odd, as I told you a long time ago, the son of Grim Shaggy-Cheek from the north of Norway."

"Are you that Odd who traveled to Bjarmaland a long time ago?"

"I'm the one who went there."

"Then it's not surprising that my high-seat companions utterly failed against you at the games."

Now the king stood up to greet him and welcomed Odd warmly, and invited him to sit next to him in the high seat. Odd said, "I won't accept that at all, unless all of us companions sit there." It's said that they brought seats for them, and Odd sat next to the king, but Harek moved his own seat to a chair in front of the king. The king honored Odd so highly that he valued no man higher than him.

CHAPTER XXVIII

Odd and Harek were always conversing together. Odd asked whether anyone had asked for the king's daughter's hand in marriage.

"That's not a good idea," he said. "The king's high-seat companions have asked for her hand."

"How did the king answer their proposal?" said Odd.

"He has given them a choice," he said.

"Let me hear it," said Odd.

"The king is supposed to receive tribute from Bjalkaland.[47] A king named Alf, known as Alf Plank, rules over that land. He is married, and his wife is named Gydja.[48] She is a great sacrificer; both of them are. They have a son named Vidgrip. They're such powerful sorcerers that they could hitch a stud-horse to a star. The king is supposed to receive tribute from that land, but it's been neglected for a long time. The king has stated that for him to betroth his own daughter to his companions, they must claim tribute from the land. But that went nowhere when they asked to take so many fighters from the land that the king thought he would be defenseless against warriors who might attack the kingdom."

"It seems to me," said Odd, "that either the tribute will never be brought home, or else it'll be brought home if a smaller force is used. What do you think? Will the king be willing to give me the same choice as the others, if I manage to fetch the tribute?"

"The king is a wise man," said Harek, "and I guess he'll realize the advantages of making this match with you."

Now the matter was brought up before the king, and whether it was discussed more or less, they all reached agreement that Odd was to make this journey to bring home the tribute, and that if he came back from the journey and brought the tribute, he should be granted the king's daughter. The woman was promised to him, with many men as witnesses.

Now Odd prepared for his journey, and the forces that he wanted to have with him were assembled. When he was ready, the king led him to the road. They were to go by land.

"Here's a treasure that I want to give you," said the king.

"What is it?" said Odd.

"This is a shield-maiden[49] who has served me for a long time," said the king, "and been a shield before me in every battle."

Odd smiled and said, "I've never been in a situation where women have been my protection. Yet I shall accept, since you think this is a good offer."

Arrow-Odd's Saga

The king and Odd parted, and Odd traveled until he came to a great swamp. He took a running start and leaped over the swamp. The shield-maiden was next to him, but she held back when she came to the swamp. Odd asked, "Why didn't you jump after me?"

"Because I wasn't ready," she said.

"Yes," he said, "now be ready."

She hitched up her skirts and rushed at the swamp a second time, and it happened again, and also a third time. Then Odd leaped back over the swamp and seized her with his hands and flung her out into the swamp and said, "Now go there, and may all trolls take you." He leaped over the swamp a third time and waited for his men—they had all had to walk around the swamp, it was so broad and hard to cross.

Now Odd traveled with his men and sent out scouts ahead of him, and he heard the news that Vidgrip had assembled huge forces and was advancing against them. They encountered each other on some fields in the evening. Both sides pitched their tents, and Odd paid attention to where Vigrip set up his own tent. When the men had made their beds and everything was still and silent, Odd stood up and went out. He was equipped with a sword in his hand and no other weapons. He didn't stop until he came to the tent in which Vidgrip was sleeping, and he stood there for a very long time and waited for someone to come out of the tent. It so happened that a man came out when it was very dark. He spoke up and said, "Why are you loitering here, neither going into the tent nor going away?"

"Well," he said, "I'm in a bad situation. I can't find the place where I slept last night."

"Do you know where that was in the tent?"

"I'm sure that I was to sleep in Vidgrip's tent, with one man between me and him, but I am far from being able to find my way there, and I'll be the laughingstock of every man if I don't get help from you."

"Yes," said the other man, "I can do that for you, to bring you to the bed that Vidgrip's in." And he did so.

"Yes," said Odd, "keep quiet. This will do quite well for me, because now I clearly see where I'm supposed to sleep."

Now the man went away, and Odd stayed behind until he thought that the man must have gone to sleep. Then Odd stuck a wooden peg out through the tent, above where Vidgrip was lying. After that he went outside and around to the back of the tent, where the peg stood. There he loosened the tent pegs and hauled Vidgrip out from under the edge and onto a tent-block, and he cut his head off against the block. He pegged the tent back together, letting the headless body collapse inside, and went to his own tent and lay down to sleep, acting as if nothing had happened.

CHAPTER XXIX

In the morning, when the raiders awoke, they found Vidgrip slain and his head missing. They found this to be such a portent and a wonder that they were all astonished. Now they held a council, and it was decided that they would take another man as their chieftain and call him by Vidgrip's name, and carry the battle-standards before him that day.

Now Odd and his men awoke and armed themselves. It occurred to Odd that he should set up a staff as a battle-standard, and he set Vidgrip's head on the staff. Now both sides deployed their forces. Odd advanced in front of his men; he had much smaller forces. Then Odd spoke up and called to the people of the land, and asked if they recognized the head that was carried in front of him. The people thought they recognized Vidgrip's head, and were completely astonished that such a thing could happen.

Now Odd gave them two choices: to battle him or submit to him. They felt that their situation was not likely to turn out well even if they were to fight, and their decision was to submit to Odd. He accepted them and all their forces, and traveled until he encountered Alf Plank. Both of them had large forces, but Odd had smaller forces than Alf. A battle broke out at once between them. There was such a fierce fight that Odd had never before seen such a slaughter, because he thought he saw terrible losses in his ranks in a short time.

"And another thing," said Odd, "I thought I could clear a path all the way to Alf's standard, but I don't see him anywhere."

Then a local man who had formerly followed Vidgrip spoke up. "I don't know what's the matter that you don't see him," he said, "because he's walking behind his standards and never leaves them. This is the proof: he shoots an arrow from each finger and hits a man with each one."[50]

"I still don't see him," said Odd.

Then the man held his arm over Odd's head and said, "Look out from underneath my hand."[51] And at once, Odd saw Alf, and also saw that everything was as he had been told.

Odd said, "Stay there for a while," and the man did so. Now Odd searched for Gusir's Gifts and took one of them and nocked it on the bowstring and shot at Alf Plank, but he brought up his palm, and the arrow didn't bite at all.

"Now you must all go," said Odd, "though it won't help." He shot all the arrows, and none of them bit. All of Gusir's Gifts dropped into the grass.

"I expect that what old man Jolf said has come true," said Odd. "Gusir's Gifts are finished, and now we'll have to test the old man's stone-tipped arrows."

He took one of them and nocked it on the string and shot at Alf Plank. When Alf heard the whizz of the arrow that was flying at him, he brought up his palm again, but the arrow pierced it through and came out the back of his neck. Odd took another arrow and nocked it and shot at Alf. He brought up his other palm and thought that it would protect his remaining eye better, but the arrow pierced his uninjured eye and came out the back of his neck. Alf still didn't fall any more than the first time. Then Odd shot the third arrow, and it pierced Alf in the belly, and this time he fell. Now the old man's stone-tipped arrows were used up, and he had stipulated previously that Odd wouldn't shoot them more than once, and they wouldn't be found.

The battle lasted only a short while longer, for the enemy host took to flight and fled to the town. There stood the priestess at the gates of the town, shooting arrows from every finger. Now the fighting ceased, and the men submitted to Odd or ran in all directions. By the town there stood temples and altars, and Odd had them set on fire and burned up all the ones near the town. Then a song came to the priestess's lips:

> Who fans the fire,
> who forces battle,
> whose arrow-points slash
> with strength of a jarl?
> The harrows are singed,
> the high places burn,

> who reddens edges
> on Yngvi's folk?

Odd replied, saying this:

> Odd burned the temples
> and broke the altars
> and laid to waste
> your wooden idols;
> your gods achieved
> no good in this world,
> they couldn't save
> themselves from the flames.

Then she said,

> My heart laughs
> that you'll have to suffer
> Frey's malice,
> mixed with harm.
> Help, Aesir
> and Asynjur,
> ye holy powers,
> help your priestess.

Then Odd said,

> Wicked woman,
> I won't be moved,
> though you menace me
> with the malice of Frey;
> I fuelled the flames
> and fed them the idols;
> may trolls take you—
> I trust in one god.

Then she said,

> Who brought you up
> to be such a fool
> that you don't want
> to worship Odin?

Odd answered back and said:

> When I was a child,
> Ingjald raised me,
> the lord over Eikund
> who lived in Jæderen.

Then she said:

> Most fortunate
> I'd find myself
> if I could meet with
> the mighty Alf;
> four farms I gave him
> and feasts I offered;
> he'll drag you all
> down into the fire.

Then Odd said this:

> Odd bent the elm,
> an arrow flew;
> Jolf's precious craft
> pierced Alf through.
> Don't offer presents
> for Plank to receive;
> crouched on his carcass
> are cawing ravens.

Then she said,

> Who helped you to come
> here from the east,
> full of falsehoods,
> filled with deceit?
> You must be planning
> to pillage everywhere,
> if you could make
> Alf lose his life.

Then Odd said,

> Arrows aided me,
> also Jolf's skill,
> strongly-made shafts
> and a stout bow,
> and you'll soon find
> that the fifth thing
> is that I've never flattered
> and fawned on the Æsir.
>
> First I allowed
> Frey and Odin,
> both of them blind,
> to burn in the flames.
> The gods were forced
> to get away from us
> wherever we found
> a flock of them.

And he also said:

> I chased two gods,
> those gutless cowards,
> like fearful goats
> facing a wolf;

it's bad to have Odin
as a bosom friend;
no more to monsters
you'll make sacrifices.

Odd rushed at the priestess with a huge oaken club. She ran away, and fled into the town with the men that followed her. Odd pursued the fleeing men, and his men killed everyone that they could get their hands on. But the priestess fled to the chief temple which stood in the town. She rushed into the temple and said this:

Help, Aesir
and Asynjur,
ye holy powers,
help your priestess.

Odd came to the temple, but didn't want to go inside after her. He went up onto the temple and looked through a window to see her lying inside. In the end, he picked up a great stone and smashed it into the window. It landed on the ogre's spine and slammed her down against the altar, and there she died.

Odd pillaged all through the town. He came to where Alf was, and he wasn't dead yet. Odd beat him with his club until he was dead. Now he collected tribute throughout the land, appointing chieftains and governors to rule it. It's said in songs that this happened in Antioch, when he killed the father and son.

When Odd was ready, he left with such immense wealth and boundless riches that they were beyond counting. Nothing is said about his journey until he came back to Greece. Meanwhile, something noteworthy had happened in that land: King Herraud had passed away, and he was carried out and a mound was raised for him. Odd had the inheritance-feast held as soon as he reached the land. When that was prepared, Harek betrothed his foster-daughter Silkisif to Odd, and men celebrated the wedding feast and King Herraud's inheritance-feast at the same time. At this feast, Odd was given the title of king, and he ruled his kingdom.

CHAPTER XXX

Something noteworthy had taken place seven years previously: the king of Novgorod in the east had died suddenly, and an unknown man named Kvillanus had seized power and become king over the land. He was rather striking in appearance because he wore a mask over his face, so that his bare face was never seen. People found that strange. No one knew his family or his native land, nor where he had come from. People talked about this a great deal. The news was heard far and wide, and it reached Odd's ears in Greece. Odd found it remarkable that, as far as he had travelled, he should never have heard him mentioned. Odd stepped up on a stump and swore this oath: that he should find out who this king was in Russia. Somewhat later, he summoned his forces and prepared to leave his home. He sent a message to his sworn brother Sirnir, and Sirnir came to meet him in the east, off the Baltic coast. He had thirty ships, and Odd had fifty. They were all well equipped with weapons and men. They sailed east to Novgorod.

Russia is such a large country that it contained many kingdoms at the time. There was a king named Marro, who ruled over Murom; that land is in Russia. One king was named Radstaf, and the land he ruled was called Rostov. One king was named Eddval; he ruled over the kingdom called Suzdal. Holmgeir was the name of the king who ruled Novgorod before Kvillanus. A king named Paltes ruled over Polotsk. There was a king named Kaenmar, and he ruled over Kiev, where Magog, the son of Japheth, the son of Noah, was first to settle.[52] All these kings that have been named had to yield tribute to King Kvillanus.

Before Odd arrived at Novgorod, Kvillanus had been assembling forces for the previous three years. People felt that he must have known in advance about Odd's arrival. All the kings that were named were there with him. Svart Geirridarson was also there; he had been called that ever since Ogmund Eythjof's Bane disappeared.[53] There was also a huge host from Karelia and Tavastia, Refaland, Virland, Estonia, Livonia, Vitland, Courland, Samland, Ermland, and Poland.[54] This host was so huge that it couldn't be counted. People were quite astonished that such a countless host should be assembled.

When Odd arrived in the land, he set men to find King Kvillanus and invited him to joust. Kvillanus didn't waste any time, and he went up against him with his forces. He was wearing a mask in front of his face, as was his custom. As soon as they encountered each other, they prepared to joust. They had long, strong lances. They broke four lances, and contested with each other for three days, and nothing came of it. Then Kvillanus said, "It seems to me now that we've put each other to the test. I say that we're equal."

"I believe you could call us that," said Odd.

"I think it's best for us to part," said Kvillanus. "Let's not fight any longer. I want to invite you home to a feast."

"There's one matter left," said Odd.

"What is it?" said Kvillanus.

"This," said Odd. "I don't know who you are, but I have sworn an oath to find out who the king of Novgorod is."

Then Kvillanus took the mask away from his face and said, "Do you recognize this hideous head at all?"

Odd clearly recognized Ogmund Eythjof's Bane, because he saw all the scars on him from where Odd had torn off his beard and face, all the way back to the middle of his skull. This was all healed, but no hair had grown on it.

Then Odd spoke. "No, Ogmund," he said, "I'll never make peace with you. You have done me much greater harm, and I challenge you to battle in the morning."

Ogmund agreed, and the next day they began fighting. The battle was savage and fierce, and there was the most terrible slaughter on both sides. Once again, Sirnir advanced most boldly, as he often had before, and he killed many men, because Snidil cut everything in front of it. Svart Geirridarson turned on him, and there was a fierce fight, but then Snidil failed to cut, although Svart had no armor. Svart wasn't lacking in either strength or wickedness, and their duel ended when Sirnir fell dead before Svart, winning great glory.

By then, Odd had killed all of Kvillanus's vassal kings, shooting some and striking others down. But when he saw the fall of Sirnir, it grieved him much, and he felt that the losses he suffered from Ogmund and his men all flowed from the same source. He nocked an arrow on the string and shot at Svart, but he blocked it with his palm and it didn't bite. The same happened to a second arrow, and a third. It occurred to Odd that he had lost a great deal when Gusir's Gifts had disappeared. He turned away from the battle and went into the forest, cut himself a huge club, and went back into battle. When he met Svart, they began to fight. Odd bashed with the club and didn't let up before he had broken every bone in Svart's body and caused his death.

Kvillanus had not been idle in the meantime, because people say that arrows flew from each of his fingers[55] and each one killed a man. With the assistance of his men, he had killed every mother's son on Odd's side. So many had also fallen on Kvillanus's side that they could hardly be counted. Odd was still standing and defended himself most bravely. He was neither weary nor wounded, thanks to his shirt. Night parted them, because there was no light for fighting. Kvillanus went to the fort with his surviving men, no more than sixty, all weary and wounded. Since then, he was called Kvillanus Blaze. He ruled Novgorod for a long time afterwards.

Odd went away into the woods and forests, all the way until he came into Gaul. Two kings ruled there, but there had been twelve realms there. One of the kings was named Hjorolf, and the other was Hroar. They were cousins. Hroar had killed Hjorolf's father to gain the kingship and ruled the kingdom alone, except Hjorolf stayed in one county. Odd came there and joined his household. The king was young and went to the archery butts for amusement, and he didn't do very well. Odd said that they shot awkwardly.

"Do you think you'll shoot better?" said the king.

"It seems simple to me," said Odd. Now he shot and always hit the target. The king was very pleased with this man, and he valued Odd highly. The king told him how he had been wronged by King Hroar. Odd encouraged him to propose an equal division of the kingdom. They sent twelve men to the king with a letter. When he had read over the letter, he answered, saying that they must not be timid to make such an offer, and the thing to do was to send the messengers back in such a way that no one else would dare to make such an offer. Then both sides summoned their forces, and Odd and Hjorolf didn't have a twelfth of the force that Hroar had. Odd ordered them to point out King Hroar. Then he took one arrow and shot it at him, and it pierced his belly. King Hroar fell dead there, and there was no battle. Hjorolf offered Odd the kingdom, but he didn't stay there long and stole away one night. He stayed out in the forests until he came to his own kingdom, and stayed there quietly.

Some time later, Kvillanus sent Odd great gifts of gold and silver, and many splendid treasures, along with words of friendship and an offer to make a settlement. Odd accepted these gifts, because he understood that Ogmund Eythjof's Bane, who was then named Kvillanus, couldn't be defeated, because he might be called a spirit no less than a human being. It isn't said that they had any dealings with each other later, and so their encounters ended.

CHAPTER XXXI

Now Odd stayed in his kingdom. He lived there for a long time, and had two sons with his wife. One was named Asmund, after his foster brother, and the other was named Herraud after his mother's father, and both of them were promising.

One evening, when Odd and his wife were getting into bed, Odd spoke up: "There's a trip away from this land that I intend to make."

"What do you intend to do?" said Silkisif.

"I intend to go north to Hrafnista," he said. "I want to find out who's in charge of the island, because I and my family have to keep it."

"It seems to me," she said, "that you have enough holdings here, since you have all of Russia, and as much as you want from other possessions and kingdoms. I wouldn't think you'd have any need to yearn for and care about this useless scrap of an island any more."

"Yes," he said, "it's true that the island is of little worth. Still, I want to decide who should have it. It won't do any good to dissuade me, because I've decided to go. I'll be gone a short time."

At once he prepared two ships to sail away, with forty men on each one. There is nothing to report about his journey until he came north to Hrafnista in Norway. The people who were there welcomed Odd warmly and held a feast in his honor, and he accepted the feasting for half a month. They invited him to take the island and all the property that went with it. He granted them all those properties and didn't want to stay there. Then he made ready to travel, and he was sent away with fine gifts.

Now Odd sailed out of Hrafnista until they came before Berurjod; men think that it lies in Jæderen. He ordered the sail to be lowered. Odd and his men landed at the place where Ingjald's farm had stood, but the old foundations there were overgrown with turf. He looked over the place and said, "It's a terrible thing, knowing that this farm must have all fallen down, and everything that was once here has been destroyed."

He went to the place where he and Asmund had had their archery targets, and he told them what a difference there had been between the sworn brothers. He also went with them to the place where they had gone swimming, and he told them all about the landmarks. When they had seen that, he said, "Now we must be on our way, and it's no use heading up onto land, but it's terrible to see such things."

Odd and his men went down to the shore, and where the earth had blossomed well when Odd had lived there before, now it had been blown away. When they went down, Odd said, "I suppose that now there's no chance of that prophecy coming true, which the wretched seeress predicted for me a long time ago. But what's that over there?" said Odd. "What's lying there? Isn't that a horse skull?"

"Yes," said his men, "and it's quite bleached and worn, huge and gray all over."

"Do you suppose that could be Faxi's skull?"

Odd went up to it, and he stuck his spear-shaft at the skull. It tipped over a bit, and an adder crawled from it towards Odd. The snake struck his leg above the ankle, so that the venom took effect, and his entire leg swelled up along with his thigh. This injury took Odd so fast that they had to lead him down to the shoreline.

When Odd came there, he sat down and said, "Now I must divide my men into two. Forty men must stay next to me; I want to compose a poem about my life. The other forty must make me a stone coffin and drag it over here. They must lay a fire inside and burn up everything together when I am dead."

CHAPTER XXXII

Now Odd began the poem. Some began their work of carving the stone coffin and carrying wood to it. But those who were meant to learn the poem did so.

Odd said this:

> Listen, warriors
> to what I must tell

you fighting folk
of friends long gone.
Now I know—
no need to conceal it—
this forest-staff°   *forest-staff:* man, i.e. Odd himself
could not strive against fate.

I was fostered early
by my father's counsel,
to be brought up
at Berurjod;
I felt no lack
of love and happiness,
of all that Ingjald
could offer me.

We both grew up
at Berurjod,
Asmund and I,
all through childhood;
shafts shaping,
and ships building,
fletching arrows
for fun as children.

The seeress told
true runes to me,
but in no way
did I want to listen;
I said to the young
son of Ingjald
that I felt like a visit
to my father's estate.

While Asmund lived,
he often said
he was eager to travel

and used to the steel-meet;°   *steel-meet*: battle
I told the old gaffer
that I'd go away
and never come back;
now I've broken my word.

We let our launch
linger on the sea;
with our own hands
we hoisted the sail;
we sailed from afar
to a steep island
where Grim once had
his home and lands.

When I got to the farm,
I was glad to see
benchmates bidding
both of us welcome.
Surely I was able
to share out gold
and fair speech
with friends of mine.

In spring I heard
the summons to attend
the byrnie-assembly°   *byrnie-assembly*: battle
of the Bjarmians;
at once I said
to Sigurd and Gudmund
that I'd make the journey
and join the bold ones.

My two kinsmen
were crafty fellows,
wise leaders
and warship captains;

the wily crewmen
wanted to claim
the takings from
the Tyrfi-Finns[56].

In a merchant ship
we made safe landfall
where the Bjarmians
had built their houses;
we ravaged their folk
with fire and flame;
we managed to capture
a careless guide.

He vowed to reveal
to our valiant men
a good place to go
to gather a hoard;
he told us to leave
by the longer road,
if we should want
to win more money.

The Bjarmians rushed out,
ready to defend
their heroes' howe,
with hosts deployed;
we made many
mighty warriors
lose their lives
before leaving the place.

We had to dash
down to the ships
after forcing our foes
to flee to the marshes;

we lost both
our boat and ships,
with the wealth and men
that we brought down.

Quickly we kindled
in the close forest
a blazing beacon
burning on land;
the hound of trees°   *hound of trees*: flames
we turned loose to frisk,
rising to the sky,
red and towering.

Soon we saw
splendid ships
and richly decked men
rushing to land;
my own kinsmen
who'd camped there
were overjoyed
at their arrival.

As the breeze blustered,
we brave fellows
let our ship
sail where it would;
it seemed as if sand
was strewn on the deck,
no hope of landfall—
I didn't lie idle.

We came from afar
to a craggy island
late in the summer,
sails all tattered;

most of the heroes
hauled up the ships,
sending them swiftly
sliding on rollers.

We pitched our tents,
and practiced archers,
wielders of the bow,
went on a bear hunt;
we landed on the island
to light a flame,
a blazing bonfire,
and the bear stood before us.

The crag-dwellers
called out and said
that they'd drive us away
if we didn't leave;
the rock-plain rulers'°   *rock-plain rulers*: giants
roaring voices
weren't so winsome
for warriors to hear.

We the warlike
weapon-trees°   *weapon-trees*: men
never cringed
since coming there;
the heroes stacked up
sturdy walls
along the cliff;
I labored at that.

I set out, going
with Gusir's Gifts
between the cliffs
and the coals burning.

I shot out the eye
of an awful troll,
and pierced the breast
of the boulder-Freyja.°   °*boulder-Freyja:* giantess

There I won the name
that I wanted to have,
which the ogres called
from the crags to me.
They said they'd gladly
give Arrow-Odd
a wind for sailing
away from here.

We said we were ready
to sail from the island
as soon as we found
a favorable wind;
we escaped from them
and came home safely,
kinfolk greeted
their gracious friends.

We were together
all winter long,
gladdened by gold
and good-hearted words;
when the frost melted,
the fighters dragged
their finest warships
to the water's edge.

Straightaway we sailed
south along the land,
truly, we travelled
in two ships and one more;

we hoped to haul in
a hoard of treasure
by searching all
of the Elfar Skerries.

There in the sound
we saw ahead of us
capable thanes,
Thord and Hjalmar;
standing before us,
the fighters asked whether
we'd accept a truce
or sail on our way.

Our band of heroes
held council together,
there seemed little hope
for a haul of wealth;
the Halogalanders
made a happier choice,
we judged it better
to join our forces.

We all set sail
from sea to land,
wherever we heroes
could hope for plunder;
we feared nothing
while fierce chieftains,
staunch commanders,
steered the warships.

We were wrathful
when we met with
a stout shield-bearer,
standing off Holmsnes;

we gathered up
the gear of all
the splendid warriors
on six ships.

We were all there
in the west with Skolli,
where a lord of men
his land was ruling;
the brave ones bore
bloody wounds,
gashed by swords,
but we gained the victory.

The jarl's warriors
laid waste the cape,
used to the fight-moot°   °*fight-moot*: battle
as foxes to hounds;
Hjalmar and I
headed right for them,
savaged the ships
with swords and flames.

Gudmund asked
if I'd go with him
and head for home
at harvest time;
I made it known
that I never wanted
to see my family
in the far-off north.

We all made a pledge
to meet in the summer,
on the Alv, in the east,
outward bound;

the bold-hearted
Hjalmar wanted
my band of fighters
as we fared south.

The cheerful ones fared
to the chainmail-meeting
by two different ways,
once the breeze was fair;
then to Sweden
we set our course,
we sought out Ingvi[57]
in Uppsala.

The bold-hearted
Hjalmar gave me
farms on the land,
five all together;
I was glad of the gift,
and was greeted by others
with the finest rings
and the fairest wishes.

We all met up
on a merry day,
Swedish sailors
and Sigurd from the north;
we rifled and robbed
riches aplenty
from those island freaks;
they faced burning.

We let the roller-steeds°   *roller-steeds*: ships
ride the billows,
setting out westwards,
sailing to Ireland;

when we came there,
we quickly saw
that lords and ladies
had left their houses.

I ran down the wide
wagon's track,
seized my sturdy
staves of the bowstring.°   *staves of the bowstring*: arrows
All of my gold
I'd give, to have
Asmund alive,
alongside me.

Later I saw
assembling there
bold warriors,
their wives as well;
there I forced four
of Olvor's folk,
though good at the edge-game,°   *edge-game*: battle
to give their lives.

From the wagon
the woman addressed me,
promising me
prized treasures;
the lady told me
to return next summer,
said that they'd seek
a suitable reward.

It did not seem
like a stout byrnie,
or frigid iron rings
falling down over me,

when this silk shirt,
sewn with gold,
fell over me firmly,
fitting my sides.

We went westwards
to win more treasure;
the crewmen called me
a cowardly wretch,
until the fighters
found in Skida
baleful brothers
and brought them death.

In the Swedish Skerries,
Soti and Halfdan
were murderers
of many folk;
when we came away,
we'd cleared the decks
of sixty ships
from stern to prow.

As we sailed away,
we saw warriors,
troublesome and spirited,
in Tronuvagar.
Ogmund's death
was not ordained yet;
three of us escaped,
and they had nine.

I could boast
before brave heroes
that I'd killed great men,
when we came to the sea;

we two suffered
the saddest loss,
when Prow-Gleam
was pierced by a spear.

The wise warriors
went home from there,
but hailed Thord
with a high gravemound.
No man dared
to defy our wills,
we lived with no lack
of luxuries.

Hjalmar and I
were happy each day,
steering our ships
and safe from harm,
until we found
fighters on Samsey;
well could they wield
the wound-flame.°   *wound-flame*: sword

We let fall into
the eagle's clutches
twelve berserks,
tainted with shame;
I was forced to part
on the fated day
from my true friend,
trusted and worthy.

Never before
had I known a man
with a better head
for bold adventure;

I hoisted on my shoulders
the helm-destroyer,°   *helm-destroyer:* warrior
and then set out
for Sigtuna.

I hadn't lingered
for a long time,
when I could see
Sæmund coming;
his men cleared
the crew from my ship;
myself, I struggled
to swim away.

I went through Gotland,
grim in my mind,
for a full six days
before finding Saemund;
I forced his followers
to face my sword,
thirteen churls
plus the chieftain himself.

Southwards on the sea
I set my course,
until I grounded
on great shallows;
I was all alone,
but on the other hand,
many I forced
to fare on the Hel-road.

I came to a country
where castles were ruled
by excellent folk
in Aquitania;

there I left four
fearless warriors'
corpses lying;
I've come here now.

Earlier, I'd sent
a short message
to the northernmost
of my near kinsmen;
I was as glad
to greet them arriving
as a hungry hawk
harrying its prey.

The men made offer
of many honors
to the heroes three
in that place, later.
I didn't want
to win such things,
but both my brothers
stayed behind.

I hurried away
from the host of the mighty,
until I found
the fortress, Jerusalem;
I went to the water
to wash all over,
then I learned to serve
and to love Christ.

I know that the waters
washed me all over,
the flood of the Jordan,
far from Greece;
nonetheless,

as is known by all,
the splendid shirt
preserved all its powers.

Near the chasms
I encountered a vulture;
he flew off with me,
far through the lands,
until we came
to craggy heights,
and in his aerie
at ease I rested.

Until Hildir
took me away
in his rowboat,
a robust giant;
freely offering
the fire of Vimur,°   *Vimur*: a river; its *fire*: gold
he let me tarry
for twelve months.

I dallied with Hild,
daughter of that giant,
wise and huge
and winsome indeed—
on her I begot
a glorious son,
a marvelous
and mighty lad,
surpassing all other
proud warriors.

Ogmund Eythjof's Bane
ended my son's life
in the harsh stony
Helluland wastes.

His nine companions
I deprived of life;
never have I known
a nastier pirate.

He slew yet more
of my sworn brothers,
Sirnir and Gardar,
but I seized the ogre's beard.
Unlike anyone
in his appearance,
he was then called
Kvillanus Blaze.

I was reckoned useful
at the rain of swords°,   *rain of swords*: battle
when battle raged
on Brávellir;[58]
Hring then ordered
Odd Far-Traveler
to have his fighters
form a wedge.

A little while later,
when lands I ruled,
I met with a pair
of proud-minded rulers:
I granted to one
of these green leaders
a stroke of good fortune
in fighting for his inheritance.

I came to where Sigurd
and Sjolf his fellow
thought themselves keenest
of the king's household;

the rank and file urged us
to ride out hunting
and show my weapon-skill
against such great men.

My shots flew
no shorter than the princes',
the smoothed linden
was light in my hand.
Then we decided
on a swimming match;
I left them both blowing
blood from their noses.

A shield-maiden
was meant for me then,
when we had
to hold the battle;
I know that our enemies
in Antioch
were robbed of life;
we reaped great wealth.

We fell on the fighting
folk with our swords,
and we wasted
their wooden idols.
I battered Bjalki
with a bludgeon of oak
within the fort gates,
until I finished him off.

Harek was loyal
and a loving friend,
when he plighted the faith
of his foster-daughter;

I wedded the ruler's
wise daughter;
we ruled our lands,
my lady and I.

In good spirits
I stayed there
for a span of time,
as I see now;
a great many tales
could be told of my journeys
to thoughtful thanes:
this is the last.

All who are hale
must hurry now,
go down to the ships;
our doom is to part.
Send to Silkisif,
and our sons as well,
my fondest greetings;
I'll go there no more.

When the poem was done, Odd was fading fast, and they led him to where the stone coffin had been built. Odd said, "Now everything the seeress told me has turned out to be true. I want to lie down in the stone coffin and die there. Then you must light a fire inside and burn everything all together." He lay down in the stone coffin and said, "You must carry my farewell home to Silkisif, and to our sons and friends."

After that, Odd died. They lit a fire inside and burned everything together, and they didn't leave until it was completely burned up. Most men say that Odd had been twelve ells[59] tall, because the stone coffin measured that long on the inside.

Odd's retainers went on their way and traveled back east. They had a favorable wind until they arrived at home. They told Silkisif what had happened on their journey, and they brought her his farewell. She felt that this was terrible news, and so did the people of the land. Afterwards, she took over the kingdom, along with her foster-father Harek. They kept watch over the land and thanes, until Odd's sons were ready to claim the kingdom.

The lineage in Russia that was descended from Odd grew up there. But the girl whom Odd left behind in Ireland, who was named Ragnhild, came from the west after her mother's passing and went north to Hrafnista, and there she was married. Many people are descended from her, and her lineage has grown up there.

And here ends the saga of Arrow-Odd, as you have now heard it told.

THE SAGA OF AN BOW-BENDER
Áns saga bogsveigis

CHAPTER I

This story begins in the days when petty kings ruled in Norway. A father and son ruled together over a certain shire. The father was named Olaf, and the son was named Ingjald, although Ingjald was fully grown when this saga takes place. The father and son weren't like each other: King Olaf was well-liked, but Ingjald was the most deceitful of men. Bjorn and Ketil were the names of their retainers; Bjorn was called Bjorn the Strong. They were of the same temperament as Ingjald, aggressive and bullying. King Olaf had a daughter named Asa, the loveliest of women, and well-accomplished. Father and son ruled the shire of Namdalen.

King Olaf was old at the time of this story. He had been married to two queens, and each one had died. His second wife was named Dis; she had previously been married to King Onund the Open-Eyed[1] from the shire of Fjordane, and had two sons by him. Both of them were named Ulf, and now they ruled Fjordane. Ingjald thought that he should have half of his brothers' kingdom, as an inheritance from his mother. He had fought two battles against them, and had lost both of them.

There was a farmer named Bjorn. He lived on Hrafnista, which lies off the coast of Namdalen. Bjorn was considered one of the most prominent farmers there in the north. His wife was named Thorgerd, the daughter of Bodmod Framarsson and Hrafnhild, the daughter of Ketil Salmon. She and Bjorn had a daughter named Thordis, who married Gaut of Hamar,[2] an excellent man. They had a son named Grim, who was both big and strong from an early age.

Bjorn and Thorgerd had more children. The older son was named Thorir, a handsome man, courtly and accomplished in every way. He was a retainer of King Olaf and was highly valued by him. As a token of his esteem, King Olaf gave Thorir the sword that his family had owned for a long time and prized as an heirloom. Its name was Thane. It was both long and broad, and it was the sharpest of all swords; it was triply polished. For a long time, Thorir would spend one winter with the king, and the next winter with his father.

Bjorn's younger son was named An. He was tall from an early age, but not handsome, and quite slow. People didn't realize how strong he was, because he had never put his strength to the test. Instead, he seemed to be a simpleton. He had little love from his father, but his mother loved him very much. People didn't think that he resembled his ancestors, such as Ketil Salmon and the other men of Hrafnista, in any way except in size. An didn't lie around in the hearth-house, but he was still called a simpleton by some people.[3] He never was in the habit of playing sports. So time passed until he was nine years old. By then he was no smaller than Thorir his brother. He was quite unfit to be seen, and he wasn't well off for clothes, because both his knees and his elbows stuck out.

When he was twelve, he disappeared for three nights, so that no one knew what had become of him. An went into a clearing in the forest. There he saw a single large stone, and a man standing next to a stream. He had heard mention of dwarves, and he'd also heard that they were more skillful than other men. An got between the stone and the dwarf, and cast a spell barring him from the stone.[4] He said that the dwarf would never be able to get back inside unless he crafted a bow for him, as large and strong as he could wield, and five arrows[5] to go with it. They should have such a nature that he would hit everything that he shot at, on the first shot, as he wished. This had to be completed within three nights, and An waited while it was done.

The dwarf complied with these terms, without placing any curses on the weapons. The dwarf was named Lit.[6] As payment, An gave him some silver coins which his mother had given him. The dwarf gave An a fine chair.

An went home, carrying the chair on his back. People laughed at him a lot. An gave the chair to his mother and said that he had to give her the best present.[7]

CHAPTER II

When An was eighteen, he was larger than anyone else in the north, but neither his wits nor his manners had increased. That winter, Thorir had settled at Hrafnista and had received a nickname on account of his sword; he was called Thorir Thane.

In the spring, Thorir prepared to travel to meet the king. An begged to go with him, but Thorir flatly refused. But when he went out to his ship, An came along. Thorir asked what he wanted then. An said that he had to go with him, whether Thorir granted him permission or not.

Thorir said that he would never go. "You don't know how to behave among chieftains," he said, "since your conduct is hardly fit for staying here at home." He took An and tied him rather tightly to an oak tree. An didn't struggle.

Thorir left, but it wasn't long before he saw that An was walking towards him, dragging the oak behind him. He had pulled it up by the roots.

Thorir said, "You're an incredible man as far as strength goes, brother. But I still don't think it's a good idea for you to go to meet the king, with a disposition such as you have." Thorir cut the bonds from him and said, "You don't value my words very highly." He drew the sword Thane, and threatened him with it: "This sword will teach you manners, which you've never had before. It won't respect you, and it will block the path before you."

An said, "You won't frighten me like a child that's in for a spanking. So that you'll know what I'm able to do to you, you'll find out now."

An gripped Thorir and lifted him up and shook him like a child, and said, "Now see how much control you have, if we don't see eye to eye." He turned him loose, and Thorir realized what the man was made of.

They went out to the ship. An considered where he could place himself so as to cause everyone the most inconvenience.[8] The merchants asked one another who this man could be.

An said, "Why don't you ask me? I can tell you. My name is An, and my family is from Hrafnista, and my brother is Thorir Thane."

They said that they didn't believe it. He said that what he had said was true. They said that he would be welcome there.

An was poorly dressed. Thorir ordered some of the ship's cargo of cloth to be cut up to dress him, so that he would not look so strange, and it was done. It wasn't much use to him, because he fastened it on himself awkwardly, and it didn't improve his dress at all. The ship's crewmen were well-disposed toward An, and he knew no other way than to be friendly in return.

CHAPTER III

Thorir and his men came to the shire of Namdalen. There they heard the news that King Olaf had died, and Ingjald was now sole king over the kingdom that they had both ruled. Thorir said, "The better man has been lost. I would not have traveled from the north if I had known about this change."

Thorir arrived at the king's estates. An had his bow with him, and when they came to the hall, An strung his bow, which was tremendously strong. Thorir asked why he had to do that. An said that they would see soon. He let the string run across his chest, and he placed the bow across his shoulders, carrying his arrows in his hands. When they came to the hall doors, the doorkeepers gave Thorir space, but there was a great commotion when An arrived, because he hadn't changed his outfit. He walked right at the doors, but the bow was sticking out beyond his shoulders, and there wasn't enough space for it in the doorway. The bow had to either break or be bent a great deal, because the doors were blocking the way. An got through into the hall; the bow bent but didn't break.

An sat down at the outer edge of the hall, but Thorir went before the king and greeted him. The king welcomed him warmly, and invited him to go to the high seat opposite himself. "You shall be welcome among us. But who was that coming with you, and why did he separate from you so quickly?"

Thorir said, "That man is my brother, and he hardly even knows how commoners behave."

The king said, "He shall be welcome here. Let him sit next to you. We will do that for your sake. We have heard An mentioned, and he is a remarkable man in many ways."

Thorir found An and told him what the king had said. "Turn this honor to your advantage, brother."

An answered, "We won't share a seat. It's more important to me to get lodging for the winter."

Thorir said that he thought that it would be readily available. Nonetheless, Thorir went before the king and said, "I want to ask for winter lodging for my brother An, at his request, though he stay in his seat."

The king said, "Winter lodging is readily available for him. But what other seat is better for him than next to you?"

Thorir said that he couldn't do anything with him. "It suits him best to have his own way. I was unwilling for him to come with me because I knew that his nature is strange."

Thorir told An what the king had said. An said, "This has turned out well now. Go to your seat, brother." Thorir did so.

An was taciturn and refused to mingle with people. He stayed in his seat for the longest time, except for when he had to go to the latrine. The retainers laughed at him a great deal, and Ketil was the leader at that. An paid no attention to it, and thus it went on until Yule. Then the king made it known that he would give Yule gifts, as his father had done. He said that thus he wanted his men to pay homage to him. And on Yule Eve, all the men were presented with gifts except for An.

The king asked why An did not receive the gifts. "Should he not accept gifts like others?"

This was told to An. He rose to his feet and said, "I think it would be good to have some gold."

The man didn't look much like a warrior when he pushed his way up to the king. He was astonishing to look at. The king said, "What twanged so loudly, An, when you came through the doors the first time?"

"My bow," said An, "because your hall doors were so small, king, that the tips bent all the way together when I had it on my shoulders, before I came in, and it howled aloud when it sprang back."

"You shall be called An Bow-Bender," said the king.

"What are you giving me for a naming-gift?" said An.[9]

"You shall have a gold ring," said the king, "as both a naming-gift and a Yule gift together, because I heard what you said before. You must be a most mighty man, as large as you are."

"I guess I'm mighty," said An, "but I don't know about that."

An accepted the ring and didn't thank the king. He played with the ring and set it on his coat of mail. He tossed it from hand to hand, and on one occasion the ring flew out of his grasp. He went to look in the latrine,[10] but when he came back, he looked as if he'd bathed in filth. His benchmates asked why he looked so awful. He didn't say much, but later, he said to one of them, "I'll tell you if you'll keep it secret."

He said that he would keep it secret.

An said, "It's true what they say, 'Wealth that stirs up envy is eager to flee.' Now the ring is lost."

His benchmate said, "Let's keep quiet about this."

An said, "So be it—but the ring isn't meant for me to have. I'll give it to the man who finds it."

This was brought up before the household, and everyone told someone else. Ketil laughed a lot at this, and said that giving a gold ring to that crazy man had gone as might have been expected. Then he went and searched for the ring with the other retainers. They squeezed together tightly in the latrine.

Then An said, "Why is it that people are crawling on hands and knees, toiling in filth? Has there been a fight?"

He was told that the men wanted to make good his mishap and find the ring.

An said, "I'm so absent-minded. Here's the ring on my hand. Now I've paid you all back this once for mocking me so often."

The retainers said that they'd been made to look ridiculous. An said that that was how it had to be. The mockery let up for a while, but it came back the same as before, and Ketil was the worst mocker.

CHAPTER IV

One day it happened that the two brothers were outside, next to the hall. The king's retainers came out and said, "You must be a strong man, An."

He answered, "Maybe, but I haven't put it to the test."

They said, "Will you wrestle Bjorn?"

He answered, "On one condition. You have to serve me and make a big fire in front of me."

They did so, and invited him to warm himself. He said that he'd have a greater need to warm up when he came from the wrestling match. Then they prepared for wrestling in the hall.

An had come there in a shaggy cape which his mother had given him.

He didn't have a belt on, but the cape was so long that it dragged more than an ell[11] behind him. The sleeves fell down over his hands. Bjorn rushed at An, but An stood before him calmly. Bjorn was the strongest of all men. He picked up An and threw him out of the hall onto the fire, so that his shoulders fell down into the flames, but his legs slammed against the fence. There was loud laughter.

An slowly stood up. The fire hadn't hurt him because of the shaggy cape. The king said, "I don't believe you're as strong as you claimed, An."

An said, "He who falls first would seem stronger to me, king." The king laughed.

An put on a belt and tucked up his cloak and rolled up his sleeves. They charged at each other a second time. An pulled Bjorn into his grip and shook him like a baby, and then turned him loose by flinging him onto the fire outside. The retainers rushed to him and pulled him out of the flames, and Bjorn was badly burned. They said that this man was quite strong. An was pleased to be called strong. He said that now it was clear that he wanted Bjorn to warm himself at the fire, and Bjorn needed it more than he did. Then An spoke this verse:

> The sneering man shouldn't have
> slammed me against the planks,
> I wasn't one whit able
> to withstand him. Damn that man.
> I flung some fuel on the fire
> when he fell into my grip;
> I denied him dignity, rather.
> Damn that man forever.

Now winter wore on, and one day the brothers were again standing outside together. Thorir said, "Aren't you unhappy with coming here, since you've found scorn and mockery here?"

An said that he wasn't unhappy. "I've received gold and good lodging over the winter, and I don't care about their mockery."

Thorir said, "I will try something that's occurred to me. I'll give you the sword Thane, so that you may kill any two of the king's men and settle the score yourself."

The Saga of An Bow-Bender

An said, "I want to see the sword, and I'll accept it, but I won't promise to pay them back."

Another day, when it was time for drinking, An stood up and faced the man who sat nearest to him, and stared at him. He did the same with everyone in the hall; he stood before the king for the longest time. Then he went up to Thorir and laid the sword on the table in front of him and said that he didn't want to have it. There was loud laughter at that, and Thorir felt that this was terrible.

On one occasion the brothers found themselves together, and Thorir asked, "Why did you act so outrageously, brother, and completely opposite from what I'd planned?"

An said, "I thought about whether to avenge myself on the king's men, and it didn't seem possible. But I stared at the king for the longest time, because that's when my mind wavered the most over my decision."

Thorir said, "You're a complete idiot, because the king is well-disposed towards you."

An said, "We don't need to discuss him, because I think that no man worse than this king will grow up in Norway."

Then they ended their conversation.

Spring came on. Then King Ingjald had an assembly summoned. He stood up in the assembly and said, "It is known to men that my father is dead and I hold the realm. I wish to proclaim that I will grant compensation to all those whom I have transgressed against, and give good laws to them and to all of you. But I require you, my thanes, to go on a journey with me and seek out my brothers, so that we may peacefully set our kingdom in order. I will provide my men with food and ale." This was greeted with cheers.

An said, "You must think that the king speaks well, brother."

Thorir said that that remained to be seen.

An said, "I can tell you that now he bears the greatest malice towards his brothers, and is planning for the worst evil to befall them somehow."

Thorir said that he hadn't stopped thinking about the king.

After that they prepared for the journey. An asked Thorir whether he wanted him to go with the king's household—"and with you and the king. It's a small matter if I go off as I am, and it's quite unclear how I'll manage to get food here in the meantime, so I'm more eager to go with you. That will take longest and turn out for the worst."

Thorir said that he wanted him to go. They set out northwards with the king and anchored along some islands. The king said that they should raise a harbor-beacon.[12] Then An spoke a verse:

> It's well for you, willow,[13]
> you wait by the sea
> quite well leafed out;
> a man shakes off you
> the morning dews,
> and I long for a thane,
> by night and day.

Thorir said, "You don't need to do that, because I'll give you the sword Thane."

An said, "I'm not longing for that thane."

Then Ketil said, "I suppose you're longing for some man, and you want to bugger him." And at this they made many jeers and jokes.[14]

"That's not it," said An. "I'm not longing for that thane, I'm longing for Thorir Thane, my brother, because he is so simple-minded that he trusts this king, but I know that the king will bring about his death."

Later on, they came to the shire of Fjordane. King Ingjald said, "I think that we have now entered my brothers' kingdom. I have heard that they do not want to reach a settlement with us, and it seems most promising to me that we should fight, and so rid ourselves of their opposition." Many men wished then that they had stayed home, rather than coming there.

When the brothers heard that, they summoned their forces to oppose King Ingjald. King Ingjald ordered his men to be served drink, so that they would set out in high spirits. A large ox-horn came to An. He spoke a verse:

> If fighters must fall,
> I would find it better
> for us to stride swiftly
> to the spear-meeting°.   °*spear-meeting*: battle
> Let's drink up all the ale from
> the ox's head-spear thief;[15]

swords will swing more sharply,
if I say aught about it.

The king said, "That is well composed. The man who has you striding by his side won't be defenseless."

An said, "I don't expect that that will be so useful today, although I'm able to offer help."

The king said that he didn't know what sort of thane he might be. An said that two possibilities would present themselves.

An lay down on the ship when the others got up to fight. Thorir said, "What you're doing is completely wretched—first to have traveled here, and now to lie on the ship when your help is needed. I thought that you'd be gifted with courage."

An said that he didn't care what he said.

The king disembarked, and a host of the men of that land came against them. They encountered each other next to a forest, and fought. An got up and went to the forest and sat on a stump. From there he looked out over both forces, and he saw two banners carried forward before King Ingjald's brothers.

An said to himself, "Why wouldn't it be a good idea to offer help to King Ingjald, even though he needs it least, yet he desires it himself? I'll shoot, and it's most likely that I'll hit my target, because the one who gave me this bow and these arrows said that I would become a good shot. That was the dwarf whom I once met in the woods on Hrafnista. People thought I had disappeared, when the dwarf and I made our bargain. Now I shall test the craftsmanship with which he redeemed himself and his head, when I once enchanted him out of the stone. He said that I would shoot three famous shots,[16] and one hit with each arrow."

He shot and aimed at one of the brothers Ulf. The arrow flew through him and into the brushwood behind his back. The banner fell at once. An recovered the arrow and dashed back to the ships. When men saw that, they told the king that he must have been laid low by a thong-spear[17] or a bow-shot.

In the evening, the men came to the ships. Everyone was talking about that shot. An heard that and said that they might succeed, "if it's half-completed now."

In the morning, the king urged his men to disembark, and said that he hoped for victory. An stayed behind, and no one called on him to disembark. It occurred to him that King Ingjald might need help. He shot a second arrow. This one hit Ulf in the chest, and it wasn't shot as hard as the previous one, so the arrow stuck fast. Men recognized the shot and thought that one man must have made both shots—which was true, although the shooter couldn't be seen.

The king said, "I knew all along that An would be a man of accomplishment." The king sent for him, saying that he would grant him a rich reward for his great deeds. The messengers saw that An had gotten into a boat and wasn't very close to them. They told him the king's message, and said that he would be honored for his exploit.

An said, "I won't go to meet the king, because he'll bestow a gallows on me as a reward for my efforts."

The men went back and told the king. He said, "He's not far wrong. I don't want him to kill any more notable men in secret.[18] I meant for my brothers to live, and for me to hold the kingdom in their name."

Thorir said, "You're doing wrong. You would rather have done the deed yourself. There hasn't been much time when you didn't want them doomed."

The king answered, "Had he disembarked with us, he would be worthy of honor. But for killing in secret, he deserves death."

Thorir said that he supposed that the king must have an equal reward for him in mind.

Ingjald claimed his brothers' landholdings, and set men to rule the shire. A burial mound was raised for his brothers, which was called Ulfahaug.

The king was on the ship and ready to sail away. Ketil said that he wanted to visit a friend of his who lived a short distance away. The king replied, "Don't delay, because we'll sail soon."

Ketil had An's arrow in his hand. He came to the farm of a certain farmer, a short distance from the ships. He didn't know this farmer. The farmer greeted him and asked his name. He answered, "I'm called An Bow-Bender, whom you must have heard of by now, on account of my shooting."

The farmer answered, "Your shooting was quite An-wanted,[19] because our chieftains were trusty men. But stay with us tonight."

The Saga of An Bow-Bender

He said that he would accept. There was no one else living there except for the farmer's wife and daughter, whose name was Drifa.

Now it must be told how An rowed up a hidden creek and came to the same farm. He hid himself and listened to the men talking. The guest spoke up: "Is that your daughter, farmer?"

"That's right," he said.

"I intend to get into bed with her tonight, and you won't get a better offer."

The man didn't say much about that. Ketil said that he had done mightier deeds than getting into her bed. When An heard that, he went to the doors and pounded on them. A slave went to the doors and went out a long way before he saw the man. He asked his name. The man said that he was named An.

The slave said, "What's going An here?[20] That's the name of the man who's inside."

An said that that might be the case, and he went inside and sat down across from Ketil. The farmer asked him his name. He gave his name as An.

The farmer said, "I've had quite An-nough of this.[21] Do you want to stay with us?"

He said that he would accept, "but I have to wait a bit before I have a meal. Has Ketil named himself An?"

Ketil said, "I did it as a joke."

An said, "I put up with this from you when we met. We both lodged together, and you asked about some aspects of my accomplishments. You didn't think to look into that, but instead you thought that I was an idiot. All the same, I am a skillful man, and I know a remedy that will cure your desire for women. I heard just now that you were trying to make the farmer's daughter your concubine."

He grabbed him by the forelock and sent him tumbling outside, and he spoke a verse:

> You'll find out,
> as you're forking dung,
> that you are no
> An Bow-Bender.

You're a bread-bender,
not a bow-bender,
a cheese-bender,
not an elm°-bender. °*elm*: bow

He tied him up, shaved off his hair, and covered him with tar, and said that anything that was feathered ought to fly. He stabbed one of his eyes out, and then he castrated him.[22] After that, he turned him loose and gave him two staffs—"but I'll take my arrow back."

An said, "When there's something that stands out from the rest, men call it a 'king's treasure.' Now you've been somewhat altered, so I'm sending you to King Ingjald as you are. I give you over to him as compensation for one of his brothers, whenever one of them is paid for."

Ketil set out for the ship and told the king. His staffs bore witness that he had been crippled, but his appearance told a more powerful story, with both his eye and his testicles missing.

"You're unfit for me," said the king, and drove him away.

CHAPTER V

Now we shall relate how An spoke with the farmer: "You've welcomed me, and you shouldn't suffer on my account. We must abandon the farm and go into the forest, because the king's men will be here shortly."

That's what they did. An's guess was right, because the king sent men there in the night. They burned down the farm and then went back.

The king said to his men, "If An has gotten away, I set a price of three marks of silver on his head, and I declare him an outlaw throughout all Norway." This was heard far and wide. The king went home to his kingdom. An stayed with the farmer and rebuilt his farm over the summer.

An was dressed every day in a white fur robe that was so long that it reached his heels. Over that, he wore a gray fur coat that came to the middle of his calves. Over that, he wore a red tunic that reached his knees. On the outside, he wore a homespun shirt that reached to the middle of his thighs.[23] He had a hood on his head and a wood-axe in his hand. The man was quite large and manly, but not very handsome.

One day, An met the farmer's daughter Drifa outside. Three women were walking with her. She was the loveliest of women, and well dressed; she wore a long-sleeved red tunic, not wide below, but long and narrow-waisted. She wore a lace ribbon around her forehead, with the finest hair of all women. The women laughed at him a lot, and made fun of his outfit.

Drifa said, "Where are you coming from now, Four-Fold?"[24]

"From smithing," said An.

Just then the farmer came up and asked them not to mock him. An spoke a verse:

> When they met me,
> the maidens asked,
> the fair-haired ones:
> "Four-Fold, where did you come from?"
> I gave a good answer
> to the Gunn of silk,°   *Gunn:* a valkyrie; *Gunn of silk:* woman
> mocking in return:
> "Mild Air,[25] where did you come from?"

"I don't believe your tunic suits you any better than my shirt," said An, "because it hangs below the bottom of your cloak." Then they parted for the time being.

When the farm was rebuilt, the farmer told An in the autumn that he had the right to stay there over the winter—"and you have worked hard for this." An said that he would accept. He was pleased with the farmer's daughter; although she had made fun of the cut of his clothes, he was patient with that.

But in the spring, An declared that he would go away and take up something else. "If it turns out that your daughter is pregnant, as I suspect, there aren't many people here whom I could fob this off on, and I'll admit to being the father. And if it's a boy, send him to me when you hear that I have settled down, and let this ring go with him as a token. But if it's a girl, look after her yourself."[26]

Then he went away and headed east into the forest. A robber named Garan lived out there. As An was going down the forest path that day, he saw a man following him, trying to conceal himself. The man had a black shield and a helmet on his head, a bow in his hand and a quiver of arrows on his back. He saw the newcomer and shot a broad arrow right into his shield, and it barely went through the shield. An took aim at him and shot an arrow through his shield, and it pierced his upper arm so that he was wounded. The robber said that he found this to be harder shooting than necessary, and he laid down his weapon and went to meet this man, and asked him his name. He said that he was called An.

Garan said that he had heard his name—"and you're famous."

An said, "I've heard your name mentioned as well, and always with a bad reputation."

Garan said, "I'll treat you well. I want to invite you to stay with me and make a pact together, and we two will accomplish many things."

An said, "There'll be quite enough to accomplish, if we want to do wrong."

They came to a hut that stood in the woods, and the door was shut. They went inside, and there was no lack of riches, weapons, or armor. An saw two stones there, one taller than the other. An asked what they might be. Garan said, "That's where I've tested the back-strength of certain men who have come for a visit."

An said, "You treat your guests cruelly. But which stone would be more convenient for you to be bent over?"

Garan said that he hadn't given that any thought, but still admitted that the taller stone was more suitable on account of its height.

By then the day was passing. Garan said, "Now we should prepare our meal. Which would you rather do: fetch water or make fire?" An said that he would take it on himself to make the fire, because he said that he was used to that task. When he had crouched down, he threw the sword that he carried as his weapon onto his back. He heard a whirring noise up over him. The robber struck at him and hit the sword, and that saved him.

An jumped up and said "You're not trustworthy. Now you want to sever our partnership quickly, but I've done nothing to you. Maybe now you'll spend the night with the taller stone."

There was a fierce fight, and each one wanted to keep away from the stones. Then Garan bore down on the stones. An stomped on Garan's instep, pinned his arms against his chest and bent him over the stone, and his back was broken.[27] An got off his dead body. He cut off his head and dragged him outside and stuck his nose in his crotch, so that he wouldn't walk after death.[28]

The night passed. An stayed there through the summer and didn't hurt anyone, and didn't let himself be seen. When autumn came, he closed up the hut and went away; he wanted to have other lodgings for the winter.

In the evening he came to the home of a certain wealthy widow named Jorunn. He stayed there through the night in hiding. But when the lady of the house came into the outbuilding, she asked her guest his name. He said something that seemed appropriate. She went out, but came back and said "Why did you come here? I think you must be An Bow-Bender."

He said that it was true.

"Why did you come here?" she said, "This won't protect you from the king."

An said that he supposed that he wouldn't need protection any more. "I'll risk staying here, if you'll allow me."

She said, "I won't withhold food from you."

He stayed there for a while, and was busy and looked after her farm, with her whole-hearted consent. An said, "I would like to stay here with you over the winter, but not quite settle here permanently."

She said that the place wasn't right for him—"the king is preoccupied with finding you, and we can't do much for you."

He said that he thought King Ingjald wouldn't do him any harm.

She said, "I won't withhold food from you," but said that he should take care of his own business. An became the best overseer.

Later, they began to talk. He said that it had occurred to him that he should propose marriage to her. She said that it would have to be done on the advice of her kinfolk, but it was very much what she wanted. No one dissuaded them, and the marriage was made.

An was the best household manager, and a very skilled man. He had a boat-shed in the woods, close to the farm, and there he built a ship. His stores of wealth and reputation quickly grew great. He owned four great farms, and there were thirty fighting men on each farm who followed him. The inhabitants of the district took him as their leader. He was well-liked and generous.

King Ingjald heard about this and searched for him. His brother Thorir often went east with offers of a settlement, and the brothers were on affectionate terms. By then, their father Bjorn had died on Hrafnista, and their brother-in-law Gaut and their sister Thordis took care of the farm. Their son Grim was tall, handsome and strong, and said that none of his kinsmen were as agreeable to him as An. He went to meet him. An welcomed him, and he stayed there for a long time. He was well-liked.

Thorir often asked An to yield to the king—"it's no use, brother, since I clearly see his hostile intentions towards you."

"Fate must decide between the king and me," said An, "but you trust him too much. I'd rather have you take care of our farm." But that didn't happen.

CHAPTER VI

There was a man named Ivar, descended from an excellent family in Oppland. He came to King Ingjald's household, and the king welcomed him warmly. He hadn't been there while An had stayed with the king. Ivar was an accomplished man. He set his heart on Asa, and asked for her hand in marriage. The king received his proposal reluctantly. They discussed the matter among themselves.

The king said, "You're trying hard for this, and I will give you a chance. You must go and find An and bring me his head, and when you return, then you may hope for this marriage that you've asked for, because you will be called a great man and a suitable brother-in-law for a king."

Ivar said that this wasn't easy to accomplish—"but do you consent to this arrangement, king's sister?"

She answered, "I intend to submit to my brother's will, if you succeed in this mission."

With that, he went inland and eastward to find An, and he pleaded for winter lodging with him. An asked who he might be, and said that he hardly knew what sort of man anyone might be at heart, but admitted that he wasn't in the habit of withholding food. "And I don't demand recompense for food, until I know how it's received or offered." Ivar was a faithful helper to him at smithing and other tasks.

One evening, as they were going home, Ivar remembered what he had to accomplish. He rushed at An and struck at him. An was moving faster than Ivar thought, taking great strides, and Ivar's stroke plunged into the earth, all the way into the roots of a tree. An noticed his attack, and turned around and said that the expense of feeding him didn't seem to have paid off very well.

An tied Ivar up with a bowstring and drove him home in front of him. He set Ivar in fetters overnight. When the people found out, they asked to kill him and let him know when it was done. An said that they must not do that: "Then it will be said that I made myself the king's enemy, if people don't know the true story. I want to have a great assembly summoned. Let the king's man tell his story, and lay bare the trouble he has caused, in front of everyone."

And so it was done. An came to the assembly, leading Ivar behind him. He said, "Now tell all about your mission." Ivar did so. They all said that he had condemned himself to death.

An said, "No, that shall not be. I know whom he had to visit at home, as you've heard." He had his legs broken all the way to the knees, and then let them heal, but he twisted his feet in the opposite direction; then his toes pointed backwards.[29] An said, "Now stand before me," and so he did.

An said, "Now you're a 'king's treasure,' since you're exceptional among men." Then he twisted Ivar's face a bit, and said, "Now you stand out from other men on both ends: your face is striking, and your feet aren't like anyone else's. Go and find King Ingjald. I compensate him for his other brother with you, and now he has no reason to come here."

Ivar found the king and said that the trip hadn't gone smoothly. The king said, "I know that men have fought and killed each other, but I never knew that such mutilation was done, or that this was called a 'king's treasure'. You don't look like much of a treasure. Go to your estates."

The king's sister said, "Don't you want to consent to his marriage to me?"

The king said that it wasn't the same thing, and said that Ivar had been overconfident that he would succeed—"and thus no flat refusals were brought forth against you."[30]

Thorir was at home then, and hadn't been there for long.

After that, the king sent twelve men to bring back An's head. He told them: "I want to send you with the intent of meeting An, so that you ask winter lodging from him. He is a generous man, and will ask why so many of you are traveling together. You should say that you've pooled all your money together, and you don't trust anyone but him to divide it amongst yourselves. If he takes you in, bring an equal number of his men over to your side with bribes. I say that then it will be easy for you to keep him from escaping."

They went at once to find An, and their conversation went as the king had guessed. He took them in, and they stayed there until after Yule.

One evening, Jorunn was talking with An. "What do you think of the guests who have come to visit our home?"

He said, "I think that they are good men, and we may expect good things from them."

She said that she didn't think that they could be called trusty men—"I suspect that they've either done wicked deeds, or else they're planning them, because every time you leave your seat, they follow you with their eyes and change their expressions."

He said that he didn't think that.

"I'm taking more trouble on your behalf than I thought," she said. "I want you to go out of the house in the morning, and if they do nothing suspicious, then what I say isn't true. Say that you'll be home in the evening and that you want to go alone. If they do anything to bring suspicion on themselves, you'll know what sort of men they are."

An said that he would do this. In the morning, An left the house, and when the winter guests saw that, they thought they had a chance to capture An, and they left the house in two groups of six men each. Six of the spies stayed home, along with six men of the household who had taken money for An's head. Six spies and six householders set an ambush. They lay in wait next to An's path.

Jorunn found Grim and said that their movements seemed suspicious to her—"go and get information." He said that he was ready, and he went into the forest with many men, so that the others didn't know and didn't see anything. Evening was now coming on, and the spies felt that their greatest need was to go home and wait for the right moment, so that nothing might go wrong with their plan of attack. They went home. An was seated in the high-seat and was frowning. Grim had also come home.

An said, "Now it's fitting for our winter guests to tell us why they've come here, and how they meant to see me dead today. I know your plan, and for a long time I have known your treachery against me, but I didn't have trusty servants." They had to confess.

The Saga of An Bow-Bender

An said, "I won't kill my servants; let them go away. But I give the king's men into the power of my kinsman Grim. May he have fun with them today."

Grim said that this was well said. He went with them to the forest and hanged them all on one gallows.

King Ingjald heard this and didn't like it at all. By that time, Thorir had returned to his household. He was taciturn and seemed very angered by something. The king asked why he might be so silent. "We wish to treat you well, as before."

Thorir said, "I'm not questioning that, but this is hardly comfortable."

The king asked, "What is lacking, compared with what my father did?"

"I'm not complaining about it," said Thorir, "but your father gave me greater gifts, such as this sword."

The king said, "Is it a great treasure?"

"See for yourself," said Thorir.

The king accepted the sword and drew it and said, "This is not the possession of a low-born man."

Thorir said, "Then accept it, lord."

The king said, "I won't do that. You must have it, and it shall be yours longest." He went up to Thorir in the high-seat and ran him through with it, and left the sword sticking in the wound. He said, "We two will take turns exchanging presents, An and I."

Then he prepared a ship, and there were sixty men on it. He ordered them to go to find An and dock at his anchorage and lure him onto the ship—"and say that his brother Thorir has arrived and wants to reach a settlement. If he comes into your clutches, kill him. If this comes about, some compensation for my brothers will have been paid. Arrive at An's home early in the day." This deed was very badly spoken of, and he was now called Ingjald the Evil by everyone.

They went on their way. The night before they landed, An had a dream, and he told Jorunn: "It appeared to me as if Thorir had come here, looking very sad. He has always come here when he's appeared to me in a dream. But I don't want the ones who bring him here, in the way that my mind warns me about, to come in vain—because he looked all bloody to me, and a sword was sticking through him."

She said that his dreams might well be clear.

An jumped up and said that men would come. He had four ships made ready; two were anchored along an outlying island, and the other two were in a hidden bay next to the anchorage by the farm. An sent messengers into the settlement to tell people to hold a welcoming feast in honor of Thorir, if he were to arrive happy and well, but otherwise to test their weapons. An stayed on the farm, but his men were on the ships, and he waited, ready for whatever was to happen.

Afterwards, they saw a ship sailing into the anchorage by the farm, with red shields on it.[31] The ship's crew sent An a message to come down and meet Thorir his brother, who had come to try to reach a settlement.

An said, "He's often considered it a small matter to walk to the house, but now he's falling a little short."

They said that Thord had become sleepy.

An said that they would come down to the ship, but no farther. They didn't dare to come to him, and they shoved Thorir out of the ship and asked An to accept King Ingjald's friendly gift.

An picked up Thorir and said, "You've paid for your credulity, since you trusted the king well. But now there's something more pressing than rebuking you."

He slipped Thorir into a cave whose mouth was jutting out, and leaped up into the ship and raised a red shield. He attacked them and they fought, and many of King Ingjald's men fell. One man was fighting on his knees. Grim attacked him, but that man struck him on the back of the knee and sliced off his calf, along with the heelbone. That made him stiff-legged, before he could be healed. They killed every last man.

An had a mound built, and he had the ship placed inside, with Thorir on the afterdeck but the king's men on both sides, so that it would appear that all of them had to serve him. Grim was healed.

The king now heard this news, and it seemed that his worth and honor still hadn't improved much.

CHAPTER VII

One morning, when An was at home on his farm, he said, "I think there are very many men in the forest. It may be that it's come to this, that 'great is a king's might and great is a king's luck', as the saying is."

An now woke up his retainers and said, "It's often clear that I married well. Jorunn has often warned me that I shouldn't stay here to face the king's enmity, but I want to confront him head-on,[32] however it may turn out."

Then he took a pole, chopped it in two, and carved a handgrip on both pieces. An said, "When we come out, we'll be surrounded, but it seems wrong to me to run away. Grim and I will do without weapons." He told him to take the other wooden cudgel, and Grim did so.

Now they headed for the sea. The king had come there with a great host of men. An and Grim cleared a path before them, swinging their cudgels right and left. The king's men felt that it was no good putting up with that. An's men attacked them and many were killed, but the women escaped to Jorunn's protection. An and Grim made their way onto a rowboat. They saw the king's fleet all around them, and out in the middle of the sound was a scout ship. An said that he thought it would be a good idea to do them some mean trick—"since they're bent on doing us harm." An flung an iron boat-hook under the ship's gunwale, and it happened that the deep blue sea flooded into the hold, and the crew called out to the king's ship for help. An slipped out from between them.

An said that Grim's rowing would be better if both his legs were the same. Grim said that nothing should be lacking on that account. An didn't notice anything until oar handles hit him between the shoulders: Grim was dead of exhaustion from rowing. Now An stepped overboard, and the last thing he wanted was for the king's men to get their hands on him. They saw that the man had stepped overboard, but another man lay dead in the bilge. They told this to the king. He said, "It was to be expected that An would begrudge us getting our hands on him. But still, it will all come to the same thing for him. We'll set a watch all along the coast, so that he can't escape to land."

This had occurred to An, and he turned and swam over to a certain outlying island, and he got up onto land. By then he was utterly exhausted. A man named Erp lived there, along with his wife. There was no one else there. Erp was searching the beach, walking with his ox-cart, and saw that a tall man was lying on the beach. The farmer supposed that he was dead and that it had gone badly for him. An told him to walk boldly.

Erp said, "You would have had a softer bed next to Jorunn." He drove him home, and his legs stuck out of the cart. His old wife told him not to drive dead men to their house. Erp said that it wasn't like that, and explained matters to her. She said that they'd be well-off for money if they were dealing with a good warrior.

An regained much strength there. King Ingjald supposed that An was dead, and he went home. An stayed with the old man, and when he was well, Erp ferried him to the mainland. An said that they had done well, and gave the old woman a gold ring, but he gave the island to Erp and said that their rewards would be even greater in good time.

Then An came home. Jorunn had kept things going rather well in the meantime, but yet many things were lacking to keep up appearances. The men welcomed An warmly, but he replied to his wife, "I haven't always been fair with you about money matters, up to now." She said that she wouldn't complain, if he would stay. It occurred to An that it wouldn't be a bad idea to go check on the money in Garan's hut, because he felt that there was need now. He had that brought home, and said to Jorunn, "Here you may see my possessions," and told everyone about his stroke of luck. He didn't seem penniless, as men had thought. Their finances became as strong as before, or better.

An now set out scouts in all directions. King Ingjald heard about this, and he kept guards around him and slept in an outbuilding, next to his retainers.

An continued his smithing, as before. One evening, as he was leaving the smithy, he saw a fire burning on a certain island. It occurred to him that the king must be visiting again, or else that vagrants must be after his money. He searched all around, and he went to the sea by himself, took a boat and rowed to the island. There he saw a man sitting by a fire, youthful and tall. The man wore a tunic and linen breeches. He was eating. A silver dish sat in front of him. He had an ivory-handled knife and used it to stab food in the kettle, and ate whatever came up, but threw it back in when it became cold and picked up something else.

An thought that this man wasn't taking precautions. He shot at him, and the arrow hit the piece of meat that he was lifting out of the kettle, and it tumbled into the ashes. He laid the arrow down at his feet and kept eating as before. An shot another arrow, and it hit the dish in front of him, and the dish fell in two pieces. The man sat and paid no attention to this. Then An shot the third arrow, and it hit the knife handle which was sticking out from his hand, and the handle flew apart into two pieces.[33]

Then the young man said, "This man did me harm, but it doesn't do

The Saga of An Bow-Bender

him much good that he ruined my knife." He seized his bow, but An realized that it wasn't clear where a badly shot arrow might fly. He got behind the far side of an oak tree and kept it between them. This young man shot the first arrow, so that An thought that it would have hit him in the stomach if he had waited. A second looked as if it would have hit him in the ribs, and the third would have hit his eye. All were left sticking in the oak where An had been standing.

The young man said, "It would be best for the man who shot at me to show himself now, and let us meet each other, if he has a claim against me."

Then An came forward, and they began to wrestle, and their struggle was very mighty. An grew tired sooner, because the other man was strong-legged and powerful. An asked that they take a rest. The young man said that he was ready for either rest or fighting, but An had his way. He asked, "What is your name?"

He said that he was named Thorir, and said that his father was named An—"but who are you?"

"I'm called An," he said.

The young man said, "It must be true, since many of your belongings are An-available, and you're An-able to recover this sheep that I stole."[34]

An said, "Let's not bother with hateful words. And that sheep wasn't worth much. But what tokens do you have, in case you find your father?"

"I suppose that signs might be found that my story is true, but I'm not obliged to show you," said Thorir.

An said that it would be better to show the tokens of his parentage, whatever they might be. Thorir showed him the ring.

An said, "These are true tokens that you've found your father here. Let's go home and get better lodgings."

They came home. His men were sitting and waiting for him with fear and dread, because they didn't know what had become of him. An sat in the high seat with Thorir by his side. Jorunn asked who this young man was. An asked him to say his name himself.

He said, "I'm called Thorir, and I am An's son."

She said, "It's come to this, that 'everyone's wealthier than he thinks,' as the saying is. You didn't tell me that you had this son. Yet I think that he's no trifle. Take off his wet shoes and socks. How old are you?"

"Eighteen years," said Thorir.

She said, "I suppose I'll call you Long-Legs, because I have never seen anyone taller at the knees."

He said, "I like that name. You must give me something as a naming-gift, so that men may call me that."

She said that she would, and gave him a great gold ring.

An asked Thorir about growing up with the old man. He said that word had gone out that a daughter was being raised there—"because King Ingjald wanted to kill me, so I fled from the north when I was able."

Thorir stayed there through the winter. An said once, "I have no mind to support you sitting here any longer, if you won't show what you're made of."

He said that he had no valuables except for the ring.

An said that he thought it was better to have some mission. "It seems to me that you might be obliged to avenge your namesake on King Ingjald. I suppose that it would be destined for you, more than our other kin, because it's been proven that the king and I will never lay hands on each other. You didn't need to visit here unless you were to carry out revenge, whether or not you're in debt to me. You shall have the sword Thane, and if you accomplish this deed, the king's sister is there. Take her with you, and give her a son to compensate for her brother."

Thorir said that it would be done. He set out raiding with a fully prepared ship, and in the autumn he had five ships, well equipped. He was a most bold man, and strong, and the greatest raider. He came to King Ingjald's estate in the dead of night and set fire to the buildings. The men awoke from the smoke.

King Ingjald asked who had started the fire. Thorir said that Thorir Long-Legs was there. The king said, "Maybe these sparks have flown from the old man's daughter Drifa, because I've long suspected that. This may turn out to be a very hot ending for us."

Thorir said that he wanted his evil deeds to come to an end. King Ingjald had the wall-beams broken up and brought to the hut door, and said that he didn't want to burn inside. Then the men rushed out. Thorir was standing nearby when the king came out, and he struck him a deadly blow. He carried off Asa and also took much wealth with him, and sent both to his father, who received Asa well.

The Saga of An Bow-Bender

Thorir set out raiding and accomplished many brave deeds. He was an excellent man and resembled his father. When Thorir had become very wealthy, he visited An and was welcomed there. He stayed there over the winter.

In the spring, An told him that he wanted to set out. "I give all my estates over to you. But don't covet the estates that King Ingjald had, because it won't be long before petty kings will be dispensed with.[35] It's better to look out for your own honor than to set yourself up in a higher station and be brought down.[36] I will go north to my estate on Hrafnista. You must provide for Erp, and your foster-father and mother."

Then An traveled north. Thorir became a great man. An came north to the island, and there he had a daughter named Mjoll, the mother of Thorstein, the son of Ketil Oaf and the father of Ingimund the Old[37] in Vatnsdal. An often had to fight skin-wearing trolls[38] there in the north, and he was thought of as the most accomplished of men.

Thorir's son was Ogmund Field-Spoiler,[39] the father of Sigurd Table-Bald, a prominent man in Norway.

And here ends the saga of An Bow-Bender.

APPENDIX: OHTHERE'S VOYAGE

Ohthere said to his lord, King Alfred, that he, of all Norsemen, lived the farthest north. He said that he lived on the land lying northwards along the Western Sea. He said that the land extends far to the north from there, but it is all wilderness, except that Finns camp at a few scattered places, hunting in winter, and in summer fishing in the sea.

He said that at one point, he wanted to investigate how far that land extends to the north, or whether any man lived to the north of the wilderness. Then he traveled northwards along the coast: all the way, he kept the wilderness to starboard, and the open sea to port, for three days. Then he was as far north as the whale-hunters ever sail. Then he traveled yet farther northwards, as far as he could, for another three days of sailing. There the shore curved to the east, or else the sea made a curved inlet in the land, he didn't know which, but he remembered that he waited there for a wind blowing from a little to the north of west, and then sailed east along the coast as far as he could in four days of sailing. Then he had to wait there for a wind directly out of the north, for the shore curved to the south, or else the sea made a curved inlet in the land, he didn't know which. Then he sailed southwards along the coast as far as he could in five days of sailing, until he reached a great river that flowed through that land. They turned and sailed upriver, for they did not dare to sail beyond that river, because of the risk of hostility, for the land was all settled on the other side of that river.[1] He had not encountered any inhabited land since he departed from his own home, but had found only wilderness to starboard all the way, except for fishermen and fowlers and hunters, and they were all Finns; and he had open sea to port. The Beormas had settled their land very well, and the crew didn't dare to come there.[2] But the Ter-Finns' land was uninhabited except for where hunters camped, or fishermen, or fowlers.

The Beormas told him many stories, both of their own land and of the lands that were all around them; but he didn't know what the truth was, for he didn't see them himself. The Finns and the Beormas, it seemed to him, spoke nearly the same language.[3] The main reason why he traveled there, in addition to exploring these lands, was for the walruses,[4] because they have such splendid ivory teeth—they brought some teeth to the king—and their hides are very good for ships' ropes. This whale is much smaller than other whales: it is no more than seven ells long.[5] But in his own land there is the best whaling; those are forty-eight ells long, and the greatest are fifty ells long.[6] Then he said that he and his group of six men killed sixty in two days.[7]

He was a very wealthy man in those possessions which their wealth is reckoned in, that is, in wild animals. By the time he visited the king, he had acquired six hundred tame deer which he had not purchased.[8] Those animals they call "reindeer".[9] There were six decoy reindeer[10], which are very precious among the Finns, for with them they catch the wild reindeer. He was among the leading men in that land: yet he had no more than twenty cattle and twenty sheep and twenty pigs, and the little that he ploughed, he ploughed with horses. But his revenue is mostly the tribute that the Finns pay him. That tribute is paid in animal skins and birds' feathers and whalebone and those ship's ropes that are made of whales' hide and sealskin. Each one pays according to his birth: the highest-born must yield fifty martens' pelts, five reindeer skins, one bearskin, ten ambers[11] of feathers, a bearskin or otterskin coat, and two ship's ropes, each sixty ells long, made either of whales' hide, or seals'.

He said that the Northmen's land was very long and very narrow. All the land that could either be pastured or plowed lies up against the sea, and even that is very rocky in some places. Wild mountains lie to the east and upland, alongside the cultivated land. On those mountains Finns dwell. And the cultivated land is broadest to the east, and gets narrower the farther north it is. Eastward it may be sixty miles across, or a little broader, and in the middle thirty or more, and to the north, he said, it was the narrowest, such that it might be three miles across to the mountains. The mountains in some places are so wide that a man might take two weeks to cross them, and in other places as wide as a man might cross in six days. Then alongside that land, on the other side of the mountains, is Sweden, extending as far north as that land; and alongside that land farther to the north is the Cwenas' land.¹² The Cwenas sometimes raid the Norsemen over the mountains, and sometimes the Norsemen raid them. And there are very many freshwater lakes beyond the mountains, and the Cwenas carry their ships over the land to the lakes, and from there they raid the Norsemen. They have very small and very light ships.¹³

Ohthere said that the shire where he lived is called Hálogaland. He said that no man lived to the north of him. There is one port to the south of that land which is called Sciringesheal.¹⁴ He says that a man might not sail there in one month, if he stopped at night, and had a favorable wind each day; and all the while he must sail along the coast. And on his starboard there is first Ireland, and then the islands that are between Ireland and this land; then there is this land,¹⁵ until he reaches Sciringesheal, and all the way there is Norway on the port side. To the south of Sciringesheal an extremely great sea flows up into the country; it is broader than any man can see across. And there is Gotland on the opposite side, and then Sillende.¹⁶ The sea extends many hundreds of miles up into that land.

And he said that from Sciringesheal, he sailed in five days to the port that is called Hæthum; it stands between the Wends,¹⁷ the Saxons, and the Angles, and belongs to the Danes. When he sailed there from Sciringesheal, he had Denmark¹⁸ to port and open sea to starboard for three days; and then, for two days before he came to Hæthum, he had to starboard Gotland and Sillende and many islands—the Angles inhabited those lands before they came here to this land—and for two days he had on the port side those islands that belong to Denmark.

NOTES

Introduction

1. *Saga Sigurðar Jórsalafara, Eysteins ok Ólafs* ch. 22; ed. Linder and Haggson, *Heimskringla*, vol. 3, p. 162. Note that the section containing the reference to Hrafnista, known as *Þinga þáttr*, is not found in all recensions of *Heimskringla*, or in other histories; *Morkinskinna*, for example, places the meeting at Þrándarnes (present-day Trondenes), well to the north, near the Lofoten Islands (ch. 70; transl. Andersson and Gade, p. 339).
2. Hughes ("Literary Antecedents", pp. 212-220) has argued that the similarities between *Áns saga* and the other Hrafnista sagas are superficial, and were added in order to graft an originally separate story into the Hrafnista cycle. However, Leslie ("Matter of Hrafnista," pp. 180-185) makes a strong case that *Áns saga* is fully a part of the Hrafnista cycle.
3. The data come from Driscoll and Hufnagel, "*Fornaldarsögur Norðurlanda*".
4. See Quinn, "Interrogating Genre", for a useful discussion.
5. Mitchell, *Heroic Sagas and Ballads*, p. 27. This definition excludes some of what have previously been called *fornaldarsögur*, such as *Friðþjófs saga ins frækna*, which despite its Scandinavian setting appears to be a retelling of an Arabic story.
6. *Egils saga* ch. 1.
7. *Egils saga* ch. 23. See also *Landnámabók* (S344, H303), transl. Pálsson and Edwards, pp. 129-130. The beginning of *Orms þáttr Stórólfssonar* gives a variation of this genealogy, expanding one generation into two: the elder Ketil Salmon's grandson is simply named Ketil, and

Notes

this younger Ketil has a son named Hængr ("Salmon"). It is this Hængr who escapes to Iceland.

8   Leslie, "Matter of Hrafnista," p. 185; see *Landnámabók* (S135, H107, M48), transl. Pálsson and Edwards, p. 66. Note that *Landnámabók* calls An Redcloak a son of Grim Shaggy-Cheek as well as a grandson of An Bow-bender through Helga, Grim's wife and An Bow-Bender's daughter; this is inconsistent with the sagas, although it does suggest that An Bow-Bender was considered to be part of the Hrafnista family from an early date.

9   See, for example, *Njorls saga*, cited in Chapman et al., *Monty Python*, vol. 2, pp. 47-50.

10 Ross, "Development of Old Norse Textual Worlds," pp. 375-376.

11 Ross, "Development of Old Norse Textual Worlds," pp. 379-380.

12 *Landnámabók*, ed. Jakob Benediktsson, p. cii; transl. Pálsson and Edwards, p. 6.

13 Ross, "Development of Old Norse Textual Worlds," pp. 374-376; Pálsson and Edwards, *Landnámabók*, p. 7.

14 *History of the Danes*, Preface 3, transl. Ellis-Davidson and Fisher, p. 5.

15 Mitchell, *Heroic Sagas and Ballads*, pp. 122-126.

16 Quinn, "From Orality to Literacy," p. 46; Tulinius, *The Matter of the North*, p. 45.

17 Hughes, "Literary Antecedents," p. 219, n43; the quote is my translation of Hughes' quotation from Björner's *Nordiska Kämpa Dater* (Stockholm, 1737).

18 Hughes, "Literary Antecedents," p. 219, n43.

19 My translation from the text in Halldór Hermannson, *Saga of Thorgils and Haflidi*, p. 14. For a full discussion of the passage and its authenticity and textual history, see Foote, "Sagnaskemtan."

20 *Fornaldarsögur Norðurlanda* vol. 2, pp. 271-286; for a discussion of the origins of this saga see Jesch, "Hrómundr Gripsson Revisited."

21 *Landnámabók* (SH6-9; transl. Pálsson and Edwards, pp. 18-21).

22 Mitchell, *Heroic Sagas and Ballads*, pp. 122-126.

23 Kristinsson, "Lords and Literature", pp. 1-17. Kristinsson primarily discusses the early "sagas of Icelanders" (*Íslendingasögur*), but his conclusions would certainly apply to the *Hrafnistasögur*, which, while not set in Iceland, do concern the ancestors of prominent Icelandic settlers and their families.

The Hrafnista Sagas

24 To give just one example, *Landnámabók* (S208, H175; Pálsson and Edwards, transl. pp. 93-94) mentions Thord of Hofdastrond, a descendant of the legendary king Ragnar Shaggy-Breeches and founder of a prominent family—his descendants included both Snorri Sturluson and Thorfinn Karlsefni, who led the expedition to settle Vinland.
25 Vésteinn Ólason, "The Marvellous North", pp. 113-115.
26 For background, see Ross, *The Old Norse–Icelandic Saga*, pp. 38-43.
27 Gísli Sigurðsson, *The Medieval Icelandic Saga and Oral Tradition*, pp. 31-32.
28 Clover, "Icelandic Family Sagas," pp. 292-294. See also Biebuyck, *The Mwindo Epic*, pp. 13-14; Finnegan, *Oral Literature in Africa*, pp. 370-371.
29 Clover, "Icelandic Family Sagas", pp. 292-294.
30 Leslie, "Matter of Hrafnista," pp. 169-173.
31 Gísli Sigurðsson, *The Medieval Icelandic Saga and Oral Tradition*, p. 42.
32 Ciklamini, "Old Norse Epic", pp. 95-98.
33 Snorri Sturluson, "Prologue", *Heimskringla*, transl. Hollander, pp. 3-5.
34 Lönnroth, "The Double Scene", p. 109.
35 Lönnroth, "Hjálmar's Death Song", pp. 1-10; Harris, "The Prosimetrum of Icelandic Saga", pp. 145-157.
36 Tolkien, *The Saga of King Heidrek the Wise*, pp. 5-10.
37 Lönnroth, "Hjálmar's Death Song", pp. 10-20.
38 Lönnroth, "Hjálmar's Death Song", p. 12.
39 Leslie, "Matter of Hrafnista," pp. 179-180.
40 Snorri Sturluson, *Skáldskaparmál* verse 466, ed. Faulkes, pp. 122, 484.
41 Snorri Sturluson, *Skáldskaparmál* verse 363, ed. Faulkes, p. 96; for Refr the Skald, see Faulkes, p. 155, notes to verse 4.
42 *Vatnsdæla saga* ch. 2; Ciklamini, "Grettir and Ketill Hængr", p. 146.
43 Righter-Gould, "Áns saga bogsveigis", pp. 265-268.
44 *Egils saga* ch. 76.
45 *History of the Danes* VI.180-181; transl. Ellis-Davidson and Fisher, pp. 168-169.
46 *History of the Danes* V.166, pp. 153-154.
47 *Hyndluljóð* stanzas 23-24.
48 Harris, "The Prosimetrum of Icelandic Saga", p. 145.
49 Quinn, "From Orality to Literacy", pp. 39-40; quote translated in

Notes

Andersson, *The Saga of Olaf Tryggvason*, p. 35.

50 For several examples, see Gísli Sigurðsson, *The Medieval Icelandic Saga and Oral Tradition*, pp. 253-302.
51 The text and a translation appear in Bately and Englert, *Ohthere's Voyages*; see the additional articles in that book for commentary.
52 Ross, *Terfinnas and Beormas*, pp. 66-68.
53 Storli, "Ohthere and His World", pp. 81-85.
54 Compare Thorolfr in *Egils saga* (ch. 10), who must set his men to work at sealing, egg-collecting and fishing, in order to have everything he needs to live well.
55 Perdikaris, "From Chieftainly Provisioning to Commercial Fishery", pp. 388-395.
56 Ross, *Terfinnas and Beormas*, pp. 56-59.
57 Chesnutt, in Ross, *Terfinnas and Beormas*, pp. 72-78.
58 Binns, "Ohthere's Northern Voyage", pp. 43-50.
59 See Hofstra and Samplonius, "Viking Expansion Northwards," pp. 238-244, for a more thorough review of Norse voyages to Bjarmaland.
60 *Haralds saga Hárfagra* ch. 32, transl. Hollander, *Heimskringla*, p. 86; see also *Egils saga* ch. 37.
61 *Haralds saga gráfeldr* ch. 14; transl. Hollander, *Heimskringla*, p. 140.
62 *Magnuss saga berfoetts* ch. 2; transl. Hollander, *Heimskringla*, p. 670.
63 *Óláfs saga helga* ch. 133; transl. Hollander, *Heimskringla*, pp. 403-408.
64 transl. Kunin, p. 3.
65 chs. 78-80; transl. Hollander, *Heimskringla*, p. 232.
66 *Egils saga Skallagrímssonar* chs. 14, 17.
67 Mundal, "Perceptions of the Saami", pp. 99-104; "Coexistence of Saami and Norse Culture", pp. 347-348; Zachrisson, "The Sámi and Their Interaction with the Nordic Peoples", pp. 34-37.
68 Tambets et al., "The Western and Eastern Roots of the Saami", p. 671, 677
69 DuBois, *Nordic Religions in the Viking Age*, pp. 24-27; Zachrisson, "The Sámi", p. 35.
70 Hofstra and Samplonius, p. 242, Zachrisson, "The Sámi", pp. 35-36.
71 Mundal, "Coexistence of Saami and Norse Culture," pp. 353-355.
72 Beach, *A Year in Lapland*, p. 5.
73 Orning, "Magical Reality," p. 6.

74 Gisli Sigurðsson, *The Medieval Icelandic Saga and Oral Tradition*, p. 127.
75 Fjalldal, *The Long Arm of Coincidence*, pp. 88-96, gives a thorough critique of the "Bear's Son" as applied to *Beowulf* and *Grettis saga*, pointing out that many features of the folktales do not appear in either *Beowulf* or *Grettis saga*, and that many of their similarities also appear in stories that have nothing to do with the "Bear's Son". *Grettis saga*, in particular, contains five different episodes that all somewhat resemble *Beowulf* and/or the "Bear's Son," none of them perfectly convincingly (Fjalldal, pp. 1-16)
76 Fjalldal, pp. 119-129, points out that almost every feature of the proposed *Beowulf* analogues in *Grettis saga* can be found in other Icelandic sagas that the *Grettis saga* author probably knew. Stitt (*Beowulf and the Bear's Son*, pp. 19-23) notes that the similarities among the various claimed "Bear's Son" texts could well come from borrowing of motifs and episodes, rather than the single origin and diffusion of an entire tale.
77 Pizarro, "Transformation of the Bear's Son Tale", pp. 269-275.
78 Pizarro, pp. 275-277. These include the encounter with Odd's bear-fetch, which corresponds to the "Bear's Son" hero being bear-like or even having bear ancestry; the episode where Odd shoots a giantess from behind a bearskin, whose significance is obscure but also seems to go with a bearish nature for the hero; and the tearing off of Ogmund's face, which matches a number of the "Bear's Son" folktales in which the supernatural villain loses his face instead of an arm.
79 McKinnell, *Meeting the Other*, pp. 126-129.
80 McKinnell, *Meeting the Other*, pp. 172-176.
81 McKinnell, *Meeting the Other*, pp. 172-173.
82 *Hversu Noregr Byggðist* ch. 1.
83 D732 in Thompson, *Motif-Index*, vol. 2, p. 84. See Folks and Lindahl, "Loathly Lady", pp. 600-602.
84 Cross and Sherbowitz-Wetzor, eds. *Russian Primary Chronicle*, p. 69.
85 Faulkes (*Two Icelandic Stories*, pp. 27-29) suggests that *Orms páttr Stórólfssonar* borrowed these motifs directly from Örvar-Odds saga. However, McKinnell (*Meeting the Other*, p. 129) suggests that it is perhaps more likely that motifs derived from Thor myths were simply common in this kind of story.

Notes

86 Ciklamini, "Grettir and Ketill Hængr", pp. 136-155.
87 Pizarro, p. 280.
88 Gísli Sigurðsson, *The Medieval Icelandic Saga and Oral Tradition*, pp. 124-128.
89 Gísli Sigurðsson, p. 128.
90 Jorgensen, "The Two-Troll Variant," pp. 40-43.
91 Battles, "Dwarfs in Germanic Literature," p. 44.
92 *Grettis saga* ch. 14.
93 *Orms þáttr Stórólfssonar* ch. 1.
94 Simek, *Altnordisches Kosmographie*, pp. 342-345.
95 See Lönnroth, "The Noble Heathen", for a discussion of the figure of the "noble heathen" in the sagas; this paper does not discuss the Hrafnista sagas but is still applicable to *Örvar-Odds saga*.
96 Details of Odd's visit to the Holy Land may have come from accounts in the "kings' sagas" of visits to Jerusalem; e.g. *Magnússona saga* ch. 10, in *Heimskringla*, transl. Hollander, pp. 695-696. See Ferrari, "Gods, Warlocks, and Monsters," p. 1.
97 Tulinius, *The Matter of the North*, pp. 159-161.
98 Hastrup, *Culture and History*, pp. 147-154. Ross (*Prolonged Echoes*, vol. 1, pp. 50-56) argues for a more complex conceptual model with multiple concentric circles, and with both vertical and horizontal dimensions. I believe that Hastrup's model is adequate, as long as it is remembered that it is fractal: the *Innangarðr/Útgarðr* division repeats itself on multiple spatial scales.
99 DuBois, *Nordic Religions*, pp. 122-138.
100 *Ynglinga saga* chs. 13, 19, transl. Hollander, *Heimskringla*, pp. 16-17, 22-23.
101 *Haralds saga hárfagra* ch. 25, transl. Hollander, *Heimskringla*, pp. 80-81.
102 *Haralds saga hárfagra* ch. 32, transl. Hollander, *Heimskringla*, pp. 86-87; see also *Egils saga* ch. 37.
103 *Óláfs saga Tryggvasonar* ch. 76, transl. Hollander, *Heimskringla*, p. 211.
104 ch. 19; transl. Andersson, *The Saga of Olaf Tryggvason*, p. 66.
105 Orning, "Magical Reality," pp. 10-12.
106 Arnold, "Við Þik Sættumsk Ek Aldri", p. 96.
107 *Völuspá*, verse 13.
108 Snorri Sturluson, *Skáldskaparmál* verse 431, ed. Faulkes, p. 114.

109 Mundal, "Coexistence of Saami and Norse Culture," pp. 348-352.
110 Straubhaar, "Nasty, Brutish, and Large", p. 110; Mundal, "Coexistence of Saami and Norse Culture," p. 352-353.
111 Straubhaar, "Nasty, Brutish, and Large", p. 106.
112 Mundal ("Coexistence of Saami and Norse Culture", pp. 349-352) has pointed out that the descendants of such mixed matches in the sagas and genealogies often go on to be heroes and leaders.
113 Arnold, "Hvat er Tröll Nema Þat?", pp. 129-139.
114 The name *óargr* is hard to translate adequately; *argr* implied not merely cowardice, but unmanliness, or the inability to follow norms of male behavior. In some contexts, although not always, it could imply passive homosexuality, which was considered shameful and degrading. Probably the most accurate translation would be something like "Ulf Not-a-Pussy".
115 *Skáldatal*, a list of the court poets of various rulers, does mention him: *Úlfr inn óargi var hersir ágætr í Nóregi, í Naumudali, faðir Hallbjarnar hálftrolls, föður Ketils hængs. Úlfr orti drápu á einni nótt ok sagði frá þrekvirkjum sínum. Hann var dauðr fyrir dag.* "Ulf No-Coward was a noble hersir in Norway, in Namdalen, the father of Hallbjorn Half-Troll the father of Ketil Salmon. Ulf created a long praise-poem in one night, telling about his own mighty deeds. He was dead before day came." (Guðni Jónsson, *Edda Snorra Sturlusonar*, p. 353) While Ulf's poem is unknown, its description seems similar to his great-grandson Odd's "death-poem" at the end of *Örvar-Odds saga*.
116 Arnold, "Við Þik Sættumsk Ek Aldri", p. 95.
117 Tulinius, *The Matter of the North*, pp. 40-43.
118 Arnold, "Við Þik Sættumsk Ek Aldri", p. 141.
119 Arnold, "Við Þik Sættumsk Ek Aldri", p. 141-143.
120 Straubhaar, "Nasty, Brutish, and Large," pp. 122-123.
121 Tulinius, *The Matter of the North*, pp. 161-163.
122 Tulinius, *The Matter of the North*, pp. 163-164.
123 Hughes, "The Saga of Án the Bow-Bender", p. 301, n. 21.
124 Orning, "Imagining the Kalmar Union", pp. 730-736.
125 Driscoll and Hufnagel, "*Fornaldarsögur Norðurlanda*".
126 Orning, "Imagining the Kalmar Union", pp. 729-730.
127 Bately, *The Old English Orosius*, I.i, pp. 13-16.
128 Simpson, *The Northmen Talk*, pp. 237-243 (this is chapter 18 of the

saga, the account of Odd's stay with the giant Hildir and his family).
129 Pálsson and Edwards, *Arrow-Odd: A Medieval Novel.*
130 Pálsson and Edwards, *Seven Viking Romances,* pp. 25-137.
131 Hughes, "The Saga of Án Bow-Bender", in Ohlgren, *Medieval Outlaws: Ten Tales in Modern English Translation,* pp. 194-215; revised and updated in Ohlgren, *Medieval Outlaws: Twelve Tales in Modern English Translation,* pp. 290-337. All references to Hughes's translation are to the revised edition.
132 Larson, *The Saga of Aun the Bow-Bender.*
133 Stitt, *Beowulf and the Bear's Son;* pp. 43-50 (*Gríms saga*); pp. 59-60 (*Ketils saga*); pp. 60-64 (*Örvar-Odds saga*).
134 Chappell, "The Saga of Ketil Trout," http://tinyurl.com/ketiltroutssaga; Tunstall, "The Saga of Grim Shaggy-Cheek," http://tinyurl.com/grimssaga. Last accessed March 11, 2012.

Saga of Ketil Salmon

1 The "hearth-fire house" or *eldahús* was an outbuilding on Norse farmsteads where the cooking was done, decreasing the risk of fire in the main house. Ketil is a typical *kolbítr* or "coal-biter"—a boy who spends all his time sitting idly by the fire. Coal-biters in the sagas often end up becoming heroes, when forced to rise to the occasion. The *kolbítr* is similar to the *askeladden* ("ash-lad") or *askefisen* ("ash-fart") of Norwegian folktales. See Larrington, "Awkward Adolescence", pp. 152-153, for an analysis of Ketil's adolescent issues, his coming to personal maturity, and his father's learning to guide him.

2 For an additional instance of this folk practice, see Chapman et al., *Monty Python,* vol. 2, p. 70.

3 *Hængr* is often translated "Trout", but can refer to the males of either trout or salmon. The word is derived from a root meaning "hooked", referring to the hooked lower jaw of mature male Atlantic salmon. (Nordal, "Icelandic Notes", pp. 149-150)

4 *Hængr* and *Hrafn* mean "Salmon" and "Raven" respectively; Ketil Salmon (*Ketill Hængr*) has the same name as his enemy. I have translated Ketil's by-name but left his enemy's name alone, to avoid confusion.

5   *Næstifjörðr* means "nearest fjord" and *Miðfjörðr* is "middle fjord." *Vitaðsgjafi* means "certain giver". In *Víga-Glúms saga*, the same name is applied to a field in Iceland whose crop never fails.
6   *Surtr*, in Norse mythology, is the name of the being whose flames will destroy the world at the end of time, at Ragnarök. In the legendary sagas, however, the name is sometimes borne by a more "ordinary" giant or troll.
7   Jorgensen ("Additional Icelandic Analogues," p. 202) points out that the giant's precognition of Ketil's presence appears in several other sagas with giant-human encounters.
8   There is a family resemblance between this episode and the account of Thorstein's killing the robber Jokul in *Vatnsdæla saga* (ch. 3), which is much more detailed.
9   This probably refers to the hearth-fires that Hallbjorn has earlier said that he left behind when he last visited the distant fjords. The implication is that Hallbjorn has a long history of visiting and befriending the giants far to the north, as the giant Surt's remarks above imply. (Ciklamini, "Grettir and Ketill Hængr", pp. 144-145)
10 A parallel episode appears in *Grettis saga* ch. 62, in which the outlaw Grim catches the giant Hallmund stealing his catch of fish, wounds him with an axe blow to the neck, and forces Hallmund to retreat to his home in a cave. See also Grim's encounter with the giantess Feima in *Gríms saga loðinkinna* ch. 1.
11 *Kaldrani* means "taunt; sarcasm". But the name may be a variant of *Kaldgrani*, "Cold Mustache", a name found in the *þulur* or poetic lists associated with Snorri Sturluson's *Edda* (*Skáldskaparmál* 431, ed. Faulkes, p 114).
12 Stitt (*Beowulf and the Bear's Son*, p. 188) notes that the motif of a hero finishing off a wounded giant by openly entering the giant's cave and pretending to be a healer also appears in the Icelandic wonder-tale "Velvakandi og bræður hans" (Jón Arnason, *Íslenzkar þjóðsögur og æfintýri*, vol. 2, pp. 471-473). "Velvakandi" is clearly related to the "Two-Troll" version of the "Bear's Son" tales.
13 In the Icelandic calendar, the Winternights fell in mid-October; they marked the beginning of winter and were celebrated with sacrifices, feasts, and games. See *Complete Sagas of Icelanders* vol 5, pp. 417, 422. Note that the codfish season in northern Norway lasts more or less

from January to April (Perdikaris, "From Chieftainly Provisioning to Commercial Fishery", pp. 388-395). Ketil's fishing expedition would seem not only needlessly dangerous but pointless, which may be why Hallbjorn objects so strongly.

14 Shape-shifting humans often retain their human eyes while in animal form, and so can be recognized (e.g. *Kormaks saga* ch. 18; *Ála flekks saga* ch. 10, transl. Bachmann and Erlingson, *Six Old Icelandic Sagas*, p. 51).

15 An ell in the Viking era ranged from 47 cm to 63 cm, or between 18 and 25 inches. (Christensen, *Norsemen in the Viking Age*, p. 333). Straubhaar ("Nasty, Brutish, and Large", p. 107) points out that the Saami are still stereotyped as "broad-faced" by non-Saami, and that this description could just as readily mark Hrafnhild as Saami as it could mark her as a giantess.

16 Several sagas depict the Finns (Saami) as being eager for butter. *Helga þáttr Þórissonar* (ch. 1) mentions traders bringing butter and pork to trade with the Saami; in *Vatnsdœla saga* (ch. 12) Ingimundr pays three Saami for their services with butter and tin. *Hauks þáttr Hábrókar* (chs. 3-4, transl. Waggoner, *Sagas of Giants and Heroes*, pp. 15-17) depicts King Harald sending bacon and butter to his giantess foster-mother; *Egils saga einhenda* (ch. 17; transl. Pálsson and Edwards, p. 256) also depicts a giantess who appreciates a gift of bacon and butter. Once again, the same traits are attributed to historical Saami and legendary giants.

17 Else Mundal points out that not only are the Saami repeatedly described as skilled archers, but that skaldic poems use *Finns gjöld* or *Finna gjöld*, "Finn's / Finns' gift", as a kenning for arrows. ("Perception of the Saami," pp. 100-103) Whether or not the skalds who used this kenning knew about the *Hrafnistumenn*, these sagas confirm the Saami's strong associations with archery.

18 Sagas and other sources strongly associate the Saami with skiing, but the *Historia Norvegiæ* adds that they travel on skis drawn by reindeer; this presumably refers to a sleigh of some sort, and may be what is intended here. (Transl. Kunin, p. 5)

19 Drangvendil will be passed down through several generations and come to Egil Skallagrimsson, who will reject it when it fails to bite in a duel (*Egils saga* ch. 61).

20 *Flaug* means "flying, the act of flight", but could also mean "flag" or "weathervane"; *Hremsa* is probably "snatcher" (cf. *hremma* or *hremsa*, "to clutch; to grab") and *Fífa* is cottongrass (*Eriophorum* spp.), a sedge with stalked seedheads tipped with tufts of white fibers, somewhat resembling arrows. All three words are poetic synonyms for an arrow (Snorri Sturluson, *Skáldskaparmál* 465-466, ed. Faulkes, pp. 122, 468).

21 It's a commonplace in the sagas that women from the Finnic peoples of the far North have powerful magic and are dangerous to take as wives; see the Introduction.

22 *Hvat er þat býsna, / er við berg stendr / ok gapir eldi yfir?* Note the similarity with a verse in "Svipdagsmál" in the *Poetic Edda*: *Hvat er þat flagða, / er stendr fyr forgörðum / ok hvarflar um hættan loga?* "Who is that ogress, / who stands before the forecourt / and wanders around the dangerous fire?"

23 The text reads *líttu á ljóðvega*, which would literally mean something like "look at the people's paths", but *ljóðvega* is probably an error for *ljósvega*, "light-ways", i.e. the sky with the sun passing across it. (Finnur Jónsson, *Lexicon Poeticum*, p. 380) This refers to the widespread belief that trolls and other such beings cannot withstand sunlight.

24 Hjalm and Stafnglam are a doublet of his Örvar-Odd's sworn brothers *Hjálmarr inn hugumstóri* (Hjalmar the Bold-Hearted) and *Þórðr stafnglámá* (Thord Prow-Glamor); see *Örvar-Odds saga* chs. 8-9.

25 Yule Eve is described in several sources as a time for swearing binding oaths; e.g. *Hervarar saga* ch. 2, transl. Tolkien, p. 3; *Helgakviða Hjörvarðssonar* in the *Poetic Edda*.

26 By the rules of the *holmgangr* or judicial duel, each contestant was allowed to have a second, who held a shield in front of him.

27 Probably the present-day Skrova, an island in the Lofoten archipelago.

28 *Forað* means "dangerous place" (such as a chasm, swamp, pit, etc.), and can also be metaphorically used for a monster or ogre in general.

29 Ketil may be using his nickname to avoid giving the troll his real name, which might give her power over him (Straubhaar, "Nasty, Brutish, and Large", p. 112).

30 This saga often uses *fóstra*, "foster-kin", for people who are not

literally the speaker's foster-kin, either affectionately or, as in this case, sarcastically—although Straubhaar ("Nasty, Brutish, and Large", p. 112) points out that since the Men of Hrafnista have giantish ancestry, Ketil may be acknowledging that he is in fact kin to the giantess.

31 There may be a pun here: *angr* means both "fjord" and "grief, trouble, sorrow." This stanza, spoken by a giantess, has the most poetic devices of any in this saga cycle, using end-rhyme as well as alliteration.

32 Forad's journey lies from the north of Norway to the southwestern tip, and then northeast to the Elfr River, probably the Gautelfr (Göta älv) near the border between Norway and Sweden.

33 The 13th-century Older Law of West Gautland lists the accusation of "riding the witch-ride with hair loose" as a slander against a woman (Mitchell, "Blåkulla", p. 90). Artistic depictions of human women in Viking-era art usually show hair tied up in knots or bound in headdresses; unkempt hair may have been seen as outside social norms and thus fitting for witches and trolls.

34 Now known as Narvik Fjord, for the modern city located on it. Ofoti is listed in the *þulur* of giants' names (Snorri Sturluson, *Skáldskaparmál* verse 431, ed. Faulkes, p. 114)

35 Several sagas mention *Þorgerðr*, nicknamed *Hölgabrúðr* ("bride of Hölgi") or *Hörgabrúðr* ("bride of the altar"). She was especially worshipped by the jarls of Hálogaland, probably as their ancestress and family protector or *fylgja* (Røthe, "Þorgerðr Hölgabrúðr"). By calling her *Hörgatröll* ("troll of the altar"), the author of *Ketils saga* is implying that he views Thorgerd as hostile and wicked.

36 *Gandreiðir*, "staff-ridings", means the nocturnal flights of witches; the earliest meaning seems to be sending one's mind or soul out of the body in non-corporeal form to gather information (Heide, "Spinning *Seiðr*," pp. 164-165; Mitchell, "Blåkulla," pp. 88-89). The *Historia Norvegiæ* uses the word *gandus* for the "familiar spirit" of a Saami seer, whose form the Saami assumes when traveling out of the body (transl. Kunin, pp. 6-7). In later texts (including this saga), the *gandreið* became an assembly of witches and trolls in physical form, perhaps influenced by the Continental tradition of the "witches' sabbat" (e.g. *Þorsteins saga bæjarmagns* ch. 3; see Mitchell,

"Blåkulla," pp. 88-89).

37 On the east coast of Sweden, along the Gulf of Bothnia.

38 *Ár-haugr* may be translated as "harvest mound" or "season-mound"; presumably the mound was understood as a place to sacrifice to ensure good harvests. As for snow not staying on the mound: *Gísla saga Súrssonar* mentions Þorgrímr Freysgoði, a devotee of the god Freyr (the giver of good harvests and fruitfulness), who was buried in a mound which stayed free of snow even in winter, because "Freyr would not want it to freeze between them."

39 Invulnerability to iron blades is a common characteristic of berserks and supernaturally-charged beings. Here it appears to be a direct gift of the god Odin; in other sources, such as the story of Ogmund in *Örvar-Odds saga* (ch. 19), it may be conferred by magical rites of some sort (reviewed in Beard, "*Á Þá Bitu Engi Járn*").

40 The Norse *röst* and English *league* both originally meant the distance a person could travel in an hour (about three miles or five kilometers, but varying depending on the terrain).

41 The Norse is much more concise: Ketil asks Soti if he is a *matníðingr*, a "food-nithing", i.e. one who has violated ethical norms of hospitality (Meulengracht Sørensen, *The Unmanly Man*, pp. 31-32).

42 Einar Sveinsson ("Celtic Elements in Icelandic Tradition", p. 13) points out that this episode parallels an episode in the Irish *Tain Bó Cualnige*, in which the emissaries of Queen Maeve approach Cú Chulaind while he is lying naked in the snow. A closer parallel is Starkather, who sits on a mountain in a snowstorm waiting for a duel against men who want to marry his friend's betrothed against her will (Saxo, *History of the Danes* VI.196, transl. Ellis-Davidson and Fisher, p. 181). There is also a resemblance to an incident in *Vatnsdæla saga* chs. 33-34, in which Ketil's distant kisnmen Thorstein and Jokull go out to fight a duel; despite a snowstorm called down by their adversary's sorcerous friend, they wait outside in the snow.

43 In several saga episodes, a hero fights an adversary who blunts swords by magical means. One solution is to bring an extra sword (e.g. Saxo, *History of the Danes* VII.223, transl. Ellis-Davidson and Fisher, p. 207); another is to conceal the sword from the enemy's gaze until the fatal blow (e.g. *History of the Danes* VI.187, p. 173; VII.244, p. 223). Here, Ketil accomplishes the same result by using

the other edge of the sword before Framar can react.

Saga of Grim Shaggy-Cheek

1 A hersir was a local military and political leader, of lesser rank than a jarl.
2 *Vík* or Viken is the present-day Oslofjord region.
3 A king named Hrolf of Berg appears in the genealogical compilation *Hversu Noregr Byggðist*, ch. 1, as the son of the giant Svadi.
4 A king named Josur appears in *Hversu Noregr Byggðist* ch. 1 and in *Hálfs saga ok Hálfsrekka*, although this king is said to rule Rogaland in the southwest of Norway and may not be the same as the Josur in this saga.
5 *Gandvík*, literally "Witchcraft Bay," is the White Sea, reachable by sailing all the way around the northern tip of Scandinavia. As the name suggests, Gandvik was associated with monsters and sorcery. See the Introduction.
6 The name *Hrímnir* is derived from *hrím*, "frost." A giant by that name is mentioned in *Skírnismál* 28 and *Hyndluljóð* 32 in the *Poetic Edda*, as well as in the *þulur* in Snorri Sturluson's *Edda* (417, ed. Faulkes, p. 110). Here his name is simply used as a metonym for giants in general, not.
7 *Feima* means "bashful girl"; *Kleima* means "blot".
8 Thjazi appears in a myth related in *Skáldskaparmál* 56, in Snorri Sturluson's *Edda* (ed. Faulkes, pp. 1-2). Again, his name is a metonym for giants in general.
9 The word translated "bewitched" is *seiddi*, the past tense of *síða*, meaning "to work *seiðr*." *Seiðr* is hard to translate simply; some sagas depict it as a magical technique of divining the future (e.g. *Örvar-Odds saga* ch. 2), but it is also commonly depicted as a means of confusing others' minds and wills, or of conferring magical protection on someone.
10 Stitt, *Beowulf and the Bear's Son* (p. 45) interprets "wave-flocks" as "boats", but no boats have gone missing in the saga; the interpretation as "fish" makes better sense. *Landnámabók* (S145, H116) mentions a woman from Hálogaland, Thurid Sound-Filler

The Hrafnista Sagas

(*sundafyllir*), who gained her byname from using *seiðr* to fill a sound with fish during a famine. The giants may simply have physically stolen Grim's catch, but it's also possible that they have worked *seiðr* to empty the seas of fish, causing the famine in Halogaland. The Saami were allegedly able to steal away Christians' catches of fish by magical means (*Historia Norvegiæ*, transl. Kunin, p. 7).

11 *Hyrja* may be derived from *hyrr*, "embers."

12 In *Hálfdanar saga Brönufóstra* ch. 6, the hero kills two giant sisters aged five and six (transl. Waggoner, *Sagas of Giants and Heroes*, p. 97); in *Jökuls þáttr Búasonar* ch. 1, the hero encounters two giant sisters, one twelve and the other thirteen (transl. Waggoner, p. 56).

13 Peter Jorgensen suggests that this episode is a variant of the "Bear's Son" folktale. In the "two-troll" variant of this tale, the hero enters a cave and decapitates a male giant, but is forced to wrestle with a female giant when his weapon proves useless. Versions of this tale are found in a number of other sagas, as well as *Beowulf*. ("Useless Weapon," p. 85) Note also the parallels with Ketil's encounter with Kaldrani in *Ketils saga hængs* ch. 2.

14 Fights over the rights to butcher beached whales are fairly common in the sagas, e.g. *Grettis saga* ch. 25.

15 Stitt (*Beowulf and the Bear's Son*, p. 49), translates this as "be there to service Hrimnir, my brother." The word *stóðrenni* normally just means "close proximity" and does not necessarily have a sexual meaning (*Dictionary of Old Norse Prose*), but the author may have been making a sexual pun, as *stóð* is cognate with English "stud".

16 The Norse expression *eigask við* is ambiguous; both the sense of "to fight with each other" and the sense of "to have sexual relations" are attested (*Dictionary of Old Norse Prose*). I've translated this with a similarly ambiguous English idiom. Stitt (*Beowulf and the Bear's Son*, p. 49) notes that a sexual interpretation of this curse parallels Skírnir's threat to Gerðr in the Eddic poem *Skírnismál* (verse 31): she will be forced to live with (and, it is implied, have sex with) a hideous giant for her husband.

17 To keep her from using magic against them; see *Eyrbyggja saga* ch. 18, *Laxdæla saga* ch. 37-38, *Gísla saga Súrssonar* ch. 10.

18 These family names appear in *Bárðar saga Snæfellsáss*, although the order of descent is altered: Thorkel is the son of Raudfeld the son

Notes

of Svadi, and the half-brother of Bard.

19 Present-day Berglyd in Sokndal, Rogaland, southwestern Norway.
20 This Asmund is a protagonist in the legendary *Egils saga einhenda ok Ásmundar berserkjabana*. His ship, the *Gnoð*, is mentioned in several sagas as one of the greatest ships of all time.
21 The prose of *Örvar-Odds saga* doesn't mention Odd's participation in the legendary Battle of Brávellir, but other accounts do; see note 58 to *The Saga of Arrow-Odd* in this book.
22 According to *Landnámabók*, Ketil the Broad settled in Iceland, claiming Berufjörð (S121, H93; transl. Pálsson and Edwards, pp. 60-61; S133, H105; transl. Pálsson and Edwards, p. 65). Hergils Knob-Arse and his son Ingjald appear in *Gísla saga Súrssonar*.
23 A story fully told in *Egils saga* ch. 23.
24 This genealogy also appears in *Landnámabók* (S344, H303), transl. Pálsson and Edwards, pp. 129-130
25 Orm the Strong is the hero of *Orms þáttr Stórólfssonar*.
26 The tragic hero of the first part of *Njáls saga*, whose chapter 19 presents another version of this genealogy.
27 Hroar appears in *Njáls saga* and *Fljótsdæla saga*; see also *Landnámabók* (S284, H245) transl. Pálsson and Edwards, pp. 114-115.
28 Vemund the Old is mentioned in *Hversu Nóregr byggðist*, in which he is called "the Protector of Sogn" (*Sygnatrausti*); he is said to be the great-grandson of the legendary Nórr who gave his name to Norway. The saga section on Vemund, Grim, and Holmfast is extremely close in wording to a section of *Landnámabók* (S388, H342), with the main differences being that *Landnámabók* has only one Vedrorm the son of Vemund where *Gríms saga* has two, and that *Landnámabók* doesn't mention any family connection with Grim Shaggy-Cheek. In this case, there has probably been direct written copying from *Landnámabók* to a manuscript of the saga.
29 Ketil the Noisy and his purchase of Arneid appear in *Landnámabók* S278, transl. Pálsson and Edwards, p. 112. The story also appears, with some differences, in *Droplaugarsona saga* and related sagas (Gísli Sigurðsson, *The Medieval Icelandic Saga*, pp. 205-211)
30 Gest Oddleifson appears in *Laxdæla saga* (ch. 33) as a kinsman of Gudrun, who interprets her foreboding dreams.
31 Hallketil's killing of Grim is told in *Landnámabók* (S389, H343);

Hallketil's descendant Otkel figures in *Njáls saga*.

Arrow-Odd's Saga

1   *Vík* or Viken is the present-day Oslofjord.
2   Now Berglyd, a small settlement in Sokndal in Rogaland, near the southern tip of Norway. Grim and Lopthaena are sailing around the south Norwegian coast.
3   *var vatni ausinn*—"he was sprinkled with water"—refers to a pre-Christian ritual of naming a child; this expression is never used for the Christian rite of baptism.
4   *Heiðr* is a stereotypical name for a prophetess (*völva*) and seeress (*seiðkona*) in the sagas. McKinnell ("Encounters with Völur", pp. 245-248) notes that this is one of several saga episodes in which a family patriarch invites a seeress to prophesy, creating antipathy between him and his foster-son. She prophesies glory and death for the foster-son, and her words always come true. He calls this "The Hostile Young Man" group of seeress encounter tales.
5   The word translated "divinations" is *seiðr*, which, as described in the sagas, could cover several kinds of magical practice. Seiðr could be used to foresee the future, but could also be used to influence people's minds and perceptions; according to *Ynglinga saga* it was unmanly for men to practice.
6   Bjarmaland was the land on the shores of the White Sea, reached by sailing all the way around the northern tip of Scandinavia. There are historically attested trading voyages between Norway and Bjarmaland; however, in the legendary sagas, Bjarmaland is the home of giants, monsters, and other rather uncanny beings. (Hofstra and Samplonius, "Viking Expansion Northward", pp. 235-247)
7   The text has *sumarlangt* here, which might be expected to mean "all summer long", but this meaning makes no sense given that this scene is taking place just before winter. *Langt* can mean "late" in modern Icelandic, and I have assumed that this is what's meant.
8   The fetch (Norse *fylgja*, literally "follower") is an aspect of a person's soul that usually takes the form of an animal. The animal's nature

resembles the person who has it: warriors' fetches are often bears or wolves, kings have "noble" fetches such as stags or lions, and so on. Rarely seen in the waking world except by persons with second sight, fetches usually appear as portents in dreams. (Turville-Petre, "Dreams in Icelandic Tradition", pp. 36-39)

9   As in most sagas, the *Finnar* are not Finns, but Saami. *Gammar*, translated "huts", specifically applies to Saami bark-thatched dwellings (Saami *gåetie*; Zachrisson, "The Sámi and their Interaction with the Nordic Peoples", p. 36).

10 This medieval explanation for thunder appears in the 13th-century *Konungs skuggsjá*: "It also happens frequently that two winds rising at the same time will go against each other; and when they meet in the air, heavy blows fall, and these blows give forth a great fire which spreads widely over the sky." (ch. 13; ed. Brenner, *Speculum Regale*, p. 32; transl. Larson, *King's Mirror*, p. 129) The wording of the saga is dissimilar enough to *Konungs skuggsjá* that it is probably not a direct copy.

11 Stitt points out that this rock-throwing episode, as well as the episode of Odd shooting giants in the eye, are elements of the Polyphemus tradition, best-known from the *Odyssey* but turning up in various folktales as well (*Beowulf and the Bear's Son*, p. 64).

12 The Elfar Skerries (*Elfarsker*), now called the Göteborg Islands, lie at the mouth of the Göta älv, off the south coast of Sweden. They appear in several sagas as a hideout for raiders (e.g. *Þorsteins saga Víkingssonar* ch. 20; transl. Waggoner, *Sagas of Fridthjof the Bold*, p. 39)

13 Old Norse *Skíða*; an old port and trading center in the present-day county of Telemark, on the southeastern coast of Norway.

14 This episode is closely paralleled in *Þorsteins saga Víkingssonar* (ch. 7; transl. Waggoner, *Sagas of Fridthjof the Bold*, pp. 13-14), in which the hero Víking encounters a noble adversary, King Njörfi, and gives up his advantage in ships so that their battle is even. Like Thord here, Víking calls for peace when he finds out that his opponents haven't won much wealth, and so they're fighting for nothing but pride. In both sagas, the battle ends with an alliance.

15 Shields often signal the bearers' intent: "war-shields" mean hostility, while "peace-shields" signal a truce. In some sagas, red shields mean

hostility and white shields mean peaceful intent (cf. *Áns saga* ch. 6)

16 "To file down to the steel" (*sverfa til stáls*) means to fight to the bitter end. The metaphor means to sharpen a tool or weapon repeatedly, until the blade is worn down to the core.

17 Women make magically protective shirts or cloaks for men in both sagas of Icelanders (e.g. *Eyrbyggja saga* ch. 18, *Vatnsdæla saga* ch. 19) and several legendary sagas.

18 Læsø (Old Norse *Hlésey*) is an island in the Kattegat, between Jutland and Norway.

19 The Norse reads *Ópjóðans móðir*. *Ópjóðann* could be a giant's name; the name would literally mean "un-ruler", but probably is better rendered as "leader of bad people" (from *ópjóð*, "bad people"). The poem has listed five specific tribes (*þjóð*); *Ópjóðann* may imply "people who don't belong to a tribe", with the connotation that these were undesirables.

20 The word translated as "weathervane" is *húsasnotra*, a rare word literally meaning "lady of the house". It's been interpreted as a cleaning tool, like a broom; a decorative carving; or a navigational device. I have followed Sayers ("Karlsefni's *Húsasnotra*", pp. 341-350) in translating it as "weathervane". However, in Saxo's version of this episode, it is the ship's rudder that breaks and has to be replaced (*History of the Danes* V.166, transl. Ellis-Davidson and Fisher, p. 154).

21 Hjalmar lists four of his recently defeated enemies as comrades of his. Inconsistencies like this occur when an orally transmitted poem is used as a source for a written text; see note 42.

22 Lars Lönnroth has compared this poem to Beowulf's death scene. In both, the hero reviews his own life and bequeaths his helmet, sword, and ring to his steadfast companion. Both scenes contrast the easy life in the mead-hall with the grim reality of death in battle, and both end with the building of a burial mound that becomes a landmark. ("Hjálmar's Death Song," pp. 14-20.)

23 This scene may have been borrowed into *Þorsteins saga Víkingssonar*, ch. 25 (transl. Waggoner, *Sagas of Fridthjof the Bold*, p. 50), in which the captured hero also asks his captors who is to entertain whom.

24 This text has *Helsingjaland*, a district on the east coast of Sweden, nowhere near France. Boer (*Örvar-Odds saga*, p. xxi) notes that the

B recension of the saga has *Flæmingjaland*, "Flanders", and I have adopted this reading since it matches Odd's verse in chapter 27.

25 The rare word *steinnökkvi* occurs almost exclusively in legendary and chivalric sagas, and is always used for a rowboat belonging to a giant or similar being (*Dictionary of Old Norse Prose*). Cleasby and Vigfusson's older *Dictionary* (p. 461) defines *steinnökkvi* as a "stained boat"—i.e. a painted boat, not a "stone boat", which is what the word looks like it should mean. But giants in folklore and legend are often associated with stone (Motz, "Giants in Folklore and Mythology," p. 71), and there seems no reason not to assume that they might use stone rowboats.

26 *Vargeyjar*, "Wolf Islands", is present-day Vardø in the extreme northeast of Norway.

27 Norse *bláflekkótt hekla*. *Bárðar saga Snæfellsáss* (ch. 18) also includes an Odinnic character wearing a "blue-flecked hooded cloak" (*bláflekkótt skauthekla*); *Harðar saga* (ch. 15) has yet another avatar of Odin in a *blárend hekla*, "blue-striped cloak", while *Völsunga saga* includes one appearance by Odin in a *hekla flekótt*, "flecked cloak" (ch. 3), and another in a *hekla blá*, "blue cloak" (ch. 11). The color *blár*, which seems to have originally meant a dark blue-black, is associated with Odin in other sources, and saga heroes who intend to kill also tend to wear this color. (Wolf, "The Color Blue", pp. 71-72)

28 *Rauðgrani*, "Red Mustache", is a name for Odin in *Bárðar saga Snæfellsáss* (ch. 18); it's related to the Odin-names *Hrosshársgrani*, "Horsehair Mustache" (*Gautreks saga*) and *Síðgrani*, "Long Mustache" (*Álvissmál* in the *Poetic Edda*).

29 Caves under waterfalls are common places for ogresses and trolls to live; e.g. *Grettis saga* chs. 65-66; *Samsons saga fagra* chs. 7-8 (McKinnell, *Meeting the Other*, p. 245).

30 A repeated theme in the legendary sagas is that a being (human or animal, living or dead) that receives sacrifices is made more powerful and dangerous, often expressed as "to be turned into a troll" (*tryllast*).

31 The Norse word *finngálkn* (also *finngálpn*) is used in a few sagas for a sort of part-human, part-animal monster (e.g. *Hjálmpés saga ok Ölvis* ch. 10). In translations of continental texts, the word is used to translate *centaurus* or *onocentaurus* ("donkey-centaur"; e.g. Halldór

Hermannsson, *The Icelandic Physiologus*, p. 18.

32 This particular combination of names is close to a sequence used in Abbot Nikulás's *Leiðarvísir (Itinerary)*, and may have been borrowed from that source (Simek, *Altnordische Kosmographie*, pp. 344-345).

33 Helluland (Slab Land) is used in the "Vinland sagas" for a barren place in the far northern Atlantic or Arctic, often identified as Baffin Island. In this case, geographic accuracy is beside the point; Helluland is simply a remote and forbidding place.

34 Both the *hafgufa* or "sea-steam" and *lyngbakr* or "heather-back" seem to be borrowed from medieval bestiaries' account of the whale (Halldór Hermannsson, *Icelandic Physiologus*, pp. 10-11, 19). *Konungs skuggsjá*, a Norwegian text from ca. 1250, describes the *hafgufa* as an enormous whale that opens its mouth "as wide as a sound or fjord" and belches to attract huge numbers of fish (ch. 12; ed. Brenner, *Speculum Regale*, pp. 29-30; transl. Larsson, p. 125). Some more recent folklore of the "heatherback" is cited in Jón Árnason, *Íslenzkar þjóðsögur og æfintýri*, vol. 1, p. 631.

35 A common remedy in the legendary sagas for dealing with enemies that are magically immune to iron blades is to bash them with clubs. See Beard, "*Á Þá Bitu Engi Járn.*"

36 Geirrod (*Geirröðr*) appears as a powerful and sinister giant ruling somewhere in the farthest north. Thor's battle with him is told in *Skáldskaparmál* 18 (ed. Faulkes, pp. 22-30), and he also appears in the legendary *Þorsteins þáttr bæjarmagns* (transl. Pálsson and Edwards, *Seven Viking Romances*, pp. 263-272), and in Saxo's *Danish History* (VIII.289-291, transl. Ellis-Davidson and Fisher, pp. 264-266).

37 Ferrari ("Gods, Warlocks, and Monsters," p. 4) points out that Geoffroy of Monmouth tells the story of an evil giant who collected the beards of defeated kings until King Arthur killed him. Translated Arthurian romances were well known in Iceland, and this motif may be borrowed from them.

38 A blow on the buttocks (*klámhögg*, "obscene strike") was considered especially humiliating; it was symbolically equated with forcing the recipient to submit to penetration and loss of manhood. Icelandic laws grouped it with castration. See Meulengracht Sørensen, *The Unmanly Man*, pp. 68-70.

39 Sorcerous villains in the legendary sagas often can sink down into

the earth and move through it at will.

40 Snorri Sturluson's *Edda* lists *Jólfs smíði*, "Jolf's handiwork", as a kenning for "arrow." (*Skáldskaparmál* verse 466, ed. Faulkes, pp. 122, 484) Evidently, this saga episode, or at least this poem, was sufficiently widely known among poets for such a kenning to be used and understood.

41 The drinking contest scene is an example of what Lars Lönnroth calls a "double scene": the scene being described mimics the circumstances in which the listeners hear it. Some version of this saga, or at least this episode, would have been recited at feasts and gatherings that resembled the gathering where the drinking-contest takes place. Such "double scenes" encourage the saga listeners to identify with the warriors in the king's hall ("Double Scene", pp. 95-109).

42 Olvir is not mentioned elsewhere in this saga; Lönnroth suggests that this poem is older than the saga itself and served as a major source for the saga, and that the episode about Olvir may have been lost in the course of oral transmission. ("Double Scene", p. 105)

43 The word *kynmálasamr* is defined in older sources as "full of strange stories", and closely related to *skrökmálasamr*, "full of false stories", which appears in the next stanza and which I have translated "brazenly lying." Pálsson and Edwards (*Seven Viking Romances*, pp. 104-105) have rendered *kynmálasamr* as "mad for sex."

44 Sigurd is called *skauð hernumin*, literally "a sheath taken in battle". Pálsson and Edwards render this as "the comical captive" (*Arrow-Odd*, p. 89) or "the comic turn" (*Seven Viking Romances*, p. 105), but the implications may be much worse: *skauð* can mean the female genitalia and could also imply the anus, and Vikings were known to rape their male captives (e.g. Christiansen, *Norsemen in the Viking Age*, pp. 26-27). The implication is that Sigurd has submitted to sodomy—one of the worst possible insults in the Norse world. See Clover, "Regardless of Sex," pp. 8-11; Meulengracht Sørensen, *Unmanly Man*. . . .

45 Jesch (*Ships and Men*, pp. 135-136) notes that the use of "ash" (*askr*) to mean a ship is rare in poetry, but there are a few examples of this usage in both Norse and in Old English texts.

46 Lönnroth ("Double Scene", p. 107) notes the similarity between

this stanza and the Old English poem *Widsith*, suggesting that both must descend from a common tradition of poetry performed in the mead-hall.

47 On the face of it, *Bjálkaland* means "plank land", but de Vries (*Altnordisches etymologisches Wörterbuch*, p. 38) locates the land somewhere in eastern Europe and derives the name from Russian *belka*, "squirrel."

48 *Gyðja* means "priestess", specifically a pagan priestess. *Álfr* means a type of supernatural being, sometimes identified with the buried dead (cognate with English *elf*).

49 *Skjaldmeyjar* or "shield-maidens", female warriors, appear in several legendary sagas, sometimes treated with much more respect than here (e.g. *Sögubrót* chs. 8-9, transl. Waggoner, *Sagas of Ragnar Lodbrok*, pp. 53-57; also Saxo's *Danish History* VII.229-230, transl. Ellis-Davidson and Fisher, pp. 211-212). It is unclear whether there is any historical truth to this tradition (Christensen, *Norsemen in the Viking Age*, pp. 21-22).

50 The ability to shoot arrows from every finger is a fairly common skill among sorcerous villains in legendary saga; for example, the two goddesses Thorgerd and Irpa do this in *Jómsvíkinga saga* ch. 21 (trans. Hollander, p. 101), and Saami sorcerors do so in *Sörla saga sterka* ch. 20 (transl. Waggoner, *Sagas of Giants and Heroes*, p. 134).

51 The ability to see invisible villains when looking underneath someone else's arm is attested in Saxo's *Danish History* (II.66; transl. Ellis-Davidson and Fisher, p. 63).

52 The identification of the Biblical figure of Magog with present-day Russia dates at least to Josephus, who claimed that Magog was the ancestor of the Scythians north of the Black Sea (*Jewish Antiquities* I.123, transl. Thackeray, pp. 58-61).

53 In Norse naming practice, a man's second name was usually patronymic, which would make Svart's name *Svartr Ögmundarson*. However, if his father died or left before his birth, or early in his life, he might bear a matronymic name, as Svart does here.

54 This list of countries seems to be copied from a list in the manuscript *Hauksbók*. All the names that can be identified are from the Baltic, and many are attested as targets of historical raids or trading expeditions on runestones. I have used familiar

Notes

English names when these exist: Karelia for *Kirjálaland*, Estonia for *Eistland*, Livonia for *Lífland*, Courland for *Kúrland*, and Poland for *Púlinaland*. The saga has *Rafastaland* in error where the *Hauksbók* list has *Tafeistaland* (Simek, *Altnordisches Kosmographie*, pp. 341-343); this is Tavastia in southern Finland (Jesch, *Ships and Men*, p. 93). *Rafaland* is the area around present-day Tallinn (Estonian *Rävala*; appears as *Rafala* in *Njáls saga* ch. 30). *Virland*, also attested in rune inscriptions, is northern Estonia, and *Vitland* may be on the east side of the Vistula. (Jesch, *Ships and Men*, pp. 90-95). The text has *Lánland* where other manuscripts have *Samland* (Simek, *Altnordisches Kosmographie*, p. 342), which may be the Sambian peninsula in what is now the Kaliningrad Oblast of Russia. *Ermland* is in present-day Poland (Polish *Warmia*).

55   See chapter 29 of this saga and note 50 on the ability to shoot arrows from every finger.

56   *Tyrfi-Finnar* are probably the same as the *Ter-Finnas* mentioned by Ohthere. The easternmost Saami people are still called the Ter Saami, and the southeast coast of the Kola Peninsula is still called *Terskij bereg*, the "Ter Coast", in Russian;, whereas the eastern Kola Peninsula is called *Tarje* in the Saami languages. (Ross, *Terfinnas and Beormas*, pp. 25-26)

57   The king of Sweden is called Hlodver in the text, but Ingvi in the poem. This discrepancy may not be a mistake; according to *Heimskringla* and several other sources, the god Ingvi or Yngvi (also known as Freyr or Yngvi-Freyr) was the mythic founder of the ruling dynasty of Sweden, and it's possible that the Swedish kings took on his name, or at least were figuratively identified with him.

58   The legendary Battle of Brávellir is described in the fragmentary *Sögubrót* (transl. Waggoner, *Sagas of Ragbar Lodbrok*, pp. 44-58) and in Saxo's *Danish History* (VIII.257-264; transl. Ellis-Davidson and Fisher, pp. 238-244); it was said to be an enormous battle in which a huge number of famous heroes fought. Both sides are said to have used the wedge formation. While this saga does not mention Odd's participation, the *Sögubrót* lists *Oddr víðförli*, "Odd the Far-Traveler", and Saxo's *History* lists "Odd the Englishman"; both sources place Odd on the side of King Hring.

59   The Viking-era ell ranged from 47 cm to 63 cm, or between 18 and

25 inches. (Christensen, *Norsemen in the Viking Age*, p. 333)

Saga of Án Bow-Bender

1. Onund's nickname *Uppsjá* literally means "look upwards"; it has been interpreted variously as "the Vigilant" (Hughes, "Literary Antecedents", p. 198) or "the Denier" (Hughes, "The Saga of Án Bow-Bender", p. 306).
2. Hamar ("crag") is located in the Hedmark district of Norway, on the shores of Lake Mjøsa.
3. As Mitchell points out (*Heroic Sagas and Ballads*, p. 56), this is a sardonic reference to the stereotypical saga *kólbítr*, the unpromising lad who lies around the hearth-fire (see note 1 to *Ketils saga hængs*).
4. The Norse *vígir hann utan steins* literally means "he consecrates him from out of the stone". The same phrase is used in one version of *Hervarar saga* to describe how King Svafrlami forced two dwarves to forge him the sword Tyrfing (on which they place a curse, unlike An's bow and arrows; transl. Tolkien, p. 68). This probably refers to some sort of magical rite, but the phrase also calls to mind Christian stories of a priest driving a being out of its home stone by prayers and holy water; e.g. *Þorvalds þáttr viðförla* ch. 3.
5. In a shorter redaction of this saga, Án gets three arrows instead of five, making these arrows resemble Gusir's Gifts more closely (Hughes, "Literary Antecedents," p. 217).
6. The dwarf-name Lit appears in Snorri Sturluson's account of Balder's funeral, in which Thor kicks a dwarf named Lit into the pyre (*Gylfaginning* 49, ed. Faulkes, p. 46). Another helpful dwarf by that name appears in the legendary *Þorsteins saga Víkingssonar*.
7. Note the parallel gift of the chair in *Ketils saga hængs* ch. 1; in that saga the origin of the chair is not explained, but Ketil, like Án, may have undergone an encounter with the non-human world. Battles ("Dwarfs in Germanic Literature", pp. 44-45) notes that this episode blends the motif of a dwarf crafting a cursed weapon (e.g. *Ásmundar saga kappabana*, *Hervarar saga*) with that of the "grateful dwarf" who richly rewards kindness from a human (e.g. *Þorsteins saga Víkingssonar*, *Þorsteins þáttr bæjarmagns*, *Egils saga einhenda*).

Notes

8   Grettir in *Grettis saga* (ch. 17), Án's distant kinsman, was also known for being an annoyance on a long sea voyage, yet winning the sailors' respect in the end.

9   It was customary to give a child, or even an adult, a naming-gift (*nafnfestr*, literally "name-fastener") upon bestowing a name or nickname, as Jorunn does for Thorir in chapter 7 of this saga.

10 The text only calls this an "antechamber" (*forstofa*), but the context makes it obvious what is meant here. In at least some Icelandic farmhouses, the latrine was probably located just off the main entrance, suggesting that the word *forstofa* could cover both (*Complete Sagas of Icelanders*, vol. 5, p. 401).

11 The Viking-era ell ranged from 47 cm to 63 cm, or between 18 and 25 inches. (Christensen, *Norsemen in the Viking Age*, p. 333).

12 A *hafnarmerki*, "harbor-mark," was a beacon or cairn, sometimes in the shape of a pyramid, but other times in human form. An's verse is an address to the *hafnarmerki*.

13 *Selja* means "willow tree" but is also used in poetry for "woman".

14 Ketil's insult makes it clear that An supposedly wants to *serða* someone—to take the active, penetrative role in a homosexual act. To say that a man had been penetrated was one of the worst insults possible; under Icelandic law, the insulted party had the right to kill the insulter (Meulengracht Sørensen, *The Unmanly Man*, pp. 15-18). The active role was not nearly as shameful, but a number of texts depict it as despicable or disgraceful—probably due to the influence of Christian teaching, which considered both partners in a homosexual act as equally sinful (Meulengracht Sørensen, pp. 26-28, 52-58). This is the background for Ketil's insult; had he said that An was or wanted to be the passive partner, An could have killed him on the spot.

15 The fourth line, *enni geira hlenni*, is hard to translate, as the word *hlenni*, "thief", does not seem to fit anywhere in the sentence. The line seems to be a blending of two kennings which share the same word: [*uxa*] *enni geira*, "spear of the forehead [of an ox]", is a kenning for "horn", while *geira hlenni*, "thief of spears", would mean King Ingjald. Hughes (p. 335, n14) suggests that this is a disguised insult, calling the oblivious Ingjald a thief. The line could be broken down in two ways: *uxa enni, geira hlenni* would mean "[let's drink ale

from] the ox's forehead [=horn], spear-thief", but *uxa enni geira, hlenni* would mean [let's drink ale from] the ox's forehead-spear, you thief".

16   This contradicts the events of Chapter 1 in which the dwarf makes five arrows for An, but as noted above in note XXX, in another redaction of this saga the dwarf makes three arrows for An (Hughes, "Literary Antecedents," p. 217). There may also be some confusion with Gusir's Gifts, the three arrows owned by Ketil Salmon, Grim Hairy-Cheek, and Arrow-Odd.

17   Norse *snærisspjót*; a throwing-spear with a thong, which was used to increase the spear's speed and/or accuracy; exactly how it was used isn't clear from saga accounts. (Short, *Viking Weapons*, p. 92)

18   Killing a man in secret, without the killer declaring openly what he had done, was a serious crime in the old Scandinavian law codes.

19   A pun on An's name; *án* means "without". The farmer says *Án mættum vér hafa verit pinna skota hér*, "We could have been without your shooting here." My attempts to translate this pun and the following ones work better if you remember that the name *Án*, with a long *á*, is pronounced more like English "on" than English "an" or "Ann".

20   Another pun on An's name. The slave says *Hér er mikit um ánagang*, "Here's a lot of *ánagangr*. *Ánagangr* could be parsed as "Áns walking around", but also means "foolishness".

21   Yet another pun: the farmer says *Hér er ánótt mjök*, "Here's a great *ánótt*." *Ánótt* could be parsed as *Án-ótt*, "full of Áns", but may also pun on *ó-nogt*, "not enough."

22   Hughes ("The Saga of Án Bow-Bender, p. 335 n16) notes that during the Third Crusade, in 1190, Richard I of England ordered that thieves were to have their heads shaved and be tarred and feathered. Removal of eyes and testicles appears in several historical sagas; such torture destroyed a man's masculinity and thus his social standing (Meulengracht Sørensen, *The Unmanly Man*, pp. 81-84). This is presumably why the king drives Ketil away, but not Ivar, whom An mutilates but does not castrate (see note 29 below).

23   The individual clothing items are of high quality, but An wears them in reverse order from inner to outer layers. This may be a deliberate reversal of courtly norms; *Konungs skuggsjá*, describing proper behavior at the 13th-century Norwegian royal court, recommends

Notes

that "your shirt should be short, and all your linen rather light. Your shirt should be cut somewhat shorter than your coat; for no man of taste can deck himself out in flax or hemp." (ch. 30; transl. Larson, *King's Mirror*, p. 181)

24 Another pun: Drifa calls An *ferfaldr*. *Ferfaldr* means "fourfold" or "four times", but *faldr* also means "hem", referring to An wearing four visible layers of clothing. Another layer of meaning may exist: the prefix *fer-* can mean "monstrous."

25 A difficult pun to translate. An calls Drifa *Logn*, which means "calm air." The name *Drífa* means "snowdrift", specifically a snowdrift that forms in calm air. (Jónsson, *Norsk-Islandske Skjaldedigtning*, vol. B2, p. 340; Hughes, "The Saga of Án Bow-Bender", p. 336 n19.)

26 A common bargain made when a hero leaves a giantess after fathering a child on her; see *Örvar-Odds saga* ch. 18 in this book, *Hálfdanar saga Brönufóstra* ch. 8 (transl. Waggoner, *Sagas of Giants and Heroes*, p. 99), and *Kjalnesinga saga* ch. 14 (transl. Waggoner, p. 44). This motif was probably borrowed from the sagas of giants, even though Drifa is apparently human.

27 Killing a wrestling opponent by breaking his body over the edge of a vertical stone appears in several sagas; usually the opponent is a troll (e.g. *Kjalnesinga saga* ch. 15, transl. Waggoner, *Sagas of Giants and Heroes*, p. 46; see also *Gunnars saga Keldugnúpsfífls* ch. 7).

28 Putting a villain's severed head between his legs ensures that he will not become a *draugr* (walking corpse); e.g. *Grettis saga* ch. 18, 35; *Fljótsdæla saga* ch. 5.

29 In *Hálfdanar saga Brönufóstra* ch. 15 (transl. Waggoner, *Sagas of Giants and Heroes*, pp. 106-107), the hero mutilates the villainous Áki using a combination of the mutilations of Ketil (eyes put out, castration, king driving victim away) and Ivar (feet twisted backwards, facial mutilation).

30 The meaning seems obscure, but the sense may be that the king had never intended to consent to the match and was setting Ivar up for failure.

31 Red shields are a token of hostility, while white shields signal peaceful intentions (e.g. *Eiríks saga rauða* chs. 10-11).

32 The Norse reads *ek vilda láta drífa um stafn*, literally "I want to let the prow drive forward", a naval metaphor.

33 Saxo Grammaticus mentions Ano Sagittarius, or An the Archer, a near translation of *bogsveigir*. Although the circumstances of his life are quite different, Ano does commit a great feat of archery by shooting his enemy's gear three times without hitting his body. This suggests a relatively early date for a part of the tradition recorded in this saga. (*History of the Danes* VI.180-181; transl. Ellis-Davidson and Fisher, pp. 168-169.)

34 Yet more puns on An's name, turning on *án* meaning "without". Thorir says *margs góðs muntu án vera, ok ertu nú án sauðarins þess*—"you must be without many goods, and now you are without this sheep."

35 A foreshadowing of the union of all Norway under King Harald Fairhair, said to have been completed in 872; this conversation is evidently set a short while before that. It may also be an allusion to Iceland's loss of independence and union with Norway in 1262.

36 *Ok er betra at gæta sinnar sæmdar en at setjast í hæra stað ok þaðan minnkast.* *Vatnsdæla saga* ch. 7 includes a proverb (spoken to An's great-great-great-grandson by his foster-father) that is worded differently, ruling out direct textual borrowing in either direction, but with much the same meaning: *Er ok þat meiri virðing at aukast af litlum efnum en at hefjast hátt ok setjast með lægingu*, "It is greater honor to increase your means little by little, than to exalt yourself and be brought low."

37 A prominent settler of Iceland; his story is told in *Landnámabók* (S179-180, H145-147; transl. Pálsson and Edwards, pp. 83-86) and in *Vatnsdæla saga* chs. 1-7. Ketil Oaf's ancestry is given in *Hversu Nóregr Byggðist* and in *Vatnsdæla saga* ch. 1.

38 The text only states that An had to fight *skinnkyrtlur*, "[people wearing] skin tunics," but skin tunics are the standard dress of giants and trolls (e.g. Forad in *Ketils saga* ch. 5; Hrimnir, Hyrja, and Geirrid in *Gríms saga* chs. 1-2; the unnamed giantess in *Örvar-Odds saga* ch. 5). Another recension of *Áns saga* states that An had much trouble from a gang of ogresses when he lived in Hrafnista (quoted in Leslie, "Matter of Hrafnista", p. 189).

39 Ogmund (or Eymund) Field-Spoiler is briefly mentioned in *Víga-Glúms saga* ch. 5 as the ancestor of several noted Icelanders, including Gizur the White (who also appears in *Njáls saga*), one of the first Icelanders to accept Christianity. Ogmund Field-Spoiler was also an ancestor of King Olaf Tryggvasson.

Ohthere's Voyage

1. The identity of this river isn't certain. Norse explorers usually sailed up the Dvina River, but Ohthere clearly states that he sailed along the coast, keeping land to starboard the whole way; to reach the Dvina River, Ohthere would have had to break away from the coast, or else loop all the way around the White Sea. Ross (*Terfinnas and Beormas*, p. 24) and Hofstra and Samplonius ("Viking Expansion Northwards," p. 239) suggest that Ohthere sailed around the Kola Peninsula into Kandalaksha Bay, stopping at the mouth of the Varzuga River or the Umba River, not the Dvina. It's also possible that what Ohthere calls the "great river" was the very long and narrow Kandalaksha Bay itself.
2. Norse accounts agree that the Bjarmians settled their land and built permanent dwellings: *Óláfs saga helga* states that the Bjarmians lived in towns and built stockades, whereas a skaldic poem quoted in *Haralds saga gráfeldr* mentions the burning of Bjarmian houses (ch. 14; transl. Hollander, *Heimskringla*, p. 140).
3. The fact that Ohthere could recognize that the Beormas' language was close to that of the Saami implies that Ohthere knew the Saami language to some degree.
4. Ohthere's word for "walrus", *horshwæl*, appears nowhere else in Old English literature, and seems to be a borrowing of Old Norse *hrosshvalr* (literally "horse-whale"). The use of Norse words, as well as the overall style, suggests that his account was originally taken by direct dictation.
5. The ell varied in length at different places and times; the Viking-era ell ranged from 47 cm to 63 cm, or between 18 and 25 inches. (Christensen, *Norsemen in the Viking Age*, p. 333). Assuming an ell of about eighteen inches, these walruses would be about 10.5 feet or 3.2 meters, which is about right (Nowak, *Walker's Mammals of the World*, vol. 2, pp. 1244-1247).
6. A fifty-ell whale would be about 75 ft or 22.9 m. This is plausible; the bowhead or Greenland right whale (*Balaena mysticetus*) can exceed 65 feet (19.8 m), and the related great right whale (*Eubalaena*

glacialis) can reach 60 feet (18 meters). Both species live or once lived in the northeast Atlantic. Right whales are relatively easy to hunt, and were or still are hunted by traditional peoples such as the Inuit; presumably the people of Finnmark were also capable of hunting it. (Nowak, *Walker's Mammals of the World*, vol. 2, pp. 1039-1042)

7   This has confused some commentators, who note that killing sixty right whales in two days would be an impossible feat. Some have suggested that Ohthere meant small "pilot whales" which can be driven onshore in herds (e.g. Bately, p. 189). However, I interpret these sixty "whales" to be walruses, which Ohthere calls *horshwæl*, "horse-whale". Walruses may haul out onto land in herds of several thousand; thus, sixty walruses killed in two days by seven men is quite believable—for comparison, in 1608, one whaling ship is known to have slaughtered 900 walruses in seven hours. (Richards, *Unending Frontier*, p. 608)

8   Old English *unbebohtra*, "unbought". I have assumed that this means that Ohthere had not bought the reindeer—i.e., he had captured them—but it could mean that no one had bought them from him—i.e. that he was selling them and had not found a purchaser yet.

9   Ohthere's word for a reindeer, *hran*, is unique in Old English and seems to be a borrowing of Old Norse *hreinn*.

10 Old English *stælhranas*, probably "steal-reindeer" or "thief-reindeer", or possibly "stall-reindeer", but in any case clearly meaning tame reindeer who act as decoys.

11 One Anglo-Saxon *ámber* was equal to four bushels. By modern standards, one *ámber* would be thirty-two gallons (141 liters), but the *ámber* varied at different places and times, and it's not clear exactly how many feathers Ohthere meant.

12 The Cwenas appear in Norse sources as the *Kvenir* (e.g. *Egils saga* chs. 14, 17). Norse texts locate Kvenland on the coast of the Gulf of Bothnia; medieval records and place names refer to a people called the *Kainu* or *Kainulaiset* in Finnish, living around the northern coasts of the Gulf of Bothnia. Most writers on the subject assume that the Kvens were Finnic, although there are other possibilities. (Ross, "Ohthere's 'Cwenas and Lakes'", p. 338; Valtonas, "Who Were the *Cwenas?*", pp. 108-109)

13 Alan Ross personally explored a possible route for the Cwenas' raids,

starting from Torneträsk or Lake Torne, crossing the mountains, and descending to the Bardu and Måls Rivers. The route is mostly navigable in light boats, and the portages are easy. ("Ohthere's 'Cwenas and Lakes'", pp. 337-343)

14 Old Norse *Skíringssalr*; identified as the archaeological site of Kaupang at the entrance to the Oslofjord. A large royal center in previous centuries, the town was no longer occupied year-round in Ohthere's town, although it continued to be used as a seasonal trading center until about 960. (Skre, "The *Sciringes healh* of Ohthere's Time", pp. 150-155)

15 "This land" is Britain, and the islands between Ireland and Britain are presumably the Hebrides, and possibly Orkney and Shetland. The placement of these islands to the west of Norway can't be literally true, but Ohthere was probably referring, not to Ireland and Britain themselves, but to known sailing lanes—to established points along the Norwegian coast where ships would turn and make for these destinations.

16 Gotland is north Jutland; Sillende is probably not Zealand, but rather south Jutland.

17 The Wends were western Slavs.

18 On a modern map, this would be the southwest coast of Sweden, but historically this was part of the Danish kingdom.

BIBLIOGRAPHY

Note that Icelandic authors have been alphabetized by first name, as is common practice. Most Icelandic sagas mentioned in the text whose publication information is not specifically cited may be found in translation in Viðar Hreinsson (ed.) *Complete Sagas of the Icelanders.* 5 vols. Reykjavík: Leifur Eiriksson Publishing, 1997.

Andersson, Theodore M., and Kari Ellen Gade (eds. transl.). *Morkinskinna: The Earliest Icelandic Chronicle of the Norwegian Kings (1030–1157). Islandica* vol. 51. Ithaca, N.Y.: Cornell University Press, 2000.

Arnold, Martin. "*Hvat er tröll nema þat?*: The Cultural History of the Troll." *The Shadow-Walkers: Jacob Grimm's Mythology of the Monstrous.* Ed. Tom Shippey. Tempe, Ariz.: Arizona Center for Medieval and Renaissance Studies, 2005, pp. 111-156.

Bachmann, W. Bryant, and Guðmundur Erlingsson. *Six Old Icelandic Sagas.* Lanham, Md.: University Press of America, 1993.

Bately, Janet (ed.) *The Old English Orosius.* Early English Text Society, Supplementary Series, vol. 6. London: Oxford University Press, 1980.

—, and Anton Englert (eds.) *Ohthere's Voyages.* Roskilde: Viking Ship Museum, 2007.

Battles, Paul. "Dwarfs in Germanic Literature: *Deutsche Mythologie* or Grimm's Myths?" *The Shadow-Walkers: Jacob Grimm's Mythology of the Monstrous*. Ed. Tom Shippey. Tempe, Ariz.: Arizona Center for Medieval and Renaissance Studies, 2005, pp. 29-82.

Beard, D. J. "*Á Þá Bitu Engi Járn*: A Brief Note on the Concept of Invulnerability in the Old Norse Sagas." *Studies in English Language and Early Literature in Honour of Paul Christophersen. Occasional Papers in Linguistics and Language Teaching*, vol. 8. Ed. P. M. Tilling. Coleraine: New University of Ulster, 1981, pp. 13-31.

Biebuyck, Daniel, and Kahombo C. Mateene (ed., transl.) *The Mwindo Epic from the Banyanga (Congo Republic)*. Berkeley: University of California Press, 1969.

Boer, Richard Constant. *Örvar-Odds Saga*. Leiden: E. J. Brill, 1888.

Brenner, Oscar (ed.) *Speculum Regale: Ein Altnorwegischer Dialog nach Cod. Arnamagn. 243 Fol. B und den Ältesten Fragmenten*. München [Munich]: Christian Kaiser, 1881.

Chapman, Graham, John Cleese, Terry Gilliam, Eric Idle, Terry Jones, and Michael Palin. *Monty Python's Flying Circus: Just The Words*. 2 vols. London: Methuen, 1989.

Christiansen, Eric. *The Norsemen in the Viking Age*. Oxford: Blackwell, 2002.

Ciklamini, Marlene. "Grettir and Ketill Hængr, the Giant-Killers." *Arv*, vol. 22 (1966), pp. 136-155.

—. "Old Norse Epic and Historical Tradition." *Journal of the Folklore Institute*, vol. 8, no. 2/3 (1971), pp. 93-100.

Cleasby, Richard and Gudbrand Vigfusson. *An Icelandic-English Dictionary*. Oxford: Clarendon Press, 1874.

Clover, Carol J. "Regardless of Sex: Men, Women, and Power in Early Northern Europe." *Speculum*, vol. 68, no. 2 (1993), pp. 363-387.

—. "Icelandic Family Sagas". *Old Norse–Icelandic Literature: A Critical Guide*. Ed. Carol J. Clover and John Lindow. Toronto: University of Toronto Press, 2005, pp. 239-315.

Cross, Samuel Hazzard and Olgerd P. Sherbowitz-Wetzor (ed. transl.) *The Russian Primary Chronicle: Laurentian Text*. Cambridge, Mass.: Mediaeval Academy of America, 1973

de Vries, Jan. *Altnordisches etymologisches Wörterbuch*. Leiden: E. J. Brill, 1961.

Dictionary of Old Norse Prose / Ordbog over det norrøne prosasprog. Copenhagen: Arnamagnæan Commission. http://www.onp.hum.ku.dk/

Driscoll, Matthew J. and Silvia Hufnagel. "*Fornaldarsögur Norðurlanda*: A Bibliography of Manuscripts, Editions, Translations and Secondary Literature." Copenhagen: Arnamagnæan Institute. http://am-dk.net/fasnl/bibl/index.php

DuBois, Thomas A. *Nordic Religions in the Viking Age*. Philadelphia: University of Pennsylvania Press, 1999.

Einar Sveinsson. "Celtic Elements in Icelandic Tradition". *Béaloideas*, vol. 25 (1957), pp. 3-24.

Faulkes, Anthony. *Two Icelandic Stories*. 2nd ed. London: Viking Society for Northern Research, 2011.

Ferrari, Fulvio. "Gods, Warlocks, and Monsters in the *Örvar-Odds saga*." *The Fantastic in Old Norse Literature: 13th International Saga Conference, Durham and York, 6th-12th August, 2006*. http://tinyurl.com/d6ntevz.

Finnegan, Ruth. *Oral Literature in Africa*. Nairobi: Oxford University Press (Eastern Africa), 1976.

Finnur Jónsson, *Norsk-Islandske Skjaldedigtning*. 4 vols. Copenhagen: Villadsen and Christensen, 1912-15.

—. *Lexicon Poeticum Antiquæ Linguæ Septentrionalis*. 2nd ed. Copenhagen: S. L. Møllers Bogtrykkeri, 1931.

Fjalldal, Magnús. *The Long Arm of Coincidence: The Frustrated Connection between* Beowulf *and* Grettis saga. Toronto: University of Toronto Press, 1998.

Folks, Cathalin B. and Carl Lindahl. "Loathly Lady." *Medieval Folklore: A Guide to Myths, Legends, Tales, Beliefs, and Customs*. Ed. Carl Lindahl, John McNamara, and John Lindow. Santa Barbara, Calif.: ABC-CLIO, 2000, pp. 245-246.

Foote, Peter G. "Sagnaskemtan: Reykjahólar 1119." *Saga-Book of the Viking Society*, vol. 14 (1953-57), pp. 226-239.

Gísli Sigurðsson. *The Medieval Icelandic Saga and Oral Tradition: A Discourse on Method*. Publications of the Milman Parry Collection of Oral Literature, no. 2. Cambridge, Mass.: Harvard University Press, 2004.

Guðni Jónsson. *Edda Snorra Sturlusonar: Nafnaþulur og Skáldatal*. Reykjavík: Islendingasagnaútgáfan, 1954.

Halldór Hermannsson. *The Icelandic Physiologus*. Islandica, vol. XXVII. Ithaca, N.Y.: Cornell University Press, 1938.

—. *The Saga of Thorgils and Haflidi*. Ithaca, N.Y.: Cornell University Press, 1945.

Harris, Joseph. "The Prosimetrum of Icelandic Saga and Some Relatives." *Prosimetrum: Cross-Cultural Perspectives on Narrative in Prose and Verse*. Eds. Joseph Harris and Karl Reichl. Suffolk / Rochester, N.Y.: D. S. Brewer, 1997. pp. 131-163.

Heide, Eldar. "Spinning *Seiðr*." *Old Norse Religion in Long-Term Perspectives*. Eds. Anders Andrén, Kristina Jennbert, and Catharina Raudvere. Lund: Nordic Academic Press, 2006, pp. 164-170.

Hollander, Lee (transl.) *The Saga of the Jómsvíkings*. Austin: University of Texas Press, 1955.

Hofstra, Tette and Kees Samplonius. "Viking Expansion Northwards: Mediæval Sources." *Arctic*, vol. 48, no. 3 (1995), pp. 235-247.

Hughes, S. F. D. "The Literary Antecedents of *Áns saga bogsveigis*." *Medieval Scandinavia* vol. 9 (1976), pp. 198-235.

—. "The Saga of Án Bow-Bender." *Medieval Outlaws: Ten Tales in Modern English*. Ed. Thomas H. Ohlgren. Thrupp, Gloucestershire: Sutton Publishing, 1998, pp. 187-215.

—. "The Saga of Án Bow-Bender." *Medieval Outlaws: Twelve Tales in Modern English*. Rev. ed. Ed. Thomas H. Ohlgren. West Lafayette, Indiana: Parlor Press, 2005, pp. 290-337.

Jakob Benediktsson (ed.) *Íslendingabók. Landnámabók. Íslenzk Fornrit*, vol. 1. Reykjavík: Hið Íslenzka Fornritafélag, 1986.

Jesch, Judith. "Hrómundr Gripsson Revisited." *Skandinavistik* 14 (1984), pp. 89–105.

—. *Ships and Men in the Late Viking Age: The Vocabulary of Runic Inscriptions and Skaldic Verse*. Woodbridge, Suffolk: Boydell and Brewer, 2001.

Jón Árnason. *Íslenzkar þjóðsögur og æfintýri*. Leipzig: J. C. Hinrich, 1862-65.

Jorgensen, Peter A. "The Two-Troll Variant of the Bear's Son Folktale in *Hálfdanar saga Brönufóstra* and *Gríms saga loðinkinna*." *Arv*, vol. 31 (1975), pp. 35-43.

—. "The Gift of the Useless Weapon in *Beowulf* and the Icelandic Sagas." *Arkiv för Nordisk Filologi*, vol. 94 (1979), pp. 82-90.

—. "Additional Icelandic Analogues to *Beowulf*." *Sagnaskemmtun: Studies in*

Honour of Hermann Pálsson. Eds. Rudolf Simek, Jónas Kristjánsson, and Hans Bekker-Nielsen. Vienna: Hermann Böhlaus, 1986, pp. 201-208.

Josephus (transl. H. St. J. Thackeray). *Josephus. Vol. IV: Jewish Antiquities, Books I-IV*. Loeb Classical Library. Cambridge, Mass.: Harvard University Press, 1930.

Kristinsson, Axel. "Lords and Literature: The Icelandic Sagas as Political and Social Instruments." *Scandinavian Journal of History*, vol. 28 (2003), pp. 1-17.

Kunin, Devra. *A History of Norway and the Passion and Miracles of the Blessed Óláfr*. London: Viking Society for Northern Research, 2001.

Larrington, Carolyne. "Awkward Adolescents: Male Maturation in Norse Literature." *Youth and Age in the Medieval North*. Ed. Shannon Lewis-Simpson. Leiden: E. J. Brill, 2008, pp. 151-166.

Larson, Laurence M. (transl.) *The King's Mirror (Speculum Regale—Konungs skuggsjá)*. New York: American-Scandinavian Foundation, 1917.

Larson, Willard (transl.) *The Saga of Aun the Bow-Bender*. Baltimore: Gateway Press, 1995.

Leslie, Helen F. "The Matter of Hrafnista". *Quaestio Insularis*, vol. 11 (2010), pp. 169-208.

Lönnroth, Lars. "The Noble Heathen: A Theme in the Sagas." *Scandinavian Studies*, vol. 41 (1969), pp. 1-29.

—. "Hjálmar's Death Song and the Delivery of Eddic Poetry." *Speculum*, vol. 46 (1971), pp. 1-20.

—. "The Double Scene of Arrow-Odd's Drinking Contest." *Medieval Narrative: A Symposium*. Ed. Hans Bekker-Nielsen. Odense: Odense University Press, 1979, pp. 91-119.

McKinnell, John. "Encounters with Völur." *Old Norse Myths, Literature, and Society: Proceedings of the 11th International Saga Conference, 2–7 July 2000, Sydney, Australia.* Ed. Geraldine Barnes and Margaret Clunies Ross. Sydney: Centre for Medieval Studies, University of Sydney, 2000, pp. 239-251.

—. *Meeting the Other in Norse Myth and Legend.* Cambridge: D. S. Brewer, 2005.

Meulengracht Sørensen, Preben (Joan Turville-Petre, transl.). *The Unmanly Man: Concepts of Sexual Defamation in Early Northern Society.* Odense: Odense University Press, 1983.

Mitchell, Stephen A. *Heroic Sagas and Ballads.* Ithaca, N.Y.: Cornell University Press, 1991.

—. "Blåkulla and its Antecedents: Transvection and Conventicles in Nordic Witchcraft." *Álvíssmál*, vol. 7 (1997), pp. 81-100.

Motz, Lotte. "Giants in Folklore and Mythology: A New Approach." *Folklore*, vol. 93, no. 1 (1982), pp. 70-84.

Mundal, Else. "The Perception of the Saamis and their Religion in Old Norse Sources." *Shamanism and Northern Ecology.* Ed. Juha Pentikäinen. Berlin: Mouton de Gruyter, 1996, pp. 97-116.

—. "Coexistence of Saami and Norse Culture—Reflected In and Interpreted By Old Norse Myths." *Old Norse Myths, Literature, and Society: Proceedings of the 11th International Saga Conference, 2–7 July 2000, Sydney, Australia.* Ed. Geraldine Barnes and Margaret Clunies Ross. Sydney: Centre for Medieval Studies, University of Sydney, 2000, pp. 346-355.

Nordal, Sigurður. "Icelandic Notes", *Acta Philologica Scandinavica*, vol. 6 (1931), pp. 144-150.

Nowak, Roland M. *Walker's Mammals of the World.* 5th ed. Baltimore: Johns Hopkins University Press, 1991.

Oddr Snorrason (Theodore Andersson, ed. transl.) *Saga of Olaf Tryggvason.* Ithaca, N.Y.: Cornell University Press, 2003.

Orning, Hans Jacob. "Imagining the Kalmar Union: Nordic Politics as Viewed from a Late 15th-century Icelandic Manuscript." *Á Austrvega: Saga and East Scandinavia. Preprint Papers of the 14th International Saga Conference, Uppsala, 9th-15th August 2009.* Ed. Agneta Ney, Henrik Williams and Fredrik Charpentier Ljungqvist. Gävle: Gavle University Press (2009), pp. 729-737.

—. "The Magical Reality of the Late Middle Ages: Exploring the World of the *Fornaldarsögur.*" *Scandinavian Journal of History,* vol. 35 (2010), pp. 3-20.

Pálsson, Hermann and Edwards, Paul. (transl.) *Arrow-Odd: A Medieval Novel.* New York: New York University Press, 1970.

—. *The Book of Settlements: Landnámabók.* Winnipeg: University of Manitoba Press, 1972.

—. *Seven Viking Romances.* London: Penguin, 1985.

Perdikaris, Sophia. "Fron Chiefly Provisioning to Commercial Fishery: Long-Term Economic Change in Arctic Norway." *Arctic Archaeology. World Archaeology,* vol. 30, no. 3. Ed. Peter Rowley-Conwy. Abingdon: Routledge, 1999, pp. 388-402.

Pizarro, Joaquín Martínez. "Transformations of the Bear's Son Tale in the Sagas of the Hrafnistumenn." *Arv,* vol. 32-33 (1976-77), pp. 263-281.

Quinn, Judy. "From Orality to Literacy in Medieval Iceland." *Old Icelandic Literature and Society.* Ed. Margaret Clunies Ross. Cambridge: Cambridge University Press, 2000, pp. 30-60.

— (ed.) "Interrogating Genre in the *Fornaldarsögur*: Round-Table Discussion." *Viking and Medieval Studies*, vol. 2 (2006), pp. 275-96.

Richards, John F. *The Unending Frontier: An Environmental History of the Early Modern World*. Berkeley: University of California Press, 2006.

Righter-Gould, Ruth. 1978-9. "*Áns saga bogsveigis*: A Legendary Analog of *Egils saga*." *Medieval Scandinavia* vol. 2, pp. 265-270.

Ross, Alan S. C. "Ohthere's 'Cwenas and Lakes'". *The Geographical Journal*, vol. 120, no. 3 (1954), pp. 337-345.

—. *The Terfinnas and Beormas of Ohthere*. London: Viking Society for Northern Research, 1981.

Ross, Margaret Clunies. "The Development of Old Norse Textual Worlds: Genealogical Structure as a Principle of Literary Organisation in Early Iceland." *Journal of English and Germanic Philology*, vol. 92, no. 3 (1993), pp. 372-385.

—. *The Cambridge Introduction to the Old Norse–Icelandic Saga*. Cambridge: Cambridge University Press, 2010.

Røthe, Gunnhild. "Þorgerðr Hölgabrúðr: The *Fylgja* of the Háleygjar Family." *Scripta Islandica* vol. 58 (2007), pp. 33-55.

Saxo Grammaticus (Hilda Ellis Davidson, ed., Peter Fisher, transl.) *History of the Danes. Books I–IX*. Cambridge: D. S. Brewer, 1996.

Sayers, William. "Karlsefni's *Húsasnotra*: The Divestment of Vinland." *Scandinavian Studies* vol. 75, no. 3 (2007), pp. 341-350.

Short, William R. *Viking Weapons and Combat Techniques*. Yardley, Penn.: Westholme Publishing, 2009.

Simek, Rudolf. *Altnordisches Kosmographie: Studien und Quellen zu Weltbild und Weltbeschreibung in Norwegen und Island vom 12. bis zum 14. Jahrhundert*.

Berlin: Walter de Gruyter, 1990.

Simpson, Jacqueline (ed., transl.) *The Northmen Talk: A Choice of Tales from Iceland.* London: Phoenix House, 1965.

Skre, Dagfinn. "The *Sciringes healh* of Ohthere's Time." *Ohthere's Voyages.* Ed. Janet Bately and Anton Englert. Roskilde: Viking Ship Museum, 2007, pp. 150-155.

Snorri Sturluson (Nils Linder and K. A. Haggson, eds.) *Heimskringla, eða Sögur Noregs Konunga.* 3 vols. Uppsala: W. Schultz, 1869-72.

— (Lee M. Hollander, transl.) *Heimskringla: History of the Kings of Norway.* Austin: University of Texas Press, 1964.

— (Anthony Faulkes, ed.) *Edda. Prologue and Gylfaginning; Skáldskaparmál. 1: Introduction, Text, and Notes; 2: Glossary and Index of Names.* 3 vols. London: Viking Society for Northern Research, 1998.

Stitt, J. Michael. *Beowulf and the Bear's Son: Epic, Saga, and Fairytale in Northern Germanic Tradition.* New York and London: Garland, 1992.

Storli, Inger. "Ohthere and His World—A Contemporary Perspective." *Ohthere's Voyages.* Ed. Janet Bately and Anton Englert. Roskilde: Viking Ship Museum, 2007, pp. 76-99.

Straubhaar, Sandra. "Nasty, Brutish, and Large: Cultural Difference and Otherness in the Figuration of the Trollwomen of the *Fornaldar sögur.*" *Scandinavian Studies*, vol. 73, no. 2 (2001), pp. 105-124.

Tambets, Kristiina, and 45 others. "The Western and Eastern Roots of the Saami—the Story of Genetic 'Outliers' Told by Mitochondrial DNA and Y Chromosomes." *American Journal of Human Genetics*, vol. 74 (2004), 661-682.

Thompson, Stith. *Motif-Index of Folk-Literature.* 5 vols. Bloomington: Indiana University Press, 1973.

Tolkien, Christopher (ed. transl.) *The Saga of King Heidrek the Wise.* London: Thomas Nelson and Sons, 1960.

Tulinius, Torfi H. (Randi C. Eldevik, transl.) *The Matter of the North: The Rise of Literary Fiction in Thirteenth-Century Iceland.* Odense: Odense University Press, 2002.

Turville-Petre, Gabriel. "Dreams in Icelandic Tradition." *Nine Norse Studies.* London: Viking Society for Northern Research, 1972, pp. 30-51.

Valtonas, Irmeli. "Who Were the Cwenas?" *Ohthere's Voyages.* Eds. Janet Bately and Anton Englert. Roskilde: Viking Ship Museum, 2007, pp. 108-109.

Vésteinn Ólason. "The Marvellous North and Authorial Presence in the Icelandic *fornaldarsaga.*" *Contexts of Pre-Novel Narrative: The European Tradition.* Ed. Roy Eriksen. Berlin: Walter de Gruyter, 1994, pp. 101-134.

Waggoner, Ben (transl.) *The Sagas of Ragnar Lodbrok.* New Haven, Conn.: The Troth, 2009.

—. *The Sagas of Fridthjof the Bold.* New Haven, Conn.: The Troth, 2009.

—. *Sagas of Giants and Heroes.* New Haven, Conn.: The Troth, 2010.

Wolf, Kirsten. "The Color Blue in Old Norse-Icelandic Literature." *Scripta Islandica,* vol. 57 (2006), pp. 55-78.

Zachrisson, Inger. "The Sámi and Their Interaction with the Nordic Peoples." *The Viking World.* Eds. Stefan Brink and Neil Price. London: Routledge, 2008, pp. 32-39.